# High Impact Quotations

# High Impact Quotations

## Compiled by
## Richard W. Pound

Fitzhenry & Whiteside

In Canada
Fitzhenry & Whiteside Limited
195 Allstate Parkway
Markham, Ontario   L3R 4T8

In the United States
Fitzhenry & Whiteside Limited
121 Harvard Avenue, Suite 2
Allston, Massachusetts 02134

www.fitzhenry.ca       godwit@fitzhenry.ca

**National Library of Canada Cataloguing in Publication**

High impact quotations / Richard W. Pound. — 1st ed.
ISBN 1-55041-847-5 (bound). — ISBN 1-55041-850-5 (pbk.)
1. Quotations, English.  I. Pound, Richard W.
PN6081.H54 2004       081       C2003-906876-5


**Publisher Cataloguing-in-Publication Data (U.S.)**

High impact quotations / selected by Richard W. Pound. — 1st ed.
[430] p. : cm.
ISBN 1-55041-847-5
ISBN 1-55041-850-5 (pbk.)
1. Quotations, English.  I. Pound, Richard W.  II. Title.
808.882 21    PN6081.H46 2004




Fitzhenry & Whiteside acknowledges with thanks the Canada Council for the Arts, the Government of Canada through its Book Publishing Industry Development Program, and the Ontario Arts Council for their support of our publishing program.

Cover design: Fortunato Design
Cover photograph: Phil Banko /Getty Images
Text design and layout: Karen Petherick

Printed in Canada

# CONTENTS

# INTRODUCTION

Several years ago, I began to keep track of quotations that appealed to me. I needed them for a broad range of speeches, introductions and observations I was called upon to give, so I could pass myself off as someone far more learned than I really am. I wore several "hats," whether as lawyer, Olympic official or member of the McGill University family. I started the project as a collection of notes and scraps of paper I kept in a filing folder, which made the exercise amusing, but almost impossible to use, since each effort required the shuffling of hundreds of pieces of paper that were in no order.

The late 20th century imposed itself upon me, as it did with almost everyone. I became, not without some reluctance and some (I lie – with major) reservations, one of the graying generation to venture into the world of the personal computer. I have the technical aptitude of the average stem of broccoli, so this was an odyssey that was undertaken in fear and trepidation. It was further complicated by the fact that, when I was in school, typing was offered only to those unwilling to try their hands at chemistry and physics, so, with great diligence, I have expanded my efforts to the full use of two fingers and partial use of four, using what has been referred to as the "Biblical" system of typing: Seek and ye shall find. I have now reached the point that I have a diffuse feeling of when I have just made a mistake, a feeling that is, unfortunately always after, and never before, the fact. I learned to deal with harsh and unappealable judgment of the computer: You have performed an illegal operation and this application will be terminated. And, most of all, I learned never, under any circumstance, to enter the "help" application. It was clear that whatever logic has been incorporated into this feature comes from a different planet.

But, to give the computer its due, entering of the quotations into some sort of order seemed, as if by magic (it is still an impenetrable mystery), to make them more accessible and, finally, useful for the very purpose for which I had begun to collect them. It is amazing how much more attention people will pay to you when you are quoting someone, rather than speaking on your own. Even quotations that border on the banal have a cachet, so listeners can be seen nodding their heads as the words roll off your tongue, instead of rolling their eyes as they would had you said the same thing without the quotation marks. Now, for the sake of completeness, I suppose I have to consider (before rejecting) the possibility that this may have had something to do with me, rather than the audience.

As the collection grew, I noticed that many of the quotations had a common theme – they triggered a reaction and they fit into a mental set that was competitive in nature and somewhat edgy. Not all did, of course, but I found that I tended not to save many that fell into the "moon, June, spoon, croon" category. These may be fine for the standard references and if I need something soothing, or a scholarly collection filled with endless cross-references, I know where to find it. The choices reflected in this collection are deliberately not meant to be the basis for some erudite work, but rather as a practical tool to help someone who needs to be able to get something started or something summed-up in a pithy manner.

At one stage, I thought that it might be a "neat" idea to put together a reference work I would dedicate to the Type "A" person. The edginess of many of the items I had chosen gave rise to a temptation to move in this direction, although not all of the quotations would necessarily appeal to such personalities. I even had a title for such a work: Useful Quotations for the Type "A" Person. It was (I freely admit) a strong temptation, since I figured that many people, whether genuine Type "A"s themselves, or just wannabes, would love to have such a handy collection. In addition, almost everyone knows Type "A" people and, what on earth can you buy for them on birthdays or holidays? This would be an obvious choice. That, I thought, would almost certainly appeal to a publisher. Plus, the collection is organic and lends itself to subsequent editions. Such a target audience simply cannot bear not being up to date, so there was a natural market and, of course, a steady stream of revenues for the publisher, not to mention the editor. I gave earnest consideration to Mark Twain's advice that, since everyone to whom a book is dedicated invariably buys a copy, one should dedicate the work to the person with the most common name, like John Smith.

Readers will be relieved to know, I am sure, that I put aside such an obvious temptation. Exploitation of the vulnerabilities of such a target market would have been like shooting fish in a barrel and I resolved not to try to take any undue advantage of them. A number of people with whom I discussed the idea of publishing the collection were barely short of snickering about my original plan. You would certainly know what a Type "A" person would want. Well, now and again, there have been occasions when uncharitable souls might have mistaken my natural desire to see that the world worked perfectly as evidence of such a tendency, such a judgment completely overlooked the soft, mushy and poetic inner self that lurks just beneath the surface. And so (not, I admit, without misgivings – after all, how can the world possibly get things right without my advice and guidance?) I changed the focus of the work to something more in the order of a self-help book for those who need to be equipped for everyday life in the fast lane.

This appeal to a kinder and gentler self should put to rest concerns about any crass commercial animus related to this work. Keeping the editor in a financial position to eat a better grade of cat food is, in itself, a worthy social undertaking for which, some day, you will undoubtedly receive your just reward, and I my just desserts, but nothing of the sort has led to publication of this work. Buy copies for every member of your family and for all your friends… .

When I began the work, I hoped to arrange quotations that had some resonance into general subject headings that appealed to me, not necessarily in a rigorous cataloguing sense, but, instead, in and around themes that I might be called upon to address in a variety of social and public circumstances. The groupings of the material are, therefore, arranged in relation to what I thought might be useful "triggers" of thought or observation on a particular theme.

In some cases, the quotations were designed to get me started on a certain train of thought. In others, to close off a line of argument, like the southern saying – you don't dig up a snake just to kill it. In others, the right quotation can be used to bridge a gap that might otherwise have been awkward or risk a conclusion of non sequitur. In many cases, I might not even need to use the quotation in a speech or article. The quotation may well have been enough to stimulate some lateral, even lineal, thinking that was all I needed to get into or to pursue a topic from a perspective that might not otherwise have been accessible, or that would have provided the initial attention-getting hook that ensures command over an audience.

I am often called upon to speak about sport. "Sport does not build character. It reveals it." This statement by Heywood Broun provides a thought-provoking lead-in to almost any consideration of the ethical foundation of sport and ranks with the famous "Damn, said the

Duchess," as an opener that attracts attention. So does Arnold Palmer's observation, "It's a funny thing: the more I practice, the luckier I get," or John Wooden's adage, "Failing to prepare is preparing to fail."

Leadership, a perennial hot topic, and especially so in recent years, can be approached from several directions. George Burns noted, "Too bad all the people who know how to run the country are too busy driving taxicabs and cutting hair," while Norman Bethune was more cerebral, "Every leader starts first by leading himself." And there is the acerbic Publilius Syrus, "Anyone can hold the helm when the sea is calm."

Lawyers are always delighted to hear about themselves and alternate between glorying in the important role they play in the defense of fundamental societal values and absorbing the public cynicism that is, in some cases, equally well merited. "Law is the backbone which keeps man erect," said S.C. Yuter, echoing Cicero, who believed that "To be completely free, one must be a slave to a set of laws," and Roscoe Pound (no relation, alas), "The law must be stable, but it must not stand still." On the other side, as the *Globe & Mail* suggested, "Whatever else their contributions may be to our society, lawyers could be an important source of protein." And for cynical social commentary, Anatole France observed, "The law, in its majestic equality, forbids the rich as well as the poor to sleep under bridges and to steal bread."

Over a period of time, a collection of this nature will result in the accumulation of many quotations from the same person and everyone will find some favourites. Mine include Mark Twain, Winston Churchill and Oscar Wilde. Twain may be the most trenchant observer of the human condition in modern time. "By trying, we can easily endure adversity. Another man's I mean." "It is easier to stay out than to get out." "Man is the only animal that blushes – or has reason to." "Suppose you were an idiot. And suppose you were a member of Congress. But I repeat myself." "It used to be a good hotel, but that proves nothing – I used to be a good boy." "Man is the creature made at the end of the week's work when God was tired."

Winston Churchill worked hard at making quotable quotes, and succeeded. "Nothing in life is so exhilarating as to be shot at without result."

"Dictators ride to and fro upon tigers, which they dare not dismount." "History will be kind to me for I intend to write it." "You make a living by what you get. You make a life by what you give." "Never end a sentence with a preposition unless you have nothing else to end it with." "It is a socialist idea that making profits is a vice; I consider the real vice is making losses." "When the war of giants is over, the wars of the pygmies will begin."

And then, the incomparable sarcasm of Oscar Wilde. "It is always a silly thing to give advice, but to give good advice is fatal." "The first duty in life is to be as artificial as possible. What the second duty is no one has yet discovered." "Bigamy is having one wife/husband too many. Monogamy is the same." "The English country gentleman galloping after a fox – the unspeakable in full pursuit of the uneatable." "It is absurd to divide people into good and bad. People are charming or tedious." "... there is much to be said in favour of modern journalism. By giving us the opinions of the uneducated, it keeps us in touch with the ignorance of the community."

There should be something for everyone in this collection and I hope the reader will enjoy browsing as much as I have had collecting and organizing it.


Richard W. Pound
2004

### Ability

Ability is a poor man's wealth. ~ Matthew Wren, English statesman

### Absence

Absence diminishes commonplace passions and increases great ones, as the wind extinguishes candles and kindles fire. ~ La Rochefoucauld

### Absent

The absent are always in the wrong. ~ Philippe Nericault Destouches

### Absolutes

No absolute is going to make the lion lie down with the lamb: unless the lamb is inside. ~ D.H. Lawrence

### Absurd

The absurd man is he who never changes. ~ Auguste Barthelemy

Look for the absurd in everything and you will find it. ~ Jules Renard

### Absurdity

Every absurdity has a champion to defend it. ~ Oliver Goldsmith

### Accommodation

He who trims himself to suit everybody will soon whittle himself away. ~ Raymond Hull

### Accomplice

He who holds the ladder is as bad as the thief. ~ German proverb

### Accomplishments

Knowledge may give weight, but accomplishments give lustre, and many more people see than weigh. ~ Lord Chesterfield

Small deeds done are better than great deeds planned. ~ Peter Marshall

The world which credits what is done,
Is cold to all that might have been. ~ Alfred, Lord Tennyson

Those who have done nothing, fancy themselves capable of everything: while those who have exerted themselves to the utmost only feel the limitation of their powers. ~ William Hazlitt

## Achievement

There is no limit to what a man can achieve as long as he doesn't care who gets the credit. ~ Bob Woodruff, Coca-Cola

It is amazing what you can accomplish if you do not care who gets the credit. ~ Harry S. Truman

There is no penalty for overachievement. ~ George Miller

We can spend our whole lives underachieving. ~ Philip Crosby

Ours is a world where people don't know what they want and are willing to go through hell to get it. ~ Don Marquis

I believe you rarely achieve more than you expect. ~ Carol Grosse

I found Rome a city of bricks and left it a city of marble.
~ Augustus Caesar

From above, we can hear the crowd below, growling and grumbling and taking it easy. ~ Robert Dollar, U.S. shipowner

The greatest pleasure in life is doing what people say you cannot do.
~ Walter Bagehot

In the long run men hit only what they aim at. ~ Henry David Thoreau

What you have become is the price you paid to get what you used to want. ~ Mignon McLaughlin

It's not what you are; it's what you don't become that hurts.
~ Oscar Levant

You're not going to get anywhere if you think you're already there.
~ Anonymous

He who would do some great thing in this short life must apply himself to work with such a concentration of his forces as, to idle spectators who live only to amuse themselves, looks like insanity.
~ Francis Parkman

Having what you want is not nearly so interesting as getting what you want. ~ Sydney Tremayne

Well done is better than well said. ~ Benjamin Franklin

## Acting

The most important thing in acting is honesty. If you can fake that, you've got it made. ~ George Burns, 1984

Acting is the art of being private in public. ~ William Hutt, 1976

Acting is standing up naked and turning around very slowly.
~ Rosalind Russell

If an actor acts it out, I hardly listen. I keep worrying about whether he's going to do something phoney every minute.
~ Holden Caulfield, *Catcher in the Rye*

If it's a good script I'll do it. And if it's a bad script, and they pay me enough, I'll do it. ~ George Burns, 1988

One of my chief regrets during my years in the theatre is that I couldn't sit in the audience and watch me. ~ John Barrymore

Just know your lines, and don't bump into the furniture. ~ Noel Coward

If at first you don't succeed, try, try, try again. Then use a stunt double.
~ Arnold Schwarzenegger

## Action

Never mistake motion for action. ~ Ernest Hemingway

Never confuse motion with action. ~ Benjamin Franklin

A good edge is good for nothing, if it has nothing to cut.
~ Thomas Fuller, M.D.

The ancestor of every action is a thought. ~ Ralph Waldo Emerson

Word is a shadow of a deed. ~ Democritus

The profit of a good action is to have done it. ~ Seneca

One starts an action,
Simply because one must do something. ~ T. S. Eliot

You can't unscramble scrambled eggs. ~ American proverb

Seize the day (Carpe diem): trust not to the morrow. ~ Horace

## Actions

Words without actions are assassins of idealism. ~ Herbert Hoover

Do what you can, with what you have, where you are. ~ Unknown

Rebellion against your handicaps gets you nowhere. Self-pity gets you nowhere. One must have the adventurous daring to accept oneself as a bundle of possibilities and undertake the most interesting game in the world – making the most of one's best. ~ Harry Emerson Fosdick

As I grow older, I pay less attention to what men say. I just watch what they do. ~ Andrew Carnegie

Don't stand shivering upon the bank; plunge in at once, and have it over. ~ Thomas Chandler Haliburton

Don't let what you cannot do interfere with what you can do. ~ Anonymous

It is no profit to have learned well, if you neglect to do well. ~ Publilius Syrus

Action springs not from thought, but from a readiness for responsibility. ~ Dietrich Bonhoeffer

A man's most open actions have a secret side to them. ~ Joseph Conrad

The best way to avoid a bad action is by doing a good one for there is no difficulty in the world like that of trying to do nothing. ~ John Clare in *Fragments*

What you do speaks so loud I cannot hear what you say. ~ Ralph Waldo Emerson

We are all inclined to judge ourselves by our ideals, others by their acts. ~ Harold Nicholson

He who means well is useless unless he does well. ~ Plautus

Action is thought tempered by illusion. ~ Elbert Hubbard

Could everything be done twice, everything would be done better. ~ German proverb

A stone thrown at the right time is better than gold given at the wrong time. ~ Persian proverb

To do certain crazy things, one must behave like a coachman who has let go of the reins and fallen asleep. ~ Jules Renard

You cannot write in the chimney with charcoal. ~ Russian proverb

Well done is better than well said. ~ Anonymous

Actions lie louder than words. ~ Carolyn Wells

It is circumstances and proper timing that give an action its character and make it either good or bad. ~ Agesilaus

He who desires but acts not breeds pestilence. ~ William Blake

The actions of men are the best interpreters of their thoughts.
~ John Locke

You don't make sheep any fatter by weighing them. ~ Scottish proverb

Strong reasons make strong actions. ~ Shakespeare

To every action there is always opposed an equal reaction.
~ Sir Isaac Newton

Men imagine that they communicate their virtue or vice only by overt actions, and do not see that virtue or vice emit a breath every moment.
~ Ralph Waldo Emerson

## Activity

Furious activity is no substitute for understanding. ~ H.H. Williams

Creative activity could be described as a type of learning process where the teacher and pupil are located in the same individual.
~ Arthur Koestler in *Drinkers of Infinity*, 1967

## Actors

We used to have actresses trying to become stars; now we have stars trying to become actresses. ~ Laurence Olivier

In the theatre, the director is God – but unfortunately, the actors are atheists. ~ Zarko Petan in *The Penguin Dictionary of Twentieth-Century Quotations*

You'd throw tomatoes at bad actors and performers and it was much more intentionally vicious. A pie might be more of a corrective....
You don't hurt anybody when you plop a pie in their face.
~ Jack Nachbar, Prof. Emeritus of popular culture at Bowling Green State Univ. in Ohio

Shakespeare is so tiring. You never get a chance to sit down unless you're a king. ~ Josephine Hull

## Adapt

Adapt or perish, now as ever, is Nature's inexorable imperative.
~ H.G. Wells

## Addiction

Addiction is a friendship without a friend. ~ Connie Palmen

## Adjourn

A motion to adjourn is always in order. ~ Robert Heinlein

## Admiration

It is better in some respects to be admired by those with whom you live, than to be loved by them. And this is not on account of any gratification of vanity, but because admiration is so much more tolerant than love. ~ Sir Arthur Helps

Admiration: Our polite recognition of another's resemblance to ourselves. ~ Ambrose Bierce

## Adolescence

In later life, we look at things in a more practical way, in full conformity with the rest of society, but adolescence is the only period in which we learn anything. ~ Marcel Proust

## Advantage

It's them as take advantage that get advantage in this world.
~ George Eliot

Move only if there is a real advantage to be gained. ~ Sun Tzu

## Adversity

A smooth sea never made a skillful mariner; neither do uninterrupted prosperity and success qualify men for usefulness and happiness. If adversity hath killed thousands, prosperity hath killed his ten thousands; therefore adversity is to be preferred. The one deceives, the other instructs; the one is miserably happy, the other happily miserable; and therefore many philosophers have voluntarily sought adversity and commended it in their precepts. ~ Richard E. Burton, U.S. author

Even after a bad harvest there must be sowing. ~ Seneca

By trying we can easily endure adversity. Another man's I mean.
~ Mark Twain

Prosperity tries the fortunate; adversity the great. ~ Pliny the Younger

Adversity reveals genius; prosperity conceals it. ~ Horace

You can't have more bedbugs than a blanketful. ~ Spanish proverb

Adversity is the first path to truth. ~ Lord Byron

The good things which belong to posterity are to be wished, but the good things that belong to adversity are to be admired. ~ Seneca

You'll never find a better sparring partner than adversity. ~ Walt Schmidt

## Advertisements

You can tell the ideals of a nation by its advertisements.
~ Norman Douglas, British novelist

Ads are the cave art of the 20th century. ~ Marshall McLuhan

When the gods wish to punish us, they make us believe our own advertising. ~ Daniel Boorstin

## Advice

"Be Yourself" is the worst advice you can give to some people.
~ Tom Mason

It is always a silly thing to give advice, but to give good advice is fatal.
~ Oscar Wilde

When we ask for advice, we are usually looking for an accomplice.
~ Marquis de la Grange

We are apt to be very pert at censuring others, where we will not endure advice ourselves. ~ William Penn

No one wants advice, only corroboration. ~ John Steinbeck

Never trust the advice of a man in difficulties. ~ Aesop

Hear the words of the wise, and apply thine heart unto my knowledge.
~ The Bible

Why should we ever go abroad, even across the way, to ask a neighbour's advice? There is a nearer neighbour within us incessantly telling us how we should behave. But we wait for the neighbour without to tell us of some false, easier way. ~ Henry David Thoreau

There are more old drunkards than old doctors. ~ Benjamin Franklin

There is some advice that is too good – the advice to love your enemies, for example. ~ Ed Howe

Advice is what we ask for when we already know the answer but wish we didn't. ~ Erica Jong

## Advocacy

It is wholly legitimate, in the pursuit of advocacy, to turn to its fullest account a knowledge of the psychology of those you seek to persuade. That – indeed – is much of what the technique of persuasion is about. ~ Sir David Napley

Just as there should be a reason for every word, there should be a reason for every sentence in the composition of written advocacy. ~ Paul M. Perell

## Affectation

Affected simplicity is an elegant imposture. ~ La Rochefoucauld

Any affectation whatsoever in dress implies … a flaw in the understanding. ~ Lord Chesterfield

## Africa

The darkest thing about Africa has always been our ignorance of it. ~ George Kimble, 1951

There is always something new out of Africa. ~ Pliny the Elder

## After-the-Fact

It's but little good you'll do a-watering the last year's crops. ~ George Eliot

## Afterlife

I don't believe in an afterlife, although I am bringing a change of underwear. ~ Woody Allen

## Age

For the unlearned, old age is winter; for the learned, it is the season of the harvest. ~ Hasidic saying

My hope is to have everybody die young as late as possible. ~ Jean Mayer

I'll never make the mistake of being 70 again. ~ Casey Stengel, fired by NY Yankees management as part of youth movement

If you want to grow old gracefully, don't try new dances. ~ Texas Bit Bender in *Just One Fool Thing After Another: A Cowfolks' Guide to Romance*

When one has reached eighty-one one likes to sit back and let the world turn by itself, without trying to push. ~ Sean O'Casey

Every age has a keyhole to which its eye is pasted. ~ Mary McCarthy, 1953

The man who views the world at 50 the same way he did at 20 has wasted 30 years of his life. ~ Muhammad Ali, 1975

One of the delights of age, and beyond the grasp of youth, is that of Not Going. ~ J.B. Priestly

Age is not important – unless you're a cheese. ~ Helen Hayes

We grow old more through indolence than age. ~ Christina of Sweden

Don't let Father Time kick sand in your face. ~ Heathcote Williams

One starts to get young at the age of 60, and then it is too late. ~ Pablo Picasso

It takes about 10 years to get used to how old you are. ~ Unknown

Old age is like a plane flying through a storm. Once you are aboard, there's nothing you can do. ~ Golda Meir

Some people reach the age of 60 before others. ~ Lord Hood

Growing old is like being increasingly penalized for a crime you never committed. ~ Anthony Powell

There is nothing more liberating than age. ~ Liz Carpenter

The worst thing that could happen to anyone is getting older. It's like drawing the ace of spades and everyone gets it. Though being very young isn't always great either. ~ Woody Allen

Ah, well, perhaps one has to be very old before one learns how to be amused rather than shocked. ~ Pearl S. Buck, "China Past and Present"

You're never too old to learn something stupid. ~ Anonymous

As one gets older, one discovers everything is going to be exactly the same with different hats on. ~ Noel Coward

I must be getting absent-minded. Whenever I complain that things aren't what they used to be, I always forget to include myself. ~ George Burns

Every age confutes old errors and begets new. ~ Thomas Fuller, M.D.

Keep on raging – to stop the aging. ~ The Deltones

The older one grows, the more one likes indecency. ~ Virginia Woolf

I'm not interested in age. People who tell their ages are silly. You're as old as you feel. ~ Elizabeth Arden

Life's tragedy is that we get old too soon and wise too late.
~ Benjamin Franklin

On balance, I find the world an entertaining place but shall be well content to leave it, holding with Horace that it is unseemly in the old and feeble to linger at the banquet, where they merely spoil the pleasure of other people. ~ Simon Raven, British novelist and hedonist

I don't need you to remind me of my age; I have a bladder to do that for me. ~ Stephen Fry

Every man over 40 is a scoundrel. ~ George Bernard Shaw

Old age is the most unexpected of all things that happen to a man.
~ Leon Trotsky

One can always tell when one is getting old and serious by the way that holidays seem to interfere with one's work.
~ Bob Edwards, *Calgary Eye Opener*, 1913

To grow old is to pass from passion to compassion. ~ Albert Camus

It doesn't matter how bold you are when the dangerous age is past.
~ Noel Coward

## Aggression

What sex was to the Victorians, aggression is to us. We deplore it, sermonize over it, criticize it publicly and practise it privately. We are in favour of peace and go to war at the drop of a hat....And we certainly talk about it and write books about it. ~ Hans Eysenck

## Agreement

Nobody agrees with anyone else anyhow, but adults conceal it and infants show it. ~ Ogden Nash

Too much agreement kills a chat. ~ Eldridge Cleaver

Agreement is brought about by changing people's minds – other people's. ~ S.I. Hayakawa

When men and women agree, it is only in their conclusions: their reasons are always different. ~ George Santayana

## Aim

It is not enough to aim – you must hit. ~ Italian proverb

## Airports

The Devil himself had probably redesigned Hell in the light of information he had gained from observing airport layouts.
~ Anthony Price in *The Memory Trap*, 1989

## Alcohol

Alcohol is a good preservative for everything but brains.
~ Mary Pettibone Poole, U.S. writer, in A *Glass Eye at a Keyhole*

## Alcoholism

The intermediate stage between socialism and capitalism is alcoholism.
~ Norman Brenner

## Alliances

We cannot enter into alliances until we are acquainted with the designs of our neighbours. ~ Sun Tzu

## Alone

To dare to live alone is the rarest courage; since there are many who had rather meet their bitterest enemy in the field, than their own hearts in their closet. ~ Charles Caleb Colton, British clergyman

When you get a thing the way you want it, leave it alone.
~ Winston Churchill

## Alternatives

Who will not feed the cats, must feed the mice and rats.
~ German proverb

Alternatives, and particularly desirable alternatives, grow only on imaginary trees. ~ Saul Bellow

The more alternatives, the more difficult the choice. ~ Abbé d'Allainville

## Amateur

Remember that Noah's ark was built by amateurs and the Titanic by professionals. ~ Sir Arthur Gold, BOA (attributed)

## Ambiguity

Give me ambiguity or give me something else. ~ Elaine Stauff

## Ambition

Ambition is in fact the avarice of power. ~ Charles Caleb Colton

All my life I wanted to be somebody. Now I realize I should have been more specific. ~ Lily Tomlin (attributed)

Well it is known that ambition can creep as well as soar. ~ Edmund Burke

If you do not raise your eyes, you will think you are the highest point. ~ Antonio Porchia

A man's feet must be planted in his country, but his eyes should survey the world. ~ George Santayana

Ah, but a man's reach should exceed his grasp – or what's a heaven for? ~ Robert Browning

He who would climb the ladder must begin at the bottom. ~ English proverb

Women who seek to be equal with men lack ambition. ~ Timothy Leary

Keep away from people who try to belittle your ambitions. Small people always do that, but the really great make you feel that you, too, can become great. ~ Mark Twain

Where none will sweat but for promotion. ~ Shakespeare

Always do one thing less than you think you can do. ~ Bernard Baruch

## America

America is a mistake, a giant mistake. ~ Sigmund Freud

The United States themselves are essentially the greatest poem. ~ Walt Whitman

It is by the goodness of God that in our country we have those three unspeakably precious things: freedom of speech, freedom of conscience, and the prudence never to practise either of them. ~ Mark Twain

America is much more than a geographical fact. It is a political and moral fact – the first community in which men set out in principle to institutionalize freedom, responsible government, and human equality. ~ Adlai Stevenson

America is the best half-educated country in the world.
~ Nicholas Murray Butler

## American Culture

We are being swallowed up by the popular culture of the United States, but then the Americans are being swallowed up by it, too. It's just as much a threat to American culture as it is to ours. ~ Northrop Frye

In America, it is sport that is the opiate of the masses. ~ Russell Baker

Very little is known about the War of 1812 because the Americans lost it. ~ Eric Nicol

America and its demons, Europe and its ghosts. ~ Le Monde

I loathe the expression "What makes him tick." It is the American mind, looking for [a] simple and singular solution, that uses the foolish expression. A person not only ticks, he also chimes and strikes the hour, falls and breaks and has to be put together again, and sometimes stops like an electric clock in a thunderstorm. ~ James Thurber

The constitution gives every American the inalienable right to make a damn fool of himself. ~ John Ciardi

## American Life

American life is a powerful solvent. It seems to neutralize every intellectual element, however tough and alien it may be, and to fuse it in the native goodwill, complacency, thoughtlessness and optimism.
~ George Santayana

## Ammunition

Praise the Lord and pass the ammunition. ~ Howell Forgy at Pearl Harbor

## Amnesia

Amnesia is not knowing who one is and wanting desperately to find out. Euphoria is not knowing who one is and not caring. Ecstasy is knowing exactly who one is – and still not caring.
~ Tom Robbins in *Another Roadside Attraction*

## Amusement

Amusement is the happiness of those who cannot think.
~ Alexander Pope

## Anachronisms

What the world needs is more anachronisms. ~ Anonymous

## Analogy

Though analogy is often misleading, it is the least misleading thing we have. ~ Samuel Butler

## Analysis

Analysis kills spontaneity. The grain once ground into flour, springs and germinates no more. ~ Henri Frédéric Amiel

## Anarchy

My political opinions lean more and more to anarchy. The most improper job of any man, even saints, is bossing other men.
~ J.R.R. Tolkien, letter to son Christopher, serving in the RAF

## Angels

Angels can fly because they take themselves lightly. ~ G.K. Chesterton

## Anger

When a man angers you, he conquers you. ~ Tom Morrison, 1993

Speak when you're angry – and you'll make the best speech you'll ever regret. ~ Laurence J. Peter (also) Ambrose Bierce, infra [Speak when you are angry and you will make the best speech you will ever regret.]

Anger is never sudden. It is born of a long, prior irritation that has ulcerated the spirit and built up an accumulation of force that results in an explosion. It follows that a fine outburst of rage is by no means a sign of a direct, frank nature.
~ Cesare Pavese in *This Business of Living: Diaries, 1935-1950*

Anger can be an expensive luxury. ~ Italian proverb

Anger blows out the lamp of the mind. ~ Robert Ingersoll

Our anger and annoyance are more detrimental to us than the things themselves which anger or annoy us. ~ Marcus Aurelius

## Animals

There are two things for which animals are to be envied: they know nothing of future evils, or of what people say about them. ~ Voltaire

I'm all for killing animals and turning them into handbags. I just don't want to have to eat them. ~ Victoria Wood, British comedy writer and vegetarian

To wear the arctic fox, you have to kill it. ~ Marianne Moore

# Answers

Bromide as it may sound, some questions don't have answers, which is a terribly difficult lesson to learn. ~ Katharine Graham, U.S. publisher

It is not every question that deserves an answer. ~ Publilius Syrus

Questions show the mind's range; answers, its subtlety. ~ Joseph Joubert

# Anticipation

Sell not the bear's skin before you have caught him. ~ Thomas Fuller, M.D.

The best part of our lives we pass in counting on what is to come.
~ William Hazlitt

Prospect is often better than possession. ~ Thomas Fuller, M.D.

If pleasures are greatest in anticipation, just remember that this is also true of trouble. ~ Elbert Hubbard

They sicken of the calm, who know the storm. ~ Dorothy Parker

Do not climb the hill until you get to it. ~ English proverb

The arrow seen before cometh less rudely. ~ Dante

Skate to where the puck is going, not to where it has been.
~ Walter Gretzky

We cannot make it rain, but we can see to it that the rain falls on prepared soil. ~ Henri Nouwen

Don't count your boobies until they are hatched. ~ James Thurber

# Ants

Ants don't go to picnics; people take picnics to them.
~ *Globe & Mail*, January 9, 1993

# Anxiety

Nothing in the affairs of men is worthy of great anxiety. ~ Plato

# Aphorisms

Someone who can write aphorisms should not fritter away his time writing essays. ~ Karl Kraus

## Apocalyptic Groups

I am more worried about after 2000 than about 2000 itself… The real problem is in the immediate period after disappointment, the first decade of the next century, one of the tendencies of disappointed apocalyptic groups is to get nasty. They look for scapegoats.
~ Richard Landes, Director of the Center for Millennial Studies, Boston University

## Apology

A stiff apology is a second insult. ~ G.K. Chesterton

Apology is only egotism wrong side out. ~ Oliver Wendell Holmes

Apologies only account for that which they do not alter.
~ Benjamin Disraeli

## Appearance

God has given you one face, and you make yourself another.
~ Shakespeare

There is no one so bound to his own face that he does not cherish the hope of presenting another to the world. ~ Antonio Machado

A clean glove often hides a dirty hand. ~ English proverb

It's not an optical illusion; it just looks that way. ~ Anonymous

Things are seldom what they seem,
Skim milk masquerades as cream. ~ William S. Gilbert

Take nothing on its looks; take everything on evidence. There's no better rule. ~ Charles Dickens

Have an open face, but conceal your thoughts. ~ Italian proverb

I was much farther out than you thought, and not waving but drowning.
~ Stevie Smith

Nothing succeeds like the appearance of success. ~ Christopher Lasch

If you would be powerful, pretend to be powerful. ~ Horne Tooke

The big drum beats fast, but does not realize its hollowness.
~ Malay proverb

Nothing is so good as it seems beforehand. ~ George Eliot

The cowl does not make a monk. ~ Latin proverb

In great affairs men show themselves as they wish to be seen, in small things they show themselves as they are. ~ Sébastien Chamfort

## Appeasement

Appeasers believe that if you keep on throwing steaks to a tiger, the tiger will become a vegetarian. ~ Heywood Broun

## Appetites

Other people's appetites easily appear excessive when one doesn't share them. ~ André Gide

## Appreciation

People generally do not appreciate what they do not suffer for. A thing is held to be cheap if it did not cost dearly. Honour is lightly worn if it was easily obtained. Inherited liberty is too often carelessly used until it is repossessed through sacrifices. ~ Fred Robert Tiffany

## Approval

A unanimous chorus of approval is not an assurance of survival; authors who please everyone at once are quickly exhausted.
~ André Gide

## Archer

The archer strikes the target partly by pulling, partly by letting go.
~ *Bits & Pieces*

## Architect

A doctor can bury his mistakes, but an architect can only advise his clients to plant vines. ~ Frank Lloyd Wright

The great thing about being an architect is you can walk into your dreams. ~ Harold E. Wagoner, 1986

Each man is the architect of his own fate. ~ Sallust

## Architecture

All architecture is great architecture after sunset; perhaps architecture is really a nocturnal art, like the art of fireworks. ~ G.K. Chesterton

Architecture is the art of how to waste space. ~ Philip Johnson

Architecture in general is frozen music. ~ Friedrich von Schelling

## Archives

Of all national assets, archives are the most precious; they are the gift of one generation to another and the extent of our care of them marks the extent of our civilization.
~ Arthur Doughty in *The Canadian Archives and Its Activities*, 1924

## Argue

It is not necessary to understand things in order to argue about them.
~ Pierre Augustin de Beaumarchais

## Argument

Arguments derived from probabilities are idle. ~ Plato

Argument seldom convinces anyone contrary to his inclinations.
~ Thomas Fuller, M.D.

If ever there could be a proper time for mere catch arguments, that time is surely not now. In times like the present, men should utter nothing for which they would not willingly be held responsible through time and eternity. ~ Abraham Lincoln

Don't take the wrong side of an argument just because your opponent has taken the right side. ~ Baltasar Gracian

Gratuitous violence in argument betrays a conscious weakness of the cause, and is usually a sign of despair. ~ Junius

Silence is argument carried on by other means. ~ Che Guevara

There is no such thing as a convincing argument, although every man thinks he has one. ~ Edgar Watson Howe

The aim of argument, or of discussion, should not be victory, but progress. ~ Joseph Joubert

The best way I know of to win an argument is to start by being in the right. ~ Lord Hailsham

An idle reason lessens the weight of the good ones you gave before.
~ Jonathan Swift

Use soft words and hard arguments. ~ English proverb

People's minds are changed through observation and not through argument. ~ Will Rogers

## Aristocracy

An aristocracy in a republic is like a chicken whose head has been cut off; it may run about in a lively way, but in fact it is dead.
~ Nancy Freeman Mitford in *Noblesse Oblige*

## Arithmetic

The different branches of arithmetic – Ambition, Distraction, Uglification and Derision. ~ Lewis Carroll

## Armageddon

Jonathan Miller: "When will it be, this end of which you have spoken?"
Peter Cook (the funny one): "In about 30 seconds time, according to the ancient pyramidic scrolls and my Ingersoll watch. ..."
(Half a minute later): "Well, it's not quite the conflagration I'd been banking on. Never mind, lads, same time tomorrow – we must get a winner one day."

## Armies

When armies are mobilized and issues joined, the man who is sorry over the fact will win. ~ Lao-tzu

Where great armies pass are calamitous years. ~ Lao-tzu

## Armour

The best armour is to keep out of range. ~ Italian proverb

## Art

Art is made by the alone for the alone. ~ Luis Barragan, 1980

Art for art's sake makes no more sense than gin for gin's sake.
~ W. Somerset Maugham

Interpretation is the revenge of the intellect upon art.
~ Susan Sontag, 1964

Art is a lie that makes us realize the truth.
Art is the lie that enables us to realize the truth. ~ Pablo Picasso, 1958

There is nothing new in art except talent. ~ Anton Chekhov

Art is a revolt against fate. ~ André Malraux

A work of art is above all an adventure of the mind.
~ Eugène Ionesco, 1960

Bad art is a great deal worse than no art at all. ~ Oscar Wilde, 1882

If people only knew as much about painting as I do, they would never buy my pictures. ~ Edwin Landseer

Art is long and life is short; let us at least do something before we die. ~ William Morris

Half of art is knowing when to stop. ~ Arthur William Radford

Art is like a border of flowers along the course of civilization. ~ Lincoln Steffens

Art is either plagiarism or revolution. ~ Paul Gauguin

Without art, the crudeness of reality would make the world unbearable. ~ George Bernard Shaw

Art is on the side of the oppressed.... For, if art is freedom of the spirit, how can it exist within the oppressors? ~ Nadine Gordimer, 1988

Art happens – no hovel is safe from it, no prince may depend upon it, the vastest intelligence cannot bring it about. ~ James Whistler

Art is the only work open to people who can't get along with others and still want to be special. ~ Alasdair Gray in *Lanark*

What I detest most of all in the arts, what sets me on edge, is the ingenious, the clever. That is not at all the same as bad taste, which is good quality gone astray. ~ Gustave Flaubert

Art is I, Science is we. ~ Claude Bernard

Great is the art of beginning, but greater the art is of ending. ~ Henry Wadsworth Longfellow

Art does not reproduce the visible; rather it makes visible. ~ Paul Klee

Art advances between two chasms, which are frivolity and propaganda. ~ Albert Camus

Art is making something out of nothing and selling it. ~ Frank Zappa

Art is vice. You don't marry it legitimately, you rape it. ~ Edgar Degas

Art is not a special sauce applied to ordinary cooking; it is the cooking itself if it is good. ~ W.R. Lethaby, *Form in Civilization*

## Artifice

Customary use of artifice is the sign of a small mind, and it almost always happens that he who uses it to cover one spot uncovers himself in another. ~ La Rochefoucauld

## Artificial

The first duty in life is to be as artificial as possible. What the second duty is no one has yet discovered. ~ Oscar Wilde

## Artists

Bad artists always admire each other's work. ~ Oscar Wilde

An artist must be a reactionary. He has to stand out against the tenor of the age and not go flopping along. ~ Evelyn Waugh

The ordinary man puts up a struggle against all that is not himself, whereas it is against himself, in a limited but all-essential field, that the artist has to battle. ~ André Malraux

Suffering is the main component of the artistic experience.
~ Samuel Beckett

No artist wants to be "understood." If he's "understood," he feels superficial. What an artist wants is not to be misunderstood.
~ Ned Rorem, 1980

An artist should be fit for the best society and keep out of it.
~ John Ruskin, British art critic

The artist is a receptacle for emotions that come from all over the place: from the sky, from the earth, from a scrap of paper, from a passing shape, from a spider's web. ~ Pablo Picasso

The musician, the painter, the poet are, in a larger sense, no greater artists than the man of commerce. ~ W.S. Maverick, cited in Useful Quotations

An artist is someone who produces things that people don't need to have but that he (for some reason) thinks it would be a good idea to give them. ~ Andy Warhol

The painter who is content with the praise of the world for what does not satisfy himself, is not an artist, but an artisan. ~ Washington Allston

The artist's egoism is outrageous. It must be: he is by nature a solipsist and the world exists only for him to exercise upon it his powers of creation. ~ W. Somerset Maugham

Too many of the artists of Wales spend too much time about the position of the artists of Wales. There is only one position for an artist anywhere: and that is upright. ~ Dylan Thomas

Every artist writes his own autobiography. ~ Havelock Ellis

An intellectual is a man who says a simple thing in a difficult way; an artist is man who says a difficult thing in a simple way. ~ Charles Bukowski

Good artists exist simply in what they make, and consequently are perfectly uninteresting in what they are. ~ Oscar Wilde

Never trust the artist. Trust the tale. ~ D.H. Lawrence

## Ask

Ask a lot, but take what's offered. ~ Russian proverb

We never reflect how pleasant it is to ask for nothing ~ Seneca

## Assessment

Look not every man on his own things, but every man also on the things of others. ~ Philippians 2:4

## Assistance

In 1784 Benjamin Franklin wrote the following letter to a man named Benjamin Webb:

Dear Sir: Your situation grieves me and I send you herewith a banknote for ten louis d'or. I do not pretend to give such a sum; I only lend it to you. When you shall return to your country, you cannot fail of getting into some business that will in time enable you to pay all your debts.

In that case, when you meet with another honest man in similar distress, you must pay me by lending the sum to him, enjoining him to discharge the debt by a like operation when he shall be able and shall meet with such another opportunity.

I hope it may thus go through many hands before it meets with a knave that will stop its progress. This is a trick of mine for doing a deal of good with a little money. I am not rich enough to afford much in good works, and so am obliged to be cunning and make the most of a little.

With best wishes for your future prosperity, I am, dear sir, your most obedient servant.

Better ask twice than lose your way once. ~ Danish proverb

## Assumptions

Assumptions are the termites of relationships. ~ Henry Winkler

Most human beings have an almost infinite capacity for taking things for granted. ~ Aldous Huxley

## Assurance

It generally happens that assurance keeps an even pace with ability.
~ Samuel Johnson

## Astronomy

Astronomy teaches us the correct use of the sun and the planets.
~ Stephen Leacock

## Atheist

An atheist is a man who has no invisible means of support.
~ John Buchan

To you, I'm an atheist; to God, I'm the Loyal Opposition. ~ Woody Allen

## Attack

The silent dog is the first to bite. ~ German proverb

I fear all I have done is awaken a sleeping giant.
~ Admiral Isoroku Yamamoto

## Attention

We despise no source that can pay us a pleasing attention.
~ Mark Twain

## Attitude

He's a man who, when he smells flowers, looks around for coffins.
~ John le Carré

Is your cucumber bitter? Throw it away. Are there briars in your path? Turn aside. That is enough. Do not go on to say, 'Why were things of this sort ever brought into the world?' ~ Marcus Aurelius

Nothing in life is so exhilarating as to be shot at without result.
~ Winston Churchill

Give me the ready hand rather than the ready tongue.
~ Giuseppe Garibaldi

You can't teach an old dogma new tricks. ~ Dorothy Parker

Man's attitude toward great qualities in others is often the same as toward high mountains – he admires them, but prefers to walk around them. ~ Moritz Saphir

Each day the world is born anew, for him who takes it rightly.
~ James Russell Lowell

About one-fifth of the people are against everything, all the time.
[20% of the people are against everything all of the time.]
~ Robert F. Kennedy

Sour grapes can ne'er make sweet wine. ~ Thomas Fuller, M.D.

There are no menial jobs, only menial attitudes. ~ William Bennett

If you can't change your fate, change your attitude. ~ Chinese proverb

Attitudes are contagious. Are yours worth catching? ~ Anonymous

Haughty, silent faces should not deceive us: these are the timid ones.
~ Jules Renard, *Journal*, 1887

And remember, no matter where you go, there you are. ~ Buckaroo Banzai

You've got to take the bitter with the sour. ~ Samuel Goldwyn

Two men look through the same bars; one sees mud and one sees the stars. ~ Frederick Langbridge

Only the game fish swims upstream. But the sensible fish swims down.
~ Ogden Nash

You've got to accentuate the positive, eliminate the negative.
~ Johnny Mercer

## Attraction

If people don't want to come, nothing will stop them. ~ Sol Hurok

## Audiences

If all the world's a stage, and all the men and women merely players, where do all the audiences come from? ~ Denis Norden

To have great poets, there must be great audiences too.
~ Walt Whitman

## Authors

What I like in a good author is not what he says, but what he whispers.
~ Logan Pearsall Smith

## Autobiographies

Autobiographies ought to begin with chapter two. ~ Ellery Sedgwick

## Automobile

The automobile changed our dress, manners, social customs, vacation habits, the shape of our cities, consumer purchasing patterns, common tastes and positions in intercourse. ~ John Keats, *The Insolent Chariots*, 1958

## Avarice

When all other sins are old, avarice is still young. ~ French proverb

Avarice, the spur of industry. ~ David Hume

## Average

Never try to walk across a river because it has an average depth of four feet. ~ Martin Friedman

The overwhelming majority of people have more than the average (mean) number of legs. ~ E. Grebenik

## Avoidance

He can best avoid a snare who knows how to set one. ~ Publilius Syrus

It is easier to stay out than get out. ~ Mark Twain

## Awake

Better to get up late and be wide awake then, than to get up early and be asleep all day. ~ Matthew Henry, English divine

## Awards

My career must be slipping. This is the first time I've been available to pick up an award. ~ Michael Caine, British actor

## Awareness

Only that day dawns to which we are awake. ~ Henry David Thoreau

## Away

Nothing ever goes away. ~ Barry Commoner

## Babies

Babies are such a nice way to start people. ~ Don Herold

## Back Door

We often get in quicker by the back door than by the front.
~ Napoleon Bonaparte

## Backwards

A step backwards is a step in the right direction if you are facing the wrong way to begin with. ~ Jaime Smith

## Bad Apples

Nineteen fresh apples do not make a single rotten apple fresh.
~ Gunnar Myrdal

## Bad Cases

He that hath the worse cause makes the worse noise. ~ Proverb

## Bad Company

Bad company ruins good morals. ~ The Bible

Bad is never good until something worse happens. ~ Danish proverb

## Bad Days

Some mornings, it's just not worth chewing through the leather straps.
~ Emo Phillips

There are days when it takes all you've got just to keep up with the losers. ~ Robert Orben

## Bad Habits

Ill habits gather by unseen degrees, as brooks make rivers, rivers run into seas. ~ John Dryden

## Bad Language

Among the middle class, especially among its more intellectually inclined members, impurity of language is taken as a symbol of purity of political and social sentiment. It is democratic to swear, and the more one does it, the more democratic one is. The frequent use of bad language demonstrates that one does not aim to set oneself apart from what is assumed to be the great mass of oppressed and suffering humanity. The use of bad language is thus – by implication – an act of compassion and solidarity. ~ Dr. Theodore Dalrymple in an article "Get Stuffed, Sunshine" from *The Independent on Sunday*

## Bad Law

The best way to get a bad law repealed is to enforce it strictly.
~ Abraham Lincoln

## Bad Men

When bad men combine, the good must associate; else they will fall one by one, an unpitied sacrifice in a contemptible struggle.
~ Edmund Burke

## Bad News

Bad news travels fast and far. ~ Plutarch

## Balance

There are many in this old world of ours who hold that things break about even for all of us. I have observed, for example, that we all get the same amount of ice. The rich get it in the summertime and the poor get it in the winter.
~ Bat Masterson, U.S. gambler, lawman and journalist

## Baldness

Baldness may indicate masculinity, but it diminishes one's opportunity to find out. ~ Cedric Hardwicke

## Baloney

No matter how thin you slice it, it's still baloney. ~ Alfred E. Smith

## Banality

Today, thanks to technical progress, the radio and television, to which we devote so many of the leisure hours once spent listening to parlour chatter and parlour music, have succeeded in lifting the manufacture of banality out of the sphere of handicraft and placed it in that of a major industry. ~ Nathalie Sarraute

Banality in the mouth of a failed businessman or an unpublished novelist sounds banal; in the mouth of David Rockefeller or Philip Roth the same words acquire the weight of oracle.
~ Lewis Lapham, *Money and Class in America*

## Banishment

Go, and never darken my towels again. ~ Groucho Marx

## Barbarians

What will become of us without the barbarians? Those people were a kind of solution. ~ Constantine Cavafy

## Baseball

Baseball is 90 per cent mental. The other half is physical. ~ Yogi Berra

## Batteries

I bought some batteries, but they weren't included. ~ Steven Wright

## Beauty

Variety of uniformities makes complete beauty. ~ Sir Christopher Wren

The perception of beauty is a moral test. ~ Henry David Thoreau

The sun would gain nothing in beauty by appearing but once a year.
~ Tom MacInnes in *Complete Poems*, 1923

The test of beauty is whether it can survive close knowledge.
~ Marjorie Kinnan Rawlings

Beauty can pierce one like a pain. ~ Thomas Mann

What is beautiful is moral, that is all there is to it. ~ Gustave Flaubert

The beauty of the world has two edges, one of laughter, one of anguish, cutting the heart asunder. ~ Virginia Woolf

At some point in life, the world's beauty becomes enough. You don't need to photograph, paint or even remember it. It is enough.
~ Toni Morrison

## Bed

No matter how big or soft or warm your bed is, you still have to get out of it. ~ Grace Slick

## Beethoven

If anybody has conducted a Beethoven performance, and doesn't have to go to an osteopath, then there's something wrong.
~ Simon Rattle, conductor, 1990

## Beetles

The Creator, if he exists, has a special preference for beetles.
~ J.B.S. Haldane

## Beginning

The beginning is the most important part of the work. ~ Plato

A good beginning makes a good ending. ~ Anonymous

You begin well in nothing except you end well. ~ Thomas Fuller, M.D.

I start where the last man left off. ~ Thomas Edison

Thus out of small beginnings greater things have been produced.
~ William Bradford

## Behaviour

Never descend to the ways of those above you.
~ George Mallanby, British diplomat

Do not do unto others as you would that they should do unto you. Their tastes may not be the same. ~ George Bernard Shaw

Men and nations behave wisely once they have exhausted all other alternatives. ~ Abba Eban

If you scatter thorns, don't go barefoot. ~ Italian proverb

With so many roosters crowing, the sun never comes up. ~ Italian proverb

When one is on one's best behaviour, one isn't always at one's best.
~ Alan Bennett

## Beings

It should not be believed that all things exist for the sake of man. On the contrary, all the other beings too have been intended for their own sake and not for the sake of someone else. ~ Moses Maimonides

## Belief

One person with a belief is equal to a force of ninety-nine who only have interests. ~ John Stuart Mill

I can believe anything, provided it is incredible. ~ Oscar Wilde

Man can believe the impossible but man can never believe the improbable. ~ Oscar Wilde

We are inclined to believe those we do not know, because they have never deceived us. ~ Samuel Johnson

The brute necessity of believing something so long as life lasts does not justify anything in particular. ~ George Santayana

There is a great deal of difference in believing something still, and believing it again. ~ W.H. Auden

I would never die for my beliefs because I might be wrong.
~ Bertrand Russell

They can conquer who believe they can. ~ Virgil

Man is what he believes. ~ Anton Chekhov

## Belief (unwarranted)

Nothing is so firmly believed as what we least know. ~ Michel de Montaigne

If there were a verb meaning "to believe falsely," it would not have any significant first person, present indicative. ~ Ludwig Wittgenstein

If you believe everything you read, better not read. ~ Japanese proverb

Everything one does enough of eventually generates its own interest and one then begins to believe in it. ~ Alan Dunn

## Belly

The belly is ungrateful – it always forgets we already gave it something.
~ Russian proverb

## Best

There is always a best way of doing everything, if it be to boil an egg.
~ Ralph Waldo Emerson

The best is the enemy of the good. ~ Voltaire

## Betrayal

Everyone has his own way of being betrayed. ~ Marcel Proust

## Better

Any time things appear to be going better, you have overlooked something. ~ Anonymous

## Biblical Tabloid Headlines

Job Outlook Dismal

Man Smites Og: Bashan king dies in battle with Israelites

Mole suspected in Apostle supper club

Salt futures dive on news of Lot's wife

Shortage of Galilean fishermen blamed on itinerant preacher

Pork futures soar in wake of Gadarene calamity

Dieticians claim loaves and fishes not a balanced meal

Social contract talks in 35th day; eight of 10 points agreed, but adultery and Sabbath shopping could be deal breakers, says source close to Moses

Red Sea parted, bridge plans on hold

God confirms change to six-day work week

More troubles at tower, management says union "doesn't speak our language."

Pharoh sets up insect task force after worst locust plague this century

Innovative rib surgery ensures gender balance

Pharoah slams Deity's "pro-Israeli bias" as threat to Mideast peace process

Man brought back to life sues village healer: "I was better off dead."

Galilean council initiates pollution probe after man walks on water

Rescued sheep protests, "I wasn't lost!"

Get haircut or go: Delilah issues ultimatum

Methusala dead at 969; sprightly patriarch attributed longevity to regular begetting

Depletion of fish stocks feared as record catch on Galilea swamps boats

God creates heavens; Earth still awaiting permit

Solomon renders split decision in custody battle

Four horsemen heading for showdown, psychic predicts

Grieving family urges ban on slings for minors

See Page 4 for revised Red Sea tide tables

One-quarter of world's population wiped out in senseless killing of brother

Jonah swears off seafood; the inside story

Miracle at wedding; wine merchants protest

Thomas casts doubt on reincarnation theory

Correction: Lazarus obituary

Social Services questions Abraham: Was sacrifice threat emotional child abuse?

David 1, Giants 0

Wine was watery, say Canaan wedding guests

Witness claims Lazarus was only holding his breath

Ark offers family mystery cruises

Burning bush; arson suspected

Ezekiel held for psychiatric examination

Salome unveiling causes heads to roll

Pests found in apple trees again, garden closed until further notice

Three Wise Men to pay customs duty on imports

Angry captive destroys Philistine temple; Samson "fit to be tied" witnesses say

Rains to stop soon, says government meteorologist; Noah's prediction "pure hokum"

King Nebuchadnezzar sues furnace-makers after three survive

Absalom not wearing protective headgear at time of riding accident

No plants registered for voyage; Noah confronts Green Party

David-Bathsheba love talk taped by Mossad

Lazarus says tomb now surplus

Unusual same-sex stalking charges laid by Naomi against Ruth

Local prophet before human rights tribunal, hires male disciples only

Animal-rights activists demand end to testing of demons on pigs

Gadarene pig farmer sues Jesus for loss of herd

Proposed environmental assessment delays Moses' sea crossing

Good-time girl was enemy agent, Jericho survivor charges

OPEC nations debate ramifications of "miracle" eight-day oil

Mess of pottage scam uncovered

Camel stuck in eye of needle in bizarre religious ritual

Ten new laws written in stone; no amending formula, says Moses

Fish lands man

Philistines demand David be tested for steroids

Money-changers demand better security

Judge orders ban on publication of evidence in case of Susannah v. Elders

"Let there be light" decree boosts sun-block stocks

Who turned on the lights? Creation enters second day

Carpenter won't fix tables damaged by errant son

Noah still dubious; plans Ark II

Gabriel Courrier Co. delivers news of miracle baby to childless couple

Eden Apple Co. opens "pick your own" orchard

Police not releasing name of young offender in "Goliath" slaying

Sodom, Gomorrah see record temperatures

Canadian plows to aid cleanup of record fall of manna from Heaven
~ from "The Challenge", *Globe and Mail*, Aug. 21 and Sept. 4, 1993

## Bigamy

Bigamy is having one wife/husband too many. Monogamy is the same.
~ Oscar Wilde

## Bigots

How it infuriates a bigot when he is forced to drag out his dark
convictions! ~ Logan Pearsall Smith

## Birds

Sir, we are a nest of singing birds. ~ Samuel Johnson

## Birth Control

Birth control is avoiding the issue. ~ Graffito

## Birthday Presents

If one doesn't get birthday presents, it can remobilize very painfully the
persecutory anxiety which usually follows birth. ~ Henry Reed

## Birthplace

The land where you were born lies lighter to your bones.
~ Emily G. Murphy

## Blame

Blame someone else and get on with your life. ~ Alan Woods

## Blind

A blind man who sees is better than a seeing man who is blind.
~ Persian proverb

I have only one eye – I have a right to be blind sometimes:
... I really do not see the signal. ~ Horatio, Lord Nelson

## Blunders

The pain others give passes away in their later kindness, but that of our
own blunders, especially when they hurt our vanity, never passes away.
~ William Butler Yeats

## Blush

Man is the only animal that blushes – or has reason to. ~ Mark Twain

## Bodies

"Imagine a child with my body and your brain." Isadora Duncan, Controversial U.S. dancer. "Yes, but suppose it had my body and your brain." George Bernard Shaw, outspoken Irish playwright

A man possesses nothing certainly save a brief loan of his own body, yet the body of man is capable of much curious pleasure. ~ J.B. Cabell

## Books

There can hardly be a stranger commodity in the world than books. Printed by people who don't understand them; sold by people who don't understand them; bound, criticized and read by people who don't understand them; and now even written by people who don't understand them.
~ Georg Christoph Lichtenberg, German physicist and writer

The failure to read good books both enfeebles the vision and strengthens our most fatal tendency – the belief that the here and now is all there is. ~ Allan Bloom

Books are the carriers of civilization. Without books, history is silent, literature dumb, science crippled, thought and speculation at a standstill. ~ Barbara Tuchman

It was books that taught me that the things that tormented me the most were the very things that connected me with all the people who were alive, or who had ever been alive. ~ James Baldwin

My books are life-affirming; that's why they don't attract the real satanists. It's all in the spirit of romance. ~ Anne Rice, writer, 1993

The reason why so few good books are written is that so few people who can write know anything. ~ Walter Bagehot

The biggest seller is cookbooks and the second is diet books – how not to eat what you've just learned how to cook. ~ Andy Rooney, 1982

Wherever they burn books they will also, in the end, burn human beings. ~ Heinrich Heine, 1823

"What is the use of a book," thought Alice, "without pictures or conversations?" ~ Lewis Carroll

The books that help you the most are those that make you think the most. The hardest way of learning is that of easy reading: but a great book that comes from a great thinker is a ship of thought, deep freighted with truth and beauty. ~ Theodore Parker

Never judge a book by its movie. ~ J.W. Eagan

Thank you so much for your book. I shall lose no time in reading it.
~ Benjamin Disraeli

Wear the old coat and buy the new book. ~ Austin Phelps

Long books, when read, are usually over-praised, because the reader wishes to convince others and himself that he has not wasted his time.
~ E.M. Forster

A book is the greatest interactive medium of all time. You can underline it, write in the margins, fold down a page, skip ahead. And you can take it anywhere. ~ Michael Lynton

Books have the same enemies as man: fire, moisture, animals, the weather – and what's inside them. ~ Paul Valéry

## Borders

Borders are not visible, or religions or nationality. This is a great advantage to mankind. ~ Yuri Gagarin, from space, April 12, 1961

## Boredom

The man who lets himself be bored is even more contemptible than the bore. ~ Samuel Butler

The effect of boredom on a large scale in history is underestimated. It is a main cause of revolutions, and would soon bring an end to all the static Utopias and the farmyard civilization of the Fabians. ~ Dean Inge

It is well-known that evils are alleviated by the fact that we bear them in common. People seem to regard boredom as one of these and therefore get together in order to be bored in common.
~ Arthur Schopenhauer

Bores bore each other, too, but it never seems to teach them anything.
~ Don Marquis

Man is the only animal that can be bored. ~ Erich Fromm

## Boundary

Boundary, *n*. In political geography, an imaginary line between two nations, separating the imaginary rights of one from the imaginary rights of another. ~ Ambrose Bierce, *The Devil's Dictionary*

## Bourgeois

"Bourgeois," I observed, "is an epithet which the riff-raff apply to what's respectable, and the aristocracy to what is decent."
~ Anthony Hope, British novelist

## Boys

Boys will be boys, and so will a lot of middle-aged men. ~ Kin Hubbard

## Bragging

A man has the right to toot his own horn to his heart's content, so long as he stays in his own home, keeps the windows closed and does not make himself obnoxious to his neighbours. ~ Tiorio

Trumpet in a herd of elephants; crow in the company of cocks; bleat in a flock of goats. ~ Malay proverb

For God hates utterly,
The bray of bragging tongues. ~ Sophocles

## Brain

The brain thinks not by adding two and two to make four, but like a sheet of wet paper on which drops of watercolour paints are being splashed, merging into unforeseen configurations.
~ Guy Claxton, British professor of psychology, author of Hare Brain, Tortoise Mind

I used to think the brain was the most important organ in the body, until I realized who was telling me that. I used to think that the human brain was the most fascinating part of the body and then I realized. "what is telling me that?" ~ Emo Phillips

Brain: an apparatus with which we think we think. ~ Ambrose Bierce

Only the man who finds everything wrong and expects it to get worse is thought to have a clear brain. ~ John Kenneth Galbraith

The brain is a wonderful organ. It starts working the moment you get up in the morning, and does not stop until you get into the office.
~ Robert Frost

The brain never stops thinking. If it has nothing else to do, it thinks of something to think about. Perhaps the question we have to ask is not why we have to dream, but why we have to think all the time.
~ Anthony Clare in The London Observer

The limit on human intelligence up to now has been set by the size of the brain that will pass through the birth canal ... but within the next 100 years, I expect we will be able to grow babies outside the human body, so this limitation will be removed. Ultimately, however, increases in the size of the human brain through genetic engineering will come up against the problem that the body's chemical messengers responsible for our mental activity are relatively slow-moving. This means that further increases in the complexity of the brain will be at the expense of speed. We can be quick-witted or very intelligent, but not both. ~ Stephen Hawking in the *Daily Telegraph*

## Brains

A good man can be stupid and still be good. But a bad man must have brains – absolutely. ~ Maxim Gorky

You can grow corn or potatoes, but you cannot grow brains. Brains come hard and they come high.
~ Sir William Osler, 1904 speech to Canadian Club, Toronto

Brains function on a need-to-know basis, and the need-to-know in order to survive on the African plains as hunter-gatherers. It's pure bonus if we manage to understand a bit about relativity and quantum theory as well. I think it's a tremendous privilege that we can understand as much as we can.
~ Richard Dawkins, British scientist, who admits there are things, such as the existence of subjective unconsciousness, that mystify him entirely

We, my Lords, may thank heaven that we have something better than our brains to depend upon. ~ The Fourth Earl of Chesterfield

## Bravery

It is easy to be brave from a safe distance. ~ Aesop

True bravery is shown by performing without witnesses what one might be capable of doing before all the world. ~ La Rochefoucauld

## Brawn

In the scale of the destinies, brawn will never weigh as much as brain.
~ James Russell Lowell

## Brevity

The fewer the words, the better the prayer. ~ Martin Luther

A multitude of words is no proof of a prudent mind. ~ Thales

## Break-Out

Everybody's always talking about people breaking into houses, but there are more people in the world who want to break out of houses.
~ Thornton Wilder

## Brilliance

It's easy to be brilliant if you are not bothered about being right.
~ Hector McNeil

## Brotherhood

Human brotherhood may be a myth, and a weak one at that, but it is the only myth that has yet to murder someone in its cause.
~ Michael Ignatieff

## Bugs

Bugs are not going to inherit the Earth, they own it now. So we might as well make peace with the landlord.
~ Thomas Eisner, professor of chemical ecology, Cornell University

## Bullets

No matter how big you are, five bullets in you are bound to do something. ~ Becky Barron, director of the Wildlife Rescue of the Florida Keys

## Bumper Stickers

There's a difference between a philosophy and a bumper sticker.
~ Charles M. Schulz

If Barbie is so popular, why do you have to buy her friends?

Everyone has a photographic memory. Some don't have film.

I owe, I owe. It's off to work I go.

If you don't believe in abortions, don't have one.

Don't like my driving? Call 1-800-BUZZ-OFF.

Hang up and drive.

So many idiots, so few comets.

Attention: driver only carries $20 in ammunition.

If evolution is outlawed, only biologists will evolve.

Circumcision is a phallusy.

They're not hot flashes, they're power surges.

Christ is coming soon. Look busy.

Born-again pagan.

Love your mother (with a picture of the Earth).

I love pygmy owls – they taste like chicken.

Ultimately, it will be up to God to decide the guilt or innocence of Osama bin Laden. It is our job to arrange the meeting. ~ U.S. Marines

## Burden

A burden in the bush is worth two on your hands. ~ James Thurber

If he has no other burden, he'll take up a load of stones. ~ Malay proverb

## Bureaucracy

I do not rule Russia; ten thousand clerks do. ~ Czar Nicholas I

Every revolution evaporates, leaving behind only the slime of a new bureaucracy. ~ Franz Kafka

The inner spirit of bureaucracy lies in the exciting interplay of nonideas and the effervescent sparkling of human personalities engaged in nondirective pursuits. ~ James H. Boren, U.S. presidential candidate

A memorandum is written not to inform the reader but to protect the writer. ~ Dean Acheson

There is only one giant machine operated by pygmies, and that is bureaucracy. ~ Honoré de Balzac

## Bureaucrat

Hell hath no fury like a bureaucrat scorned. ~ Milton Friedman

A bureaucrat is a Democrat who holds some office that a Republican wants. ~ Alben W. Barkley

## Burglars

I am laughing to think what risks you take, to try to find money in a desk by night, where the legal owner can never find any by day.
~ Honoré de Balzac, on awakening to find a burglar in his room

## Business

Business is the combination of sport and war. ~ André Maurois

My rule always was to do the business of the day in the day.
~ The Duke of Wellington

The only true battlefield of business is the mind of your constituents:
the people you serve directly; your superiors and personal clients; and
those you serve indirectly through your organization's products and
services. ~ Donald G. Krause, *The Art of War for Executives*

If people ask, "How's business?" you must tell the truth, but you must
be excited. Say: "Unbelievable!" because that'll cover it either way.
~ Tom Hopkins, a U.S. college dropout, multimillionaire owner of an Arizona mansion,
and motivational speaker

All the business of war, and indeed, all the business of life, is to find
out what you do not know by what you do. ~ The Duke of Wellington

## Business (Minding One's Own)

We cannot be wrong in leaving other people's business alone.
~ Franco Sacchetti

## Business (and Pleasure)

Business and pleasure, rightly understood, mutually assist each other,
instead of being enemies, as silly or dull people often think them. No
man tastes pleasures truly who does not earn them by previous
business; and few people do business well who do nothing else.
~ Lord Chesterfield

## Busy

If you want work well done, select a busy man: the other kind has no
time. ~ Elbert Hubbard

The bee isn't really that busy – it just can't buzz any slower.
~ Elbert Hubbard

## Busyness

Extreme busyness, whether at school, or college, kirk or market, is a
symptom of deficient vitality; and a faculty for idleness implies a
catholic appetite and a strong sense of personal identity.
~ Robert Louis Stevenson

Nowadays, people don't ask how you are, they say, "Are you busy?," meaning, "Are you well?" If someone actually does ask how you are, the most cheerful answer, of course, is a robust "Busy!" to which the person will reply, "Good!" "Busy" used to be a negative sort of word. It meant having no time for yourself, no leisure. "No, I can't come out this weekend, I'm too busy." Sorry about that, you poor stiff. Now, though, busyness is bullish. Conspicuous industriousness is the rule.
~ Richard Stengel, 1997

## Butlers

Ice formed on the butler's upper slopes.
~ P.G. Wodehouse, *Pigs Have Wings*, 1952

## Butterfly Effect

Tiny differences in input could quickly become overwhelming differences in output. In weather, this (is) known as the Butterfly Effect – the notion that a butterfly stirring the air today in Peking can transform storm systems next month in New York. ~ James Gleick in *Chaos*

## Calamity

Every calamity is a spur and a valuable hint. ~ Ralph Waldo Emerson

## Canada

You know what you need in Canada? You need a dozen or so educated Englishmen to come and teach you how to write. ~ J.B. Priestly

The planet is full of collective apparitions, like Canada, Brazil, the Swiss Congo, and the Common Market. ~ Jorge Luis Borges, 1975

What we do should have a Canadian character. Nobody looks his best in somebody else's clothes. ~ Vincent Massey

Canadians look down on the United States and consider it Hell. They are right to do so. ~ Irving Layton, 1969

I learned nothing about Canada in school. Canada was to the north; Mexico was to the south. The dumb kids got it wrong.
~ Larry King, talk show host

Canadians do not even share myths – those imagined truths that find acceptance because they illuminate the soul and galvanize the national will. ~ Laurier LaPierre, 1990

Canada is one of the most fortunate of countries in that she has not had a battle on home ground for more than a century.
~ Mary Beacock Fryer, Battlefields of Canada, 1986

If I were asked by some stranger to North American culture to show him the most important religious building in Canada, I would take him to Toronto's Maple Leaf Gardens. ~ William Kilbourn, 1984

Geographically speaking, the average Canadian, according to a weighted centre of gravity for the population, lives in Alpena, Michigan, two hundred miles north of Detroit. ~ William Kilbourn, 1988

When I stand on a street in a Canadian city and look across the street, it couldn't be anywhere else but Canada, but how can I prove it? ~ Margaret Mead

The force of Canadian niceness, like the force of Canadian ennui, can be disconcerting to the foreigner. ~ Jan Morris, 1988

Canada has no cultural unity, no linguistic unity, no religious unity, no economic unity, no geographic unity. All it has is unity. ~ Kenneth Boulding

Canada is the only country in the world where being a nationalist automatically disqualifies someone – in media eyes – as a serious person. ~ Michael Valpy, Canadian journalist

Now I don't want you behaving like normal restrained Canadians. ~ Mick Jagger

When I first came to Canada, I had to say my backup boys were from Nashville or Memphis or somewhere – instead of Canadians, which is what they were....This country's got everything but confidence. ~ Rompin' Ronnie Hawkins

Canada is a country so square, even the female impersonators are women. ~ Richard Benner

I don't even know what street Canada is on. ~ Al Capone

When they said Canada, I thought it would be up in the mountains somewhere. ~ Marilyn Monroe

Canada is an interesting place – the rest of the world thinks so, even if Canadians don't. ~ Terence Green, Canadian science fiction writer

As Bytown [Ottawa] is not overrun with Americans it may probably turn out a moral, well-behaved town, and afford a lesson to its neighbours. ~ John MacTaggart, *Three Years in Canada*, 1829

There is no authentic report of wolves ever having killed a human being in the Canadian North; although there must have been times when the temptation was well-nigh irresistible. ~ Farley Mowat, *Never Cry Wolf*

Canadians are generally indistinguishable from Americans and the surest way of telling the two apart is to make this observation to a Canadian. ~ Richard Starnes

No matter how the nation's books are finally audited, one asset outweighs all the liabilities – Canadian society is as free as any ever known in the record of an always tormented world. ~ Bruce Hutchison, *The Unfinished Country*

A Canadian is someone who knows how to make love in a canoe.
~ Pierre Berton

I have to say here that Canadian literature, coast to coast, is literally squirming with fish. I could have done a whole anthology of fish stories alone. Seems they're as important in the minds of writers as they are in those of government negotiators, a rare overlap.
~ Margaret Atwood, *The CanLit Foodbook*

Americans are benevolently ignorant about Canada, while Canadians are malevolently well informed about the United States.
~ J. Bartlet Brebner

This is the only country in the world where, in thousands of gardens, tomato plants are held up with broken hockey sticks. This is a unique Canadian happening.
~ Robert Harney, director, Multicultural Historical Society of Ontario, 1987

Yet this is also Canada, my friend, yours to absolve of ruin, or make an end. ~ Malcolm Lowry

## Candle

A candle loses nothing by lighting another candle. ~ Unknown

## Candour

Candour and generosity, unless tempered by due moderation, lead to ruin. ~ Tacitus

## Capital Market

The capital market has the memory of an elephant, the legs of a hare, and the heart of a deer. ~ *Globe and Mail*, August 20, 1993

If the market falls several hundred points, the experts speak of a correction, but nobody ever calls a hundred point rise an error.
~ Walter Goodman in *The New York Times* writing about Wall Street Pundits

## Capital Punishment

Rich people do not go to death row. The saying in America is that with capital punishment, it is those without capital who get the punishment.
~ Michael Radelet, Univ. of Florida sociologist

## Capitalism

What kind of society isn't structured on greed? The problem of social organization is how to set up an arrangement under which greed will do the least harm; capitalism is that kind of a system. ~ Milton Friedman

War is capitalism with the gloves off. ~ Tom Stoppard

The inherent vice of capitalism is the unequal sharing of the blessings. The inherent blessing of socialism is the equal sharing of misery.
~ Winston Churchill

## Car

The car has become a secular sanctuary for the individual, his shrine to the self, his mobile Walden Pond.
~ Edward McDonaugh, California sociologist, 1963

## Care

If you think nobody cares, miss a couple of payments. ~ Anonymous

If you make a slip in handling us, you die. ~ Rudyard Kipling

## Careers

Do not keep company with people who speak of careers. Not only are such people uninteresting in themselves; they also have no interest in anything interesting. ... Keep company with people who are interested in the world outside themselves. The one who never asks you what you are working on; who never inquires as to the success of your latest project; who never uses the word career as a noun – he is your friend.
~ Roger Rosenblatt

## Cases

He who knows only his own side of the case, knows little of that.
~ John Stuart Mill

## Catholics

Catholics and Communists have committed great crimes, but at least they have not stood aside, like an established society, and been indifferent. I would rather have blood on my hands than water like Pilate. ... If you have abandoned one faith, do not abandon all faith. There is always an alternative to the faith we lose. Or is it the same faith under another name? ~ Graham Greene

## Cats

Dogs come when they are called; cats take a message and get back to you. ~ Missy Dizick and Mary Bly in Dogs Are Better Than Cats, 1985

The Cat. He walked in by himself, and all places were alike to him.
~ Rudyard Kipling

I think one reason we admire cats, those of us who do, is their proficiency in one-upmanship. They always seem to come out on top, no matter what they are doing – or pretend they do. Rarely do you see a cat discomfited. They have no conscience, and they never regret. Maybe we secretly envy them. ~ Barbara Webster

When I play with my cat, who knows whether I do not make her more sport than she makes me? We mutually divert one another with our monkey-tricks. ~ Michel de Montaigne

Cruel, but composed and bland,
Dumb, inscrutable and grand,
So Tiberius might have sat,
Had Tiberius been a cat. ~ Matthew Arnold

## Cause

I would rather discover one true cause than gain the kingdom of Persia.
~ Democritus

I would rather fail in a cause that will ultimately succeed than succeed in a cause that will ultimately fail. ~ Abraham Lincoln

## Caution

If thou canst not see the bottom, wade not. ~ English proverb

He that handles a nettle tenderly is soonest stung. ~ Thomas Fuller, M.D.

The most beaten paths are certainly the surest; but do not hope to scare up much game on them. ~ André Gide

Better one safe way than a hundred on which you cannot reckon.
~ Aesop

Fear to let a drop fall and you will spill a lot. ~ Malay proverb

In waking a tiger, use a long stick. ~ Mao Tse-tung

Wait until it is night before saying that it has been a fine day.
~ French proverb

I will walk on eggs. ~ Thomas Heywood

One should not wear earmuffs in the land of the rattlesnake.
~ Warner Winter

## Cautious

The cautious seldom err. ~ Confucius

I would rather worry without need than live without heed.
~ Pierre de Beaumarchais

The policy of being too cautious is the greatest risk of all.
~ Jawaharlal Nehru

He was cautious, but he was careful not to show it. ~ Frederic Raphael

## Cemeteries

When you live next to the cemetery, you cannot weep for everyone.
~ Russian proverb

## Censorship

Censorship is the height of vanity. ~ Martha Graham

I believe in censorship. I made a fortune out of it. ~ Mae West

## Censure

They have a right to censure that have a heart to help. ~ William Penn

## Certainty

I have lived in this world just long enough to look carefully the second time into things that I am the most certain of the first time.
~ Josh Billings

To be uncertain is to be uncomfortable, but to be certain is to be ridiculous. ~ Chinese proverb

Certainty generally is illusion, and repose is not the destiny of man.
~ Oliver Wendell Holmes, Jr.

There is only one thing about which I am certain, and this is that there is very little about which one can be certain. ~ W. Somerset Maugham

He is no wise man who will quit a certainty for an uncertainty.
~ Samuel Johnson, 1775

Certainties are arrived at only on foot. ~ Antonio Porchia

In these matters, the only certainty is that nothing is certain.
~ Pliny the Elder

There is one thing certain, namely, that we can have nothing certain; therefore it is not certain that we can have nothing certain.
~ Samuel Butler

Nothing is settled. Everything can still be altered. ~ Claude Levi-Strauss

It is not certain that everything is uncertain. ~ Blaise Pascal

An acre in Middlesex is better than a principality in Utopia.
~ Lord Macaulay

What men really want is not knowledge, but certainty. ~ Bertrand Russell

There are only three things in life that are certain: death, taxes and
computer upgrades. ~ Garth Wallbridge

Doubt is not a pleasant condition, but certainty is an absurd one.
~ Voltaire

## Challenge

What's too hard for a man must be worth looking into. ~ Kenyan proverb

We never know how high we are, till we are called to rise.
~ Emily Dickinson

## Chance

How can you say luck and chance are the same thing? Chance is the
first step you take, luck is what comes afterwards.
~ Amy Tan, U.S. writer, *The Kitchen God's Wife*, 1991

Our wisdom and deliberation for the most part follow the lead of
chance. ~ Michel de Montaigne

There is a 50/50 chance of anything, because either it will or it won't.
~ Hank Phillippi

## Change

If you want to make enemies, try to change something. ~ Woodrow Wilson

If we don't change, we don't grow. If we don't grow, we aren't really
living. ~ Gail Sheehy

Things do not change; we change. ~ Henry David Thoreau

Things don't change but by and by our wishes change. ~ Marcel Proust

Change is one thing, progress is another. "Change" is scientific,
"progress" is ethical; change is indisputable, whereas progress is a
matter of controversy. ~ Bertrand Russell, *Unpopular Essays*, 1950

Taking a new step, uttering a new word is what people fear most.
~ Fyodor Dostoevsky

It is easier for us to erect monuments and rename expressways and light eternal flames than it is for us to change. ~ Stephen Rose

One of the greatest pains to human nature is the pain of a new idea. ~ Walter Bagehot

There is rarely any way to make people like change. You can only make them feel less threatened by it. ~ Unknown

The main dangers in this life are the people who want to change everything – or nothing. ~ Nancy Astor

When you can't change the direction of the wind – adjust your sails. ~ Anonymous

The only sense that is common in the long run, is the sense of change – and we all instinctively avoid it. ~ E.B. White

There is nothing more difficult to carry out, nor more doubtful of success, nor more dangerous to handle, than to institute a new order of things. ~ Machiavelli

Learn to love change. Feel comfortable with your own creative intuition. Make compassion, care, harmony and trust the foundation stones of business. Fall in love with new ideas. ~ Anita Roddick, The Body Shop

Change is good, but dollars are better. ~ Anonymous

When you're through changing, you're through. ~ Bruce Barton

You must be the change you wish to see in the world. ~ Mahatma Gandhi

You cannot step twice into the same river, for other waters are continually flowing in. ~ Heraclitus

Old ways will always remain unless someone invents a new way and then lives or dies for it. ~ Elbert Hubbard

I wish to say what I think and feel today, with the proviso that tomorrow perhaps I shall contradict it all. ~ Ralph Waldo Emerson

No great improvements in the lot of mankind are possible, until a great change takes place in the fundamental constitution of their modes of thought. ~ John Stuart Mill

If we want things to stay as they are, things will have to change. ~ Giuseppe di Lampedusa

RICHARD W. POUND

Change is not without inconvenience, even from worse to better.
~ Samuel Johnson

It rarely happens that Saul becomes Paul. ~ Max Planck

The old order changeth, yielding place to new. ~ Alfred, Lord Tennyson

## Character

A nation's character is the sum of its deeds; they constitute one common patrimony, the nation's inheritance. ~ Henry Clay

Character is what you are in the dark. ~ Dwight Moody

Little things affect little minds. ~ Benjamin Disraeli

You can tell a lot about a fellow's character by the way he eats jellybeans. ~ Ronald Reagan

Character is much easier kept than recovered. ~ Thomas Paine

A man never discloses his own character so clearly as when he describes another's. ~ Jean Paul Richter

As we are, so we do; and as we do, so it is done to us; we are the builders of our fortunes. ~ Ralph Waldo Emerson

The ultimate measure of a man is not where he stands in moments of comfort and convenience, but where he stands at times of challenge and controversy. ~ Martin Luther King, Jr.

A man is not good or bad for one action. ~ Thomas Fuller, M.D.

If you stand straight, do not fear a crooked shadow. ~ Chinese proverb

Character is simply habit long continued. ~ Plutarch

Nothing characterizes an individual more clearly than what he finds pleasurable – and nothing is better suited to show up his lack of character. ~ Hans Keller

## Charity

No one would remember the Good Samaritan if he'd only had good intentions. He had money as well. ~ Margaret Thatcher

Charity downgrades those who receive it and hardens those who dispense it. All that is not a true change will disappear in the future society. ~ George Sand, *Consuelo*, 1842

One hand opened in charity is worth two closed in prayer. ~ Anonymous

Charity begins at home, but should not end there. ~ Thomas Fuller, M.D.

## Charlatan

Surely nobody would be a charlatan who could afford to be sincere.
~ Ralph Waldo Emerson

## Chauvinism

Remember, my boy, that you are an Englishman and have consequently won first prize in the lottery of life. ~ Cecil Rhodes, British imperialist

## Cheating

I used to play golf with a guy who cheated so badly that he once had a hole in one and wrote down zero on the scorecard.
~ Bob Bruce, PGA Senior golfer, 1991

Better be cheated in the price than in the quality of [the] goods.
~ Baltasar Gracian

A thing worth having is a thing worth cheating for. ~ W.C. Fields

The world is like a game in which there are honest and dishonest players, so that a prince who plays in this game must learn how to cheat, not in order to do it, but in order not to be the dupe of others.
~ Frederick the Great of Prussia

## Cheer

The best way to cheer yourself is to cheer someone else up.
~ Mark Twain

## Cheerfulness

Early morning cheerfulness can be extremely obnoxious.
~ William Feather

Cheerfulness is a quiet condition; glee, on the other hand, is only desperation on a good day. ~ Aidan Mathews

## Cheese

Anecdote in At the Highest Levels, by Michael R. Beschloss and Strobe Talbott: Gorbachev lunching with Margaret Thatcher, recalls Charles de Gaulle's comment about it being very difficult to preside over a country that manufactures 120 kinds of cheese. "Imagine," Gorbachev says, "how much harder it is to run a country with over 120 different nationalities?" "Yes," interjects his Deputy Prime Minister, Leonid Abalkin, "Especially if there is no cheese."

What happens to the hole when the cheese is gone? ~ Bertolt Brecht

## Cheops Law

No project was ever completed on time and within budget.

## Chicago

I think that's how Chicago got started. A bunch of people in New York said, "Gee, I'm enjoying the crime and the poverty, but it just isn't cold enough. Let's go west." ~ Richard Jeni

## Chicken or Egg

The chicken must have come first – can you imagine God sitting on an egg? ~ Unknown

## Childhood

It's not a bad thing that children should occasionally, and politely, put parents in their place.
~ Colette (Sidonie-Gabrielle Claudine Colette), French novelist

A happy childhood is poor preparation for human contacts. ~ Colette

I have a big house – and I hide a lot.
~ Mary Ure, British actress, on coping with children

Childhood – a period of waiting for the moment when I could send everyone and everything connected with it to hell.
~ Igor Stravinsky

A child becomes an adult when he realizes he has a right not only to be right but also to be wrong. ~ Thomas Szasz

Childhood is the kingdom where nobody dies. Nobody that matters.
~ Edna St. Vincent Millay

There is always one moment in childhood when the door opens and lets the future in. ~ Graham Greene

## Children

Children have never been very good at listening to their elders, but they have never failed to imitate them. ~ James Baldwin

We do our best for our children, and hope they return the favour.
~ Anonymous

Children may close ears to advice, but open their eyes to example.
~ Anonymous

Children need models more than they need critics. ~ Joseph Joubert

Never lend your car to anyone to whom you have given birth.
~ Erma Bombeck

If you have a lot of tension and you get a headache, do what it says on the Aspirin bottle: "Take two tablets" and "Keep away from children."
~ Unknown

My husband and I are either going to buy a dog or have a child. We can't decide whether to ruin our carpet or ruin our lives. ~ Rita Rudner

Children are all foreigners. ~ Ralph Waldo Emerson

I love my kids, but I wouldn't want them for friends. ~ Janet Sorensen

Give a little love to a child and you get a great deal back. ~ John Ruskin

We want our children to fit in and to stand out. We rarely address the conflict between these goals. ~ Ellen Goodman

It is the securely attached child who is the most able to leave the mother's side in order to explore the environment and investigate the objects which it contains. ~ Anthony Storr

There are two great gifts you can give your children: one is roots, the other, wings. ~ Chinese proverb

## Children's Fancy

It is, in some ways, but a pedestrian fancy that the child exhibits. It is the grown people who make the nursery stories; all the children do is jealously to preserve the text. ~ Robert Louis Stevenson

## Chinese

Nothing and no one can destroy the Chinese people. They are relentless survivors. They are the oldest civilized people on Earth. Their civilization passes through phases but its basic characteristics remain the same. They yield, they bend to the wind, but they never break.
~ Pearl S. Buck

## Choice

You have a choice of two things in life; remembering and hoping.
~ Paul Villeneuve

He who does anything because it is the custom, makes no choice.
~ John Stuart Mill

There's small choice in rotten apples. ~ Shakespeare

Nobody can honestly think of himself as a strong character because, however successful he may be in overcoming them, he is necessarily aware of the doubts and temptations that accompany every important choice. ~ W.H. Auden

If we were not provided with the knack of being wrong, we could never get anything useful done. We think our way along by choosing between right and wrong alternatives, and the wrong choices have to be made as frequently as the right ones. ~ Lewis Thomas

Two roads diverged in a wood, and I – I took the one less traveled by, And that has made all the difference. ~ Robert Frost

If you come to a fork in the road, take it. ~ Yogi Berra

I see the better things, and approve; I follow the worse. ~ Ovid

The Other Line moves faster. ~ Barbara Ettore

## Christian

Scratch the Christian and you find the pagan – spoiled. ~ Israel Zangwill

## Christmas

Christmas will soon be at our throats. ~ P.G. Wodehouse

A Merry Christmas to all my friends except two. ~ W.C. Fields

To perceive Christmas through its wrappings becomes more difficult with every year. ~ E.B. White, U.S. author and essayist

## Circles

We all of us live too much in circles. ~ Benjamin Disraeli

## Circumstances

Circumstances alter cases. ~ Sam Slick (Thomas Chandler Haliburton)

## Circumstantial Evidence

Some circumstantial evidence is very strong, as when you find a trout in the milk. ~ Henry David Thoreau

## Citizen

The job of a citizen is to keep his mouth open. ~ Gunther Grass

## City

The city is not a concrete jungle, it is a human zoo. ~ Desmond Morris

## Civilization

When people ask me to compare the 20th century to older civilizations, I always say the same thing; "The situation is normal." ~ Will Durant, 1968

The end of the human race will be that it will eventually die of civilization. ~ Ralph Waldo Emerson

Civilization is nothing more than the effort to reduce the use of force to the last resort. ~ José Ortega y Gasset

To be able to fill leisure intelligently is the last product of civilization. ~ Bertrand Russell

The civilized are those who get more out of life than the uncivilized, and for this the uncivilized have not forgiven them. ~ Cyril Connolly

Civilizations die from philosophical calm, irony, and the sense of fair play quite as surely as they die of debauchery. ~ Joseph Wood Krutch

A decent provision for the poor is the true test of civilization. ~ Samuel Johnson

The path of civilization is paved with tin cans. ~ Elbert Hubbard

## Clarity

I see but one rule: to be clear. If I am not clear, all my world crumbles to nothing. ~ Stendahl (Henri Beyle)

Clearness is so eminently one of the characteristics of truth that often it even passes for truth itself. ~ Joseph Joubert

## Class

I'll go through life either first class or third, but never in second. ~ Noel Coward, 1973

At the bottom, people tend to believe that class is defined by the amount of money you have. In the middle, people grant that money has something to do with it, but think education and the kind of work you do almost equally important. Nearer the top, people perceive that taste, values, ideas, style and behaviour are indispensable criteria of class, regardless of money or occupation or education. ~ Paul Fussell, *Class*, 1983

## Classic

A classic is something that everybody wants to have read and nobody wants to read. ~ Mark Twain

## Cleanliness

Man's partial good resolutions that always succumb to ingrained habit are like the cleaning, scrubbing and adorning that we practise on Sundays and feast days. We always get dirty again, to be sure, but such a partial cleaning process has the advantage of upholding the principle of cleanliness. ~ Goethe

## Clever

Here is a good rule of thumb: Too clever is dumb. ~ Ogden Nash

All clever men are birds of prey. ~ English proverb

## Clichés

Let's have some new clichés. ~ Samuel Goldwyn

## Clothes

We should distrust any enterprise that requires new clothes.
~ Henry David Thoreau

## Clubs

It is easier for a man to be loyal to his club than to his planet; the by-laws are shorter, and he is personally acquainted with the other members. ~ E.B. White

## Cold

'Tis bitter cold and I am sick at heart. ~ Shakespeare

## Collaboration

I wanted to collaborate because, you know, I get lonely. ~ Woody Allen

Every sin is the result of a collaboration. ~ Stephen Crane

## College Degrees

If you have a college degree, you can be sure of one thing … you have a college degree. ~ Donna Blaurock in *Cheatnotes on Life*

Colleges hate geniuses, just as convents hate saints.
~ Ralph Waldo Emerson

## Comedy

What's the secret of great com–? Timing.
~ Richard Curtis and Rowan Atkinson

## Comfort

When the stomach is full, it is easy to talk of fasting. ~ St. Jerome

## Comment

Comment is free but facts are on expenses. ~ Tom Stoppard

## Commercials

Nothing's so apt to undermine your confidence in a product as knowing that the commercial selling it has been approved by the company that makes it. ~ Franklin P. Jones

## Commitment

If you dip your arm into the pickle-pot, let it be up to the elbow. ~ Malay proverb

## Committees

A committee saves minutes and wastes hours. ~ Anonymous

A committee is a *cul-de-sac* down which ideas are lured, and quietly strangled. ~ Barnett Cocks

No monument is dedicated to a committee. ~ Lester J. Pourciau

What is a committee? A group of the unwilling, picked from the unfit, to do the unnecessary. ~ Richard Harkness, *The New York Times*, 1960

A committee of one gets things done. ~ Joe Ryan

A camel is a horse designed by a committee. ~ Alec Issigonis

The committee was divided between the theorists, who had done all their thinking long ago, or had had it done for them, and the pragmatists, who hoped to discover what it was they thought in the process of saying it. ~ Ian McEwan, *The Child in Time*, 1987

Committees of twenty deliberate plenty,
Committees of ten act now and then,
But most jobs are done by committees of one. ~ Old Rhyme

Nothing is impossible until it is sent to a committee. ~ James H. Boren

There is a tendency for the person in the most powerful position in an organization to spend all of his time serving on committees and signing letters. ~ William Osler

If a committee is allowed to discuss a bad idea long enough, it will inevitably vote to implement the idea simply because so much work has already been done on it. ~ Ken Cruickshank

## Common links

Our most basic common link is that we all inhabit this planet.
~ John F. Kennedy

## Common Sense

Everybody gets so much information all day long that they lose their common sense. ~ Gertrude Stein

It is a thousand times better to have common sense without education than to have education without common sense. ~ Robert G. Ingersoll

Nothing astonishes men so much as common sense and plain dealing.
~ Ralph Waldo Emerson

Good intentions are useless in the absence of common sense. ~ Jami

Pedantry prides herself on being wrong by rules, while common sense is contented to be right without them. ~ Charles Caleb Colton

Logic is one thing and common sense another.
~ Elbert Hubbard, *Thesaurus*

## Communication

To effectively communicate, we must realize that we are all different in the way we perceive the world and use this understanding as a guide to our communication with others. ~ Anthony Robbins

Think like a wise man but communicate in the language of the people.
~ William Butler Yeats

What we've got here is failure to communicate.
~ Frank R. Pierson, *Cool Hand Luke*

After all, when you come right down to it, how many people speak the same language even when they speak the same language?
~ Russell Hoban

## Communist

A communist is one who has nothing and wishes to share it with the world. ~ Anonymous

The Communist Party USA today announced the transfer of its financial portfolio from Merrill Lynch, effective immediately.
~ A party press release, cited in Harper's magazine, August 1998

Every year, humanity takes a step towards communism. Maybe not you, but at all events your grandson will surely be a communist.
~ Nikita Khrushchev, 1956

Communism is like one big phone company. ~ Lenny Bruce

## Community

We didn't all come over on the same ship, but we're all in the same boat. ~ Bernard Baruch

## Comparison

Comparison, more than reality, makes men happy or wretched.
~ Thomas Fuller, M.D.

Nothing is good or bad but by comparison. ~ Thomas Fuller, M.D.

## Competition

Know ye not that they which run in a race run all, but one receiveth the prize? ~ The Bible

Competition brings out the best in products and the worst in people.
~ David Sarnoff

If you think squash is competitive, try flower arranging. ~ Alan Bennett

A horse never runs so fast as when he has other horses to catch up and outpace. ~ Ovid

Man is a gaming animal. He must always be trying to get the better in something or other. ~ Charles Lamb

If you can't lick 'em in the alley, you can't lick 'em on the ice.
~ Conn Smythe

A competitor will find a way to win. Competitors take bad breaks and use them to drive themselves just that much harder. Quitters take bad breaks and use them as reasons to give up. ~ Golfer Nancy Lopez

## Competitor's Creed

Every morning when the sun comes up, the gazelle wakes.
He knows that he must outrun the fastest lion or he will be eaten.

When the sun comes up, the lion also wakes.
He knows that he must outrun the slowest gazelle or he will starve.

In the end, it doesn't really matter whether you are a lion or a gazelle.
When the sun comes up, you'd better be running.
~ Management Proverb, quoted by Joe Martin, Deloitte & Touche, published in
*Globe & Mail*, July 7, 1992

## Complain

I can't complain, but sometimes I still do. ~ Joe Walsh

## Complaining

Behold I was without shoes and complained until I met a man who had
no feet. ~ Arabic saying

Complaint is the sincerest part of our devotion ~ Jonathan Swift

It will generally be found that men who are constantly lamenting their
ill luck are only reaping the consequences of their own neglect,
mismanagement, and improvidence, or want of application.
~ Samuel Smiles, Victorian self-improvement guru

Sir, Saturday morning, although recurring at regular and well-foreseen
intervals, always seems to take this railway by surprise.
~ William S. Gilbert, British dramatist, letter to Baker Street stationmaster.

Why, since we are always complaining of our ills, are we constantly
employed in redoubling them? ~ Voltaire

The worst wheel of the cart makes the most noise. ~ Benjamin Franklin

## Complexes

A man should not strive to eliminate his complexes, but to get into
accord with them: they are legitimately what directs his conduct in the
world. ~ Sigmund Freud

## Complications

There's no limit to how complicated things can get, on account of one
thing always leading to another. ~ E.B. White

## Compliments

Never let a day go by without giving at least three people a
compliment. ~ Anonymous

When you cannot get a compliment in any other way, pay yourself one.
~ Mark Twain

To say a compliment well is a high art, and few possess it. ~ Mark Twain

Compliments cost nothing, yet many pay dear for them.
~ German proverb

The paying of compliments is a middle-class convention, for this class needs the assurance compliments provide. In the upper class, there's never any doubt of one's value, and it all goes without saying.
~ Paul Fussell

## Composers (Speaking of Each Other)

I played over the music of that scoundrel Brahms. What a giftless bastard! ~ Peter Tchaikovsky, in his diary for 1886

[Bruckner's symphonies are] symphonic boa-constrictors.
~ Johannes Brahms

Berlioz composes by splashing his pen over the manuscript and leaving the issue to chance. ~ Frederick Chopin

Wagner is evidently mad. ~ Hector Berlioz

Rossini would have been a great composer if his teacher had spanked him enough on the backside. ~ Ludwig van Beethoven

Arnold Schonberg would be better off shovelling snow. ~ Richard Strauss

## Comprehension

Grasp the subject, the words will follow. ~ Cato the Elder

## Compromise

Don't compromise yourself. You're all you've got. ~ Janis Joplin

You might as well fall flat on your face as lean over too far backward.
~ James Thurber

## Computers

The real danger is not that computers will begin to think like men, but that men will begin to think like computers.
~ Sydney J. Harris, cited in *Peter's Quotations: Ideas for Our Time*

Not even computers will replace computers, because committees buy computers. ~ Edward Shepherd Mead, 1964

Electronic aids, particularly domestic computers, will help the inner migration, the opting out of reality. ~ J.G. Ballard

Electronic computers are just a cheap imitation of the original, which is the brain. And as we develop the technology of biology, I think we'll have to start thinking of our own bodies as machines. That's because we'll be able to understand how they work, replace broken parts and fix malfunctioning systems. At the same time, it will be possible to build machines out of the same components our bodies are built out of....I'm as fond of my body as anyone else, but if I can be 200 with a body of silicon, I'll take it. ~ Dr. W. Daniel Hillis

You can't fail to get along with a computer; it will never turn on you, it will never insist on talking about what it wants to talk about or doing what it wants to do. It will never find you boring, never forget to call, never ask for a favour. ~ Greg Easterbrook

Computers are useless. They can only give you answers. ~ Pablo Picasso

What do people mean when they say the computer went down on them? ~ Marilyn Pittman

Computers can figure out all kinds of problems, except the things in the world that just don't add up. ~ James F. Magary

In a few seconds a computer can make a mistake so great that it would take many men many months to equal it. ~ Merle M. Meacham

## Conceit

The conceited man relates only to his own great deeds, and only the evil ones of others. ~ Baruch Spinoza

Try not to despise yourself too much – it's only conceit. ~ P. J. Kavanagh

What renders us so bitter against those who trick us is that they believe themselves to be more clever than we are. ~ La Rochefoucauld

## Concentration

To do two things at once is to do neither. ~ Publilius Syrus

When a man knows he is to be hanged in a fortnight, it concentrates his mind wonderfully. ~ Samuel Johnson

The principles of war, not merely one principle, can be condensed into a single word – "concentration." But for truth this needs to be amplified as the "concentration of strength against weakness..."
~ Basil H. Liddell Hart

## Concessions

The concessions of the weak are the concessions of fear.
~ Edmund Burke

## Conclusion

A conclusion is the place where you got tired thinking. ~ Martin H. Fischer

## Condemnation

I wonder how anyone can have the face to condemn others when he reflects upon his own thoughts. ~ W. Somerset Maugham

If it is the devil that tempts the young to enjoy themselves, is it not, perhaps, the same personage that persuades the old to condemn their enjoyment? And is not condemnation perhaps merely the form of excitement appropriate to old age? ~ Bertrand Russell

## Conduct

Conduct is more convincing than language. ~ John Woolman

## Conductor

Show me an orchestra that likes its conductor and I'll show you a lousy conductor. ~ Goddard Lieberson, 1969

## Confidence

As is our confidence, so is our capacity. ~ William Hazlitt

## Confidentiality

The ship of state is the only one that leaks from the top.
~ John F. Kennedy

The ship of state is the only known vessel that leaks from the top.
~ James Reston

## Conflict

What sets us against one another is not our aims – they all come to the same thing – but our methods, which are the fruit of our varied reasoning. ~ Antoine de Saint-Exupéry

## Conformity

The faces of men, while sheep in credulity, are wolves for conformity.
~ Carl Van Doren

Never forget that only dead fish swim with the stream.
~ Malcolm Muggeridge

I dance to the tune that is played. ~ Spanish proverb

I think the reward for conformity is that everyone likes you except yourself. ~ Rita Mae Brown

We are half-ruined by conformity, but we should be wholly ruined without it. ~ Charles Dudley Warner

Avoid the reeking herd;
Shun the polluted flock. ~ Elinor Wylie

Where all think alike, no one thinks very much. ~ Walter Lippman

If they give you ruled paper, write the other way. ~ Juan Ramon Jiminez

## Confusion

A confused army leads to another's victory. ~ Sun Tzu

If you're not confused, you're not paying attention. ~ Anonymous

I'm not confused. I'm just well mixed. ~ Robert Frost

## Congress

Suppose you were an idiot… And suppose you were a member of Congress… But I repeat myself. ~ Mark Twain

There is no distinctly American criminal class save Congress.
~ Mark Twain

Talk is cheap – except when Congress does it. The government is like a baby's alimentary canal, with a happy appetite at one end and no responsibility at the other. ~ Ronald Reagan

## Conquer

Conquer but don't triumph.
~ Marie von Ebner-Eschenbach, Austrian novelist

You must either conquer and rule or serve and lose, suffer or triumph, be the anvil or the hammer. ~ Goethe

## Conscience

Conscience is a mother-in-law whose visit never ends. ~ H.L. Mencken

The difficulty is to know conscience from self-interest. ~ W.D. Howells

A guilty conscience is the mother of invention. ~ Carolyn Wells

Conscience is that inner voice that warns us someone may be looking.
~ H.L. Mencken

Conscience gets a lot of credit that belongs to cold feet. ~ Anonymous

A lot of people mistake a short memory for a clear conscience.
~ Doug Larson

Conscience is the perfect interpreter of life. ~ Karl Barth

## Consciousness

My consciousness is fine – it's my pay that needs raising. ~ Phyllis Diller

Consciousness is defined as that annoying time between naps.
~ Anonymous

## Consequences

He that will keep a monkey should pay for the glass that he breaks.
~ John Selden, English statesman

In nature there are neither rewards nor punishments – there are
consequences. ~ Robert Green Ingersol, 1896

A great flame follows a little spark. ~ Dante

I wear the chain I forged in life.
~ Charles Dickens (Jacob Marley, A *Christmas Carol*)

## Conservative

A conservative is a man who is too cowardly to fight and too fat to run.
~ Elbert Hubbard

I am not even sure what it means when one says he is a conservative in
fiscal affairs and a liberal in human affairs. I assume it means that you
will strongly recommend the building of a great many schools to
accommodate the needs of our children, but not provide the money.
~ Adlai Stevenson

A conservative is a worshipper of dead radicals. ~ Anonymous

## Consistency

Consistency is contrary to nature, contrary to life. The only completely
consistent people are the dead. ~ Aldous Huxley, *Do What You Will*

Consistency is the last refuge of the unimaginative. ~ Oscar Wilde

We cannot remain consistent with the world save by growing inconsistent with our past selves. ~ Havelock Ellis

Consistency requires you to be as ignorant today as you were a year ago. ~ Bernard Berenson

## Conspiracy theories

We who are mere dots used to believe it was God's plan when a dot that was a precious child or spouse ceased moving, and we found some relief from pain in that. We couldn't know the plan, but our faith told us there was a plan. Now we've subtracted God from the plan, but the plan remains, and lacking clear evidence to the contrary, we take some pleasure from ascribing our misfortune and our tragedy to dark agencies. Thinking of them makes it much easier to abide the dot lifestyle. ~ Stephen Hunter, *Washington Post*, on the popularity of conspiracy theories

## Consumerism

To some degree, the triumph of consumerism is the triumph of the popular will. You may not like what is manufactured, advertised, packaged, branded and broadcast, but it is far closer to what most people want most of the time than at any other period of modern history. ~ J. Twitchell, Florida professor

## Contemplation

The contemplative life is often miserable. You should do more, think less and not watch yourself living. ~ Sébastien Chamfort

## Contention

Better little with content than much with contention. ~ Benjamin Franklin

## Contentment

To be content with little is difficult; to be content with much, impossible. ~ Marie von Ebner-Eschenbach

How is it, Maecenas, that no one lives contented with his lot, whether he has planned it for himself or fate has flung him into it, but yet he praises those who follow different paths? ~ Horace

## Contingencies

Oh to be self-balanced for contingencies. ~ Walt Whitman

## Contingency

Consider the little mouse, how sagacious an animal it is which never entrusts its life to one hole only. ~ Plautus

## Continuity

Continuity does not rule out fresh approaches to fresh situations.
~ Dean Rusk

Continuity in everything is unpleasant. Cold is agreeable, that we may get warm. ~ Blaise Pascal

## Contradict

Do I contradict myself?
Very well then I contradict myself,
(I am large, I contain multitudes.) ~ Walt Whitman

## Controversy

I am continually fascinated at the difficulty intelligent people have in distinguishing between what is controversial from what is merely offensive. ~ Nora Ephron

## Conversation

For good or ill, your conversation is your advertisement. For every time you open your mouth, you let men look into your mind. ~ Bruce Barton

A subtle conversation, that is the Garden of Eden. ~ Caliph Ali Ben Ali

There are only two things in ordinary conversation which ordinary people dislike – information and wit.
~ Stephen Leacock in *The Boy I Left Behind Me*, 1947

If other people are going to talk, conversation is simply impossible.
~ James Abbott McNeill Whistler

## Conviction

Some men are just as firmly convinced of what they think as others of what they know. ~ Aristotle

The strength or weakness of our conviction depends more on our courage than on our intelligence. ~ Marquis de Vauvenargues

## Cooperation

Great discoveries and improvements invariably involve the cooperation of many minds. ~ Alexander Graham Bell

## Corruption

All things may corrupt when minds are prone to evil. ~ Ovid

# Cost

Nothing costs so much as what is given us. ~ Thomas Fuller, M.D.

Costs merely register competing attractions. ~ Frank H. Knight

# Cost of Living

The high cost of living hasn't affected its popularity. ~ Anonymous

In spite of the cost of living, it's still popular. ~ Laurence J. Peter

# Counsel

For by wise counsel thou shall make thy war. ~ Proverbs 24, 6

# Count

One has to be able to count if only so that at fifty one doesn't marry a girl of twenty. ~ Maxim Gorky

# Country

God made the country, and man made the town.
~ William Cowper

It is my belief, Watson, founded upon my experience, that the lowest and vilest alleys of London do not present a more dreadful record of sin than does the smiling and beautiful countryside.
~ Sir Arthur Conan Doyle, *Copper Beaches*

Anyone can be good in the country.
~ Oscar Wilde, *The Picture of Dorian Gray*

I'd rather wake up in the middle of nowhere than in any city on Earth.
~ Steve McQueen, U.S. actor

There is virtue in country houses, in gardens and orchards, in fields, streams and groves, in rustic recreations and plain manners, that neither cities nor universities enjoy.
~ Amos Bronson Alcott, U.S. educator

# Courage

He who loses wealth loses much; he who loses a friend loses more; but he who loses courage loses all. ~ Miguel de Cervantes

There is plenty of courage among us for the abstract but not for the concrete. ~ Helen Keller

This is courage in a man: to bear unflinchingly what heaven sends.
~ Euripides

The secret of happiness is freedom; the secret of freedom, courage.
~ Thucydides

Any danger spot is tenable if men – brave men – will make it so.
~ John F. Kennedy

Two-thirds of help is to give courage. ~ Irish proverb

Sometimes, even to live is an act of courage. ~ Seneca

Courage is the ladder on which all other virtues mount.
~ Clare Booth Luce

Life shrinks or expands in proportion to one's courage. ~ Anais Nin

Courage is being scared to death but saddling up anyway. ~ John Wayne

Courage is the price that life exacts for granting peace. ~ Amelia Earhart

To persevere, trusting in what hopes he has is courage in a man.
The coward despairs. ~ Euripides

## Court

When you go into court you are putting your fate into the hands of 12
people who weren't smart enough to get out of jury duty.
~ Norm Crosby, comedian

## Coward

The coward calls the brave man rash; the rash man calls him a coward.
~ Aristotle

All men would be cowards if they durst. ~ John Wilmot, Earl of Rochester

Everyone considered him the coward of the county. ~ Kenny Rogers

## Cradle

The hand that rocks the cradle is the hand that rules the world.
~ William Ross Wallace

## Crank letters (reply)

Dear Sir:
This is to inform you that some crackpot is using your name and has
recently written to me over your signature putting forth views so
eccentric in nature and so much at variance with your usual logical
style that the letter could not possibly be from you. I felt I owed it to
you to bring this to your attention. ~ John Diefenbaker, Canadian Prime
Minister, to correspondents who annoyed him

## Creation

Every successful creative person creates with an audience of one in mind. ~ Kurt Vonnegut

I don't think anybody in our business is creative. What we do is copy something better than the next person.
~ Henry Siegel, chairman, LBS Communications, 1985

## Creative Thinking

Creative thinking may mean simply the realization that there's not particular virtue in doing things the way they've always been done.
~ Rudolph Feesch

Think before you speak is criticism's motto; speak before you think, creation's. ~ E.M. Forster

## Creativity

Creativity…is mankind's ultimate capital asset, and the only one with which man has been endowed. ~ Arnold Toynbee

Creativity is the ability to see relationships where none exist.
~ Thomas Disch

Another word for creativity is courage. ~ George Prince

Creativity is the power to connect the seemingly unconnected.
~ William Plomer

Creativity is piercing the mundane to find the marvelous. ~ Bill Moyers

When Alexander the Great visited Diogenes and asked whether he could do anything for the famed teacher, Diogenes replied, "Only stand out of my light." Perhaps one day we shall know how to heighten creativity. Until then, one of the best things we can do for creative men and women is to stand out of their light. ~ John Gardner

## Credit

The world is divided into people who do things and people who get the credit. ~ Dwight Morrow

## Creditors

Creditors have better memories than debtors. ~ Benjamin Franklin

## Credo

You were born knowing all you need to know, and don't you forget it. Avoid getting any education that smacks of the ordinary and the mundane. You're not ordinary ... It's vital that you know that your uniqueness will get you through every crisis. You'll get by just by being *you*. Training is for the masses, not for classy folk like yourself. You're fated to be rich and famous, and you don't have to do one more thing to get it other than what you've already done. Just sit back and be your own uniquely great and lovable self. ~ Ben Stein, *How to Ruin Your Life*

## Credulity

The most positive men are the most credulous. ~ Alexander Pope

## Crime

The study of crime begins with the knowledge of oneself.
~ Henry Miller

It is worse than a crime: it is a blunder. ~ Joseph Fouche

Really premeditated crimes are those that are not committed.
~ Leonardo Sciascia

Obviously, crime pays, or there'd be no crime. ~ G. Gordon Liddy

A first impulse was never a crime. ~ Pierre Corneille

No man was ever more than about nine meals away from crime or suicide. ~ Eric Sevareid

## Criticism

A fly, Sir, may sting a stately horse and make him wince; but one is still an insect, and the other is a horse still. ~ Samuel Johnson

The fight against Communism diminished us. That's why we were unable to rejoice at our victory. It left us in a false and corrosive orthodoxy. It licensed our excesses, and we didn't like ourselves the better for them. It dulled our love of dissent and our sense of life's adventure.

In my country, and perhaps in yours, the service industries of criticism have almost drowned the magic of creation. Our intellectuals hate too much: our press revels in public executions. We are poisoning ourselves with malice. Yet we take no risks. We are not brave. Our orthodoxy still gives us no way out.

Yet we have never been so free. We no longer need to clip the wings of our humanity. It's time we flew again. ~ John le Carré

Criticism should not be querulous and wasting, all knife and root-puller, but guiding, instructive, inspiring – a south wind, not an east wind.
~ Ralph Waldo Emerson

If you hear someone is speaking ill of you, instead of trying to defend yourself you should say: "He obviously does not know me very well, since there are so many other faults he could have mentioned."
~ Epictetus, Stoic philosopher

To avoid criticism – do nothing, say nothing, be nothing. ~ Elbert Hubbard

Honest criticism is hard to take, particularly from a relative, a friend, an acquaintance, or a stranger. ~ Franklin P. Jones

It is much easier to be critical than to be correct. ~ Benjamin Disraeli

Doubt is an element of criticism, and the tendency of criticism is necessarily skeptical. ~ Benjamin Disraeli

People ask you for criticism, but they only want praise.
~ W. Somerset Maugham

I do not resent criticism, even when, for the sake of emphasis, it parts for the time with reality. ~ Winston Churchill

I have never found, in a long experience of politics, that criticism is ever inhibited by ignorance. ~ Harold Macmillan

Criticism is prejudice made plausible. ~ H.L. Mencken

Criticism often takes from the tree caterpillars and blossoms together.
~ Jean-Paul Richter, German humorist

A better mousetrap, or a better automobile, or a better concept of freedom, may *seem* to occur as inspiration; but no such "inspiration" is possible unless the inspired mind has first perceived the existing mousetrap, automobile or concept to be inadequate. Criticism, that is to say, and the *doubt* out of which it arises, are the prior conditions to progress of any sort. ~ Philip Wylie, *Generation of Vipers*

## Critics

Asking a working writer what he feels about critics is like asking a lamppost what it feels about dogs. ~ John Osborne

It is not the critic who counts, not the man who points out how the strong man stumbled or where the doer of deeds could have done better.

The credit belongs to the man who is actually in the arena; whose face is marred by dust and sweat and blood; who strives valiantly; who errs and comes short again and again; who knows the great enthusiasms, the great devotions, and spends himself in a worthy cause; who, at the best, knows in the end the triumph of high achievement; and who, at the worst, if he fails, at least fails while daring greatly, so that his place shall never be with those cold and timid souls who know neither victory nor defeat. ~ Theodore Roosevelt

A critic is a man who prefers the indolence of opinion to the trials of action. ~ John Mason Brown

Insects sting, not from malice, but because they want to live. It is the same with critics – they desire our blood, not our pain. ~ Friedrich Nietzsche

The critics are right nine times out of 10. ~ H.L. Mencken

No degree of dullness can safeguard a work against the determination of critics to find it fascinating. ~ Harold Rosenberg

A drama critic is a man who leaves no turn unstoned. ~ George Bernard Shaw

Critics search for ages for the wrong word which, to give them credit, they eventually find. ~ Peter Ustinov

A critic is a man created to praise greater men than himself, but he is never able to find them. ~ Richard Le Gallienne

A critic is a man who knows the way but can't drive the car. ~ Kenneth Tynan

## Crowd

Every crowd has a silver lining. ~ Phineas Taylor Barnum

The crowd gives the leader new strength. ~ Evenius

## Crown

A crown is merely a hat that lets the rain in. ~ Frederick the Great

## Crows

Most people dislike crows because they are just like we are. They hang around in groups and make a lot of noise. They're troublemakers who like to take the easy way out. ~ Dr. Carolee Caffrey, crow researcher

## Crystal Ball

There's an old Newfoundland saying: he who lives by the crystal ball must learn to eat ground glass. ~ Michael Walker, director, Fraser Institute, 1981

## Cult

A cult is a religion with no political power. ~ Tom Wolfe

## Culture

One of the fatalities of our culture is that it has idealized immaturity.
~ H.A. Overstreet

The only culture you want to preserve is bacterial. Real culture is something you strive to attain, not something you keep in a pickle jar.
~ Louis Dudek

A culture is no better than its woods. ~ W.H. Auden

A culture is in its finest flower before it starts to analyze itself.
~ Alfred North Whitehead

## Cunning

A man has made great progress in cunning when he does not seem too clever to others. ~ Jean de la Bruyère

The weak in courage is strong in cunning. ~ William Blake

## Curiosity

Curiosity will conquer fear even more than bravery will.
~ James Stephens, Irish poet and novelist

Curiosity has its own reason for existing. ~ Albert Einstein

The cure for boredom is curiosity. There is no cure for curiosity.
~ Ellen Parr

Curiosity is one of the permanent and certain characteristics of a vigorous mind. ~ Samuel Johnson

Curiosity being one of the forms of self-revelation, a systematically incurious person remains always partly mysterious. ~ Joseph Conrad

## Current

When a thing is current, it creates currency. ~ Marshall McLuhan

## Custom

Custom may lead a man to many errors, but it justifies none.
~ Henry Fielding

Customs are made for customary circumstances, and customary characters. ~ John Stuart Mill

How many things, both just and unjust, are sanctioned by custom!
~ Terence (Publius Terentius Afer)

There is no conceivable human action which custom has not at one time justified and at another condemned. ~ Joseph Wood Krutch

An old custom is so sacred when it is bad! ~ Hector Berlioz

A custom without truth is but an old error. ~ Thomas Fuller, M.D.

The perpetual obstacle to all human advancement is custom.
~ John Stuart Mill

## Cut

Never cut what you can untie. ~ Joseph Joubert

## Cynicism

If I'm realistic at all, people translate that into cynicism. ~ Woody Allen

The opposite of creativity is cynicism. ~ Esa Saarinen

The power of accurate observation is commonly called cynicism by those who have not got it. ~ George Bernard Shaw

Cynicism is an unpleasant way of saying the truth. ~ Lillian Hellman

## Cynics

The cynic never grows up, but commits intellectual suicide.
~ Charles Reynolds Brown

It takes a clever man to turn cynic and a wise man to be clever enough not to. ~ Fannie Hurst

What is a cynic? A man who knows the price of everything and the value of nothing. ~ Oscar Wilde

## Dance

The man who can't dance thinks the band is no good. ~ Polish proverb

For children and youth, dancing in the parlour or on the green may be a very pleasant and healthful amusement, but when we see older people dancing we are ready to ask with the Chinese: "Why don't you have your servants do it for you?" ~ Sir Joshua Reynolds

Lighter than a cork, I danced on the waves. ~ Arthur Rimbaud

## Danger

Don't think there are no crocodiles just because the water is calm.
~ Malaysian proverb

Our safety is not in blindness, but in facing our dangers.
~ Johann von Schiller

Those who'll play with cats must expect to be scratched.
~ Miguel de Cervantes

Dangers, by being despised, grow great. ~ Edmund Burke

Water can be good and bad, useful and dangerous. To the danger, however, a remedy has been found: learning to swim. ~ Democritus

## Daring

All serious daring starts from within. ~ Eudora Welty

## Dark Ages

In the future the so-called Dark Ages will perhaps be lengthened to include our own. ~ Georg Christoph Lichtenberg

### Dark Side

Everyone is a moon, and has a dark side which he never shows to anybody. ~ Mark Twain

### Data

Data data everywhere but not a thought to think. ~ Theodore Roszak

### Dates

I was on a date recently, and the guy took me horseback riding. That was kind of fun, until we ran out of quarters. ~ Susie Loucks

I've been on so many blind dates, I should get a free dog.
~ Wendy Liebman

### Daughters

To a father waxing old, nothing is dearer than a daughter. Sons have spirits of higher pitch, but less inclined to sweet, enduring fondness.
~ Euripides

### Days

Why are our days numbered and not, say, lettered? ~ Woody Allen

### Dead

The dead don't die. They look on and help. ~ D.H. Lawrence

We owe respect to the living; to the dead we owe only truth. ~ Voltaire

### Death

One dies only once, and it's for such a long time! ~ Molière

When I die, I want to die like my grandfather, peacefully, in my sleep and with a smile on my face, not terrified and screaming, like the passengers in his car. ~ Unknown

Death does determine life....Once life is finished it acquires a sense; up to that point it has not got a sense; its sense is suspended and therefore ambiguous. ~ Pier Paolo Pasolini, filmmaker

He who lives more lives than one
More deaths than one must die. ~ Oscar Wilde

Death is not the greatest loss in life. The greatest loss is what dies inside us while we live. ~ Norman Cousins

A useless life is an early death. ~ Goethe

True, you can't take it with you, but then, that's not the place where it comes in handy. ~ Brendan Francis

It's not that I'm afraid to die. I just don't want to be there when it happens. ~ Woody Allen

If Mr. Selwyn calls again, show him up; if I am alive I shall be delighted to see him; and if I am dead he would like to see me. ~ Lord Holland

After your death you will be what you were before your birth. ~ Arthur Schopenhauer, *Parerga and Paralipomena*

"No, it is better not. She would only ask me to take a message to Albert." ~ Benjamin Disraeli, when dying and asked whether Queen Victoria should visit him

Once you're dead, you're made for life. ~ Jimi Hendrix

In the long run, we are all dead. ~ John Maynard Keynes

Those who welcome death have only tried it from the ears up. ~ Wilson Mizner

It is a good thing to escape from death. ~ Sophocles

If there wasn't death, I think you couldn't go on. ~ Stevie Smith

The moment you're born you're done for! ~ Arnold Bennett

After the first death, there is no other. ~ Dylan Thomas

## Death Beam

They called me crazy in 1896 when I announced the discovery of cosmic rays. Again and again they jeered me when I discovered something new. Years later, they would admit that I was right. I suppose it will be the same old story now when I say that I have discovered a hitherto unknown source of energy – the Death Beam. ~ Nicola Tesla, circa 1940

## Debt

In the midst of life we are in debt. ~ Ethel Watts Mumford et al.

## Debts

We pay the debts of the last generation by issuing bonds payable by the next generation. ~ Laurence J. Peter

My father taught me never to owe anyone anything, not even a kindness. ~ Hetty Green, whose father had her keeping her own accounts by the time she was 8 years old

## Decadence

Decadence can find agents only when it wears the mask of progress.
~ George Bernard Shaw

## Deceit

Our distrust justifies the deceit in others. ~ La Rochefoucauld

Everything that deceives may be said to enchant. ~ Plato

One deceit needs many others, and so the whole house is built in the air and must soon come to the ground. ~ Baltasar Gracian

## Deceivers

There are three kinds of deceivers: *fools*, those who deceive themselves but not others; *knaves*, those who deceive others but not themselves, and *philosophers*, those who deceive both themselves and others.
~ Anonymous (cited in *Quotationary*, Leonard Frank)

It is a double pleasure to deceive the deceiver. ~ Jean da La Fontaine

## Deception

We are never so easily deceived as when we imagine we are deceiving others. ~ La Rochefoucauld

Who will not be deceived must have as many eyes as hairs on his head.
~ German proverb

People always overdo the matter when they attempt deception
~ Charles D. Warner

It is more tolerable to be refused than deceived. ~ Publilius Syrus

## Decide

Decide, *v.i.* To succumb to the preponderance of one set of influences over another set. ~ Ambrose Bierce

## Decision

It is vain to hope to please all alike. Let a man stand with his face in what direction he will, he must necessarily turn his back on one half of the world. ~ George Dennison Prentice

The man who is denied the opportunity of taking decisions of importance begins to regard as important the decisions he is allowed to take. He becomes fussy about filing, keen on seeing that pencils are sharpened, eager to ensure that windows are open (or shut) and apt to use two or three different-coloured inks. ~ C. Northcote Parkinson

Be willing to make decisions. Don't fall victim to what I call the "ready-aim-aim-aim syndrome." You must be willing to fire. ~ T. Boone Pickens

Give your decisions, never your reasons; your decisions may be right, your reasons are sure to be wrong. ~ Earl of Mansfield

When it is not necessary to make a decision, it is necessary not to make a decision. ~ Lord Falkland

Don't be afraid to take a big step if one is indicated; you can't cross a chasm in two small jumps. ~ David Lloyd George

# Deeds

Our deeds determine us, as much as we determine our deeds.
~ George Eliot

When all is said and done, more is said than done. ~ Unknown

# Defeat

Victory has a hundred fathers, but defeat is an orphan.
~ Count Galeazzo Ciano

Like snatching defeat from the jaws of victory. ~ Abraham Lincoln

# Defence

Isn't the best defence always a good attack? ~ Ovid

# Deficit

The deficit is big enough to take care of itself. ~ Ronald Reagan

# Degradation

Gurowski asked, "Where is this bog? I wish to earn some money. I wish to dig peat." "Oh no, indeed, sir, you cannot do this kind of degrading work." "I cannot be degraded. I am Gurowski." ~ Ralph Waldo Emerson

# Delay

One of these days is none of these days. ~ English proverb

Delay is preferable to error. ~ Thomas Jefferson

## Delegation

That man is great who can use the brains of others to carry out his work. ~ Donn Platt

## Deliberation

Deliberation, *n*. The act of examining one's bread to determine which side it is buttered on. ~ Ambrose Bierce

## Demands

Walking into a noisy classroom, the instructor slapped a hand on the desk and ordered sharply: "I demand pandemonium!" The class quieted down immediately.

"It isn't what you demand," explained the instructor, "but the way you demand it." ~ Unknown

## Demagogues

In every age, the vilest specimens of human nature are to be found among demagogues. ~ Thomas Babington Macaulay

It is an easy and vulgar thing to please the mob, and not a very arduous task to astonish them; but to benefit and improve them is a work fraught with difficulty and teeming with danger.
~ Charles Caleb Colton

## Democracy

Democracy means government by the uneducated, while aristocracy means government by the badly educated. ~ G.K. Chesterton

You don't have a democracy. It's a photocracy. ~ Robert G. Menzies, 1954

Democracy means the bludgeoning of the people by the people for the people. ~ Oscar Wilde

Democracy is also a form of religion; it is the worship of jackals by jackasses. ~ H.L. Mencken

Democracy is a process by which people choose who will get the blame. ~ Bertrand Russell

Democracy is only an experiment in government and it has the obvious disadvantage of counting votes instead of weighing them. ~ Dean Inge

People who want to understand democracy should spend less time in the library with Aristotle and more time in the buses and in the subway.
~ Simeon Strunsky

Democracy is measured not by its leaders doing extraordinary things, but by its citizens doing ordinary things extraordinarily well.
~ John Gardner

Democracy is the recurrent suspicion that more than half of the people are right more than half of the time. ~ Elwyn Brooks White

Democracy must be something more than two wolves and a sheep voting on what to have for dinner. ~ James Bovard, 1994

Democracy passes into despotism. ~ Plato

All the ills of democracy can be cured by more democracy.
~ Alfred Emanuel Smith

It's not the voting that's democracy, it's the counting. ~ Tom Stoppard

## Denial

To deny all is to confess all. ~ Spanish proverb

Never believe anything until it has been officially denied.
~ Claud Cockburn

## Dependence

Dependence entails vulnerability. The relationship between the hunter and the hunted, therefore, has a certain equality. Ultimately, no one can be superior to that upon which he depends. ~ Hugh Brody

## Depravity

No one ever suddenly became depraved. ~ Juvenal

## Design

Never design anything the plant is not already equipped to build.
~ Raymond Hull

## Desire

There is nothing like desire for preventing the thing one says from bearing any resemblance to what one has in mind. ~ Marcel Proust

If your desires be endless, your cares and fears will be so too.
~ Thomas Fuller, M.D.

Where there is no desire, there will be no industry. ~ John Locke

The desire for imaginary benefits often involves the loss of present blessings. ~ Aesop

Having the fewest wants, I am nearest to the gods. ~ Socrates

Remember that not getting what you want is sometimes a wonderful stroke of luck. ~ Dalai Lama

No one can have all he wants, but a man can refrain from wanting what he has not, and cheerfully make the best of a bird in the hand. ~ Seneca

Great desire obtains little. ~ Burmese proverb

Modern man lives under the illusion that he knows what he wants, while he actually wants what he is *supposed* to want. ~ Erich Fromm

## Despair

Despair, in short, seeks its own environment as surely as water finds its own level. ~ A. Alvarez, 1971

## Despise

It is easy to despise what you cannot get. ~ Aesop

We often despise what is most useful to us. ~ Aesop

## Despots

A despot easily forgives his subjects for not loving him, provided they do not love each other. ~ Alexis de Tocqueville

## Destiny

There are born victims, born to have their throats cut, as the cut-throats are born to be hanged. ~ Aldous Huxley, 1928

We are not permitted to choose the frame of our destiny. But what we put into it is ours. ~ Dag Hammarskjold

## Details

It has long been an axiom of mine that the little things are infinitely the most important. ~ Sir Arthur Conan Doyle

Our life is frittered away by detail... Simplify, simplify.
~ Henry David Thoreau

## Detection

Detection is, or ought to be, an exact science, and should be treated in the same cold and unemotional manner. ~ Sir Arthur Conan Doyle

## Deterrence

One sword keeps another in the sheath. ~ George Herbert

## Detractors

Next to the joy of the egotist is the joy of the detractor. ~ Agnes Repplier

## Development (new)

The "silly" question is the first intimation of some totally new development. ~ Alfred North Whitehead

## Devil

The devil's most devilish when respectable. ~ Elizabeth Barrett Browning

## Diamonds

No pressure, no diamonds. ~ Mary Case

## Dictators

Dictators ride to and fro upon tigers, which they dare not dismount. ~ Winston Churchill

## Die

The idea is to die young as late as possible. ~ Ashley Montague

## Diets

Diets are for those who are thick and tired of it. ~ Anonymous

## Differences

It were not best that we should all think alike; it is difference of opinion that makes horse races. ~ Mark Twain

Resemblances are the shadows of differences. Different people see different similarities and similar differences. ~ Vladimir Nabokov

The shoe that fits one person pinches another. ~ Carl Jung

One man's poison ivy is another man's spinach. ~ George Ade

## Difficulties

In youth we run into difficulties; in old age, difficulties run into us. ~ Josh Billings

He who accounts all things easy will have many difficulties. ~ Lao-tzu

All things are difficult before they are easy. ~ Thomas Fuller, M.D.

By heaven methinks it were an easy leap. ~ Shakespeare

## Digital

The days of the digital watch are numbered. ~ Tom Stoppard

## Dignity

Dignity does not consist in possessing honours, but deserving them.
~ Anonymous

Where is there dignity unless there is honesty? ~ Cicero

## Diligence

Few things are impossible to diligence and skill. ~ Samuel Johnson

## Dining Room

A dining room table with children's eager, hungry faces around it,
ceases to be a mere dining room table, and becomes an altar.
~ Simeon Strunsky, U.S. journalist

## Dinner

Everything ends this way in France. Weddings, christenings, duels,
burials, affairs of state – everything is a pretext for a good dinner.
~ Jean Anouilh

## Diplomacy

Diplomacy is to do and say the nastiest thing in the nicest way.
~ Isaac Goldberg

To say nothing, especially when speaking, is half the art of diplomacy.
~ Will Durant

## Diplomats

A diplomat is a man who thinks twice before he says nothing.
~ Anonymous

## Direction

It is no longer clear which way is up, even if one wants to rise.
~ David Riesman

What is the use of running when we are not on the right road?
~ German proverb

Rowing harder doesn't help if the boat is headed in the wrong
direction. ~ Kenichi Ohmae

When you don't know where you're going, any road will take you there.
~ Lewis Carroll

## Dirt

Dirt is not dirt, but only something in the wrong place. ~ Lord Palmerston

It is almost impossible to throw a little dirt on someone without getting a little on yourself. ~ Abigail Van Buren

## Disarmament

The Venus de Milo is the Goddess of Disarmament. ~ Al Boliska

## Disaster

The man does better who runs from disaster than he who is caught by it. ~ Homer

Even if it is to be, what end do you serve by running to meet distress? ~ Seneca

If the sky falls, hold up your hands. ~ Spanish proverb

The sky was too delicate a blue, the sea too green, the breeze too gentle. ~ Paul Verlaine

## Disco Dancing

Disco dancing is … just the steady thump of a giant moron knocking in an endless nail. ~ Clive James, 1978

## Discovery

Discovery consists of looking at the same thing as everyone else and thinking something different. ~ Albert Szent-Gyorgi

People cannot discover new oceans until they have the courage to lose sight of the shore. ~ Anonymous

We often discover what *will* do, by finding out what will not do; and probably he who never made a mistake never made a discovery. ~ Samuel Smiles

The greatest obstacle to discovery is not ignorance – it is the illusion of knowledge. ~ Daniel Boorstin

People who read a great deal rarely make great discoveries. I do not say this in excuse of laziness, but because invention presupposes an extensive independent contemplation of things. ~ Georg Christoph Lichtenberg

## Discretion

A dram of discretion is worth a pound of wisdom. ~ German proverb

Judgment is not upon all occasions required, but discretion always is.
~ Lord Chesterfield

The better part of valour is discretion. ~ Shakespeare

## Discussion (Free)

Men are never so likely to settle a question rightly as when they discuss it freely. ~ Thomas Babington Macaulay

We believe it is better to discuss a question even without settling it than to settle a question without discussing it. ~ Adlai Stevenson

## Disease

Is not disease the rule of existence? ~ Henry David Thoreau, 1851

Disease generally begins that equality which death completes.
~ Samuel Johnson, 1750

He who conceals his disease cannot expect to be cured.
~ Ethiopian proverb

If a lot of cures are suggested for a disease, it means the disease is incurable. ~ Anton Chekhov

## Dishonesty

I have known a vast quantity of nonsense talked about bad men not looking you in the face. Don't trust that idea. Dishonesty will stare honesty out of countenance any day in the week, if there is anything to be got from it. ~ Charles Dickens

## Dismissal

You have good leave to leave us; when we need
Your use and counsel we shall send for you.
~ Shakespeare, *King Henry IV, Part* 1

## Disputants

True disputants are like true sportsmen: their whole delight is in the pursuit. ~ Alexander Pope

## Dispute

In a philosophical dispute, he gains most who is defeated, since he learns most. ~ Epicurus

## Distance

If a man makes me keep my distance, the comfort is, he keeps his at the same time. ~ Jonathan Swift

Distance doesn't matter. It is only the first step that is difficult. ~ Marquise du Deffand

## Distrust

Distrust all in whom the impulse to punish is powerful. ~ Friedrich Nietzsche

## Diversion

Only two things does (the modern citizen) anxiously wish for – bread and the big game. ~ Juvenal

## Divorce

No one ever filed for divorce on a full stomach. ~ Mama Leone

Ah, yes, divorce, .... from the Latin word meaning to rip out a man's genitals through his wallet. ~ Robin Williams

## Doctors

There are more old drunkards than old physicians. ~ Rabelais

The reason doctors are so dangerous is that they believe in what they are doing. ~ Robert Mendelsohn, U.S. physician

Medicines cure diseases, but doctors cure patients. ~ Carl Jung

## Dogma

Every dogma has its day, but ideals are eternal. ~ Israel Zangwill

## Dogmatism

There are two kinds of people in the world: the conscious dogmatists and the unconscious dogmatists. I have always found myself that the unconscious dogmatists were by far the most dogmatic. ~ G.K. Chesterton

## Dogs

I loathe people who keep dogs. They are cowards who haven't got the guts to bite people themselves. ~ August Strindberg, Swedish playwright

You can say any foolish thing to a dog, and the dog will give you a look that says. "My God, you're right! I never would have thought of that!" ~ Dave Barry

Nothing in the world is friendlier than a wet dog. ~ Dan Bennett

A dog teaches a boy fidelity, perseverance, and to turn around three times before lying down. ~ Robert Benchley

If you pick up a starving dog and make him prosperous, he will not bite you. This is the principal difference between a dog and a man. ~ Mark Twain

If dogs could talk, perhaps we would find it as hard to get along with them as we do with people. ~ Josef Capek, painter

Never buy a dog and do your own barking. ~ Humphrey Bourne

## Doing Good

Do not wait for extraordinary circumstances to do good; try to use ordinary situations. ~ Jean Paul Richter

## Door

A door is what a dog is perpetually on the wrong side of. ~ Ogden Nash

## Doublethink

Doublethink is the power of simultaneously holding two contradictory beliefs in one's mind, and accepting both of them. ~ George Orwell

## Doubts

His doubts are better than most people's certainties.
~ Philip Yorke, Earl of Hardwick

Ten thousand difficulties do not make one doubt.
~ John Henry Cardinal Newman

You are never dedicated to something you have complete confidence in. No one is fanatically shouting that the sun is going to rise tomorrow. They *know* it's going to rise tomorrow. When people are fanatically dedicated to political or religious faiths or any other kind of dogmas or goals, it's always because these dogmas or goals are in doubt.
~ Robert Pirsig, *Zen and the Art of Motorcycle Maintenance*

I respect faith, but doubt is what gets you an education. ~ Wilson Mizner

Doubts are more cruel than the worst of truths. ~ Molière

If a man will be content to begin with doubts, he shall end in certainty.
~ Francis Bacon

## Drama

Drama is life with the dull bits cut out. ~ Alfred Hitchcock

## Dreams

Dreams are true while they last, and do we not live in dreams?
~ Alfred, Lord Tennyson

His life was a sort of dream, as are most lives with the mainspring left
out. ~ F. Scott Fitzgerald

People who remember dreams in the morning are probably having very
disturbed sleep at night. ~ James Horne, British sleep researcher

You see things: and you say "Why?"
But I dream things that never were:
and say "Why not?" ~ George Bernard Shaw, *Back to Methusala*

If you can dream it, you can do it. ~ Walt Disney

If you can build castles in the air, your work need not be lost; that is
where they should be. Now put the foundations under them.
~ Henry David Thoreau

The best way to make your dreams come true is to wake up.
~ J.M. Power

You don't need anyone's permission to pursue your dreams. Don't let
anyone tell you it can't be done. Learn to pilot your life.
~ Ron Hall, *Pilot Your Life*

If there were dreams to sell, what would you buy? ~ Thomas Lovell Beddoes

## Drinking

I feel sorry for people who don't drink. When they wake up in the
morning, that's as good as they are going to feel all day. ~ Frank Sinatra

An intelligent man is sometimes forced to be drunk to spend time with
his fools. ~ Ernest Hemingway

When I read about the evils of drinking, I gave up reading.
~ Henny Youngman

## Driving

Drive slowly and enjoy the scenery – drive fast and join the scenery.
~ Doug Horton

If you drink, don't drive. Don't even putt. ~ Dean Martin

The problem with the designated driver program, it's not a desirable job, but if you ever get sucked into doing it, have fun with it. At the end of the night, drop them off at the wrong house. ~ Jeff Foxworthy

## Dropout

If one defines "dropout" to mean a person who has given up serious effort to meet his responsibilities, then every business office, government agency, golf club and university faculty would yield its quota. ~ John Gardner

## Drugs

I hate to advocate drugs, alcohol, violence or insanity to anyone, but they've always worked for me. ~ Hunter S. Thompson

## Drunkenness

Sobriety diminishes, discriminates, and says no; drunkenness expands, unites and says yes. Not through mere perversity do men run after it. ~ William James

## Dull

It is to be noted that when any part of this paper appears dull, there is a design in it. ~ Sir Richard Steele

Mr. Zola is determined to show us that, if he has not got genius, he can at least be dull. ~ Oscar Wilde

## Dumb Blondes

I'm not offended by all the dumb blonde jokes because I know I'm not dumb ... and I also know that I'm not blonde. ~ Dolly Parton

I am a marvelous housekeeper. Every time I leave a man I keep his house. ~ Zsa Zsa Gabor

## Duplication

We must avoid duplication of effort, because that is being done by others. ~ Arthur Mitchell, on retirement as President of Britain's Machine Tool Technology Assoc., 1990

## Duty

A sense of duty is moral glue, constantly subject to stress. ~ William Safire, 1986

When I'm not thanked at all, I'm thanked enough;
I've done my duty, and I've done no more. ~ Henry Fielding

I ought, therefore I can. ~ Immanuel Kant

It is easier to do one's duty to others than to one's self. If you do your duty to others, you are considered reliable. If you do your duty to yourself, you are considered selfish. ~ Thomas Szasz

If we believe a thing to be bad, ... it is our duty to try to prevent it and to darn the consequences. ~ Lord Milner

Make it a point to do something every day that you don't want to do. This is the golden rule for acquiring the habit of doing your duty without pain. ~ Mark Twain

## Dyslexia

DAM = Mothers Against Dyslexia

Then there was the dyslexic agnostic insomniac who lay awake at night pondering the existence of Dog.

The dyslexic cop who spent Saturday nights handing out IUDs.

## E-Mail

Yes, your company reads your E-mail. ~ *Time* magazine

## Earth

Viewed from the distance of the Moon, the astonishing thing about the Earth...is that it is alive. ... Aloft, floating free beneath the moist, gleaming membrane of bright blue sky, is the rising earth, the only exuberant thing in this part of the cosmos. ... It has the organized, self-contained look of a live creature, full of information, marvellously skilled in handling the Sun. ~ Lewis Thomas in *The Lives of a Cell*, 1974

The whole Earth is the tomb of famous men. ~ Pericles

## East

Oh, East is East, and West is West, and never the twain shall meet.
~ Rudyard Kipling

## Eat

There's nothing on Earth to do here but look at the view and eat. You can imagine the result since I do not like to look at views.
~ Zelda Fitzgerald, in a letter to her daughter

## Eccentric

We might define an eccentric as a man who is a law unto himself, and a crank as one who having determined what the law is, insists on laying it down to others. ~ Louis Kronenberger

Eccentricity has always abounded when and where strength of character has abounded; and the amount of eccentricity has generally been proportional to the amount of genius, mental vigour and moral courage it contained. That so few dare to be eccentric marks the chief danger of the time. ~ John Stuart Mill

## Economic Outlook

Put all your eggs in one basket and watch that basket. ~ Mark Twain

## Economics

He who will not economize will have to agonize. ~ Confucius

I learned more about economics from one South Dakota dust storm than I did in all my years in college. ~ Hubert H. Humphrey

The stoical scheme of supplying our wants, by lopping off our desires, is like cutting off our feet when we want shoes. ~ Jonathan Swift

## Economists

We have two classes of forecasters: Those who don't know – and those who don't know they don't know. ~ John Kenneth Galbraith

If all the economists were laid end to end, they would not reach a conclusion. ~ George Bernard Shaw

If the masses are confused by their ignorance, the economists seem to be equally confused by their learning. ~ Fraser Robertson

If economists could manage to get themselves thought of as humble, competent people, on a level with dentists, that would be splendid!
~ John Maynard Keynes in *Economic Possibilities for Our Grandchildren*

Once economists were asked: "If you're so smart, why ain't you rich?" Today they're asked: "Now you've proved you ain't so smart, how come you got so rich?" ~ Edgar Fiedler, U.S. economist, circa 1978

## Economy

Mere parsimony is not economy....Expanse, and great expense, may be an essential part of true economy. ~ Edmund Burke

Economy is a distributive virtue, and consists not in saving but selection. Parsimony requires no providence, no sagacity, no powers of combination, no comparison, no judgment. ~ Edmund Burke

## Editors

Some editors are failed writers, but so are most writers. ~ T.S. Eliot

## Education

Education is what you must acquire without any interference from your schooling. ~ Mark Twain

We must reject that most dismal and fatuous notion that education is a preparation for life. ~ Northrop Frye

Human history becomes more and more a race between education and catastrophe. ~ H.G. Wells, 1920

Should we force science down the throats of those that have no taste for it? Is it our duty to drag them kicking and screaming into the 21st century? I am afraid that it is. ~ George Porter, British chemist

Only the educated are free. ~ Epictetus

To repeat what others have said, requires education; to challenge it, requires brains. ~ Mary Pettibone Poole, U.S. writer, A Glass Eye at a Keyhole, 1938

One of the chief objects of education should be to widen the windows through which we view the world. ~ Arnold Glasgow

Creative minds always have been known to survive any kind of bad training. ~ Anna Freud

Between the semieducated, who offer simplistic answers to complex questions, and the overeducated, who offer complicated answers to simple questions, it is a wonder that any questions get satisfactorily settled at all. ~ Sydney J. Harris

Soap and education are not so sudden as a massacre, but they are more deadly in the long run. ~ Mark Twain

Education consists mainly in what we have unlearned. ~ Mark Twain

No pleasure, no learning. No learning, no pleasure.
~ Wang Ken, Chinese philosopher, in Song of Joy

When you don't have an education, you've got to use your brains.
~ Anonymous, New Webster Dictionary of Quotations and Famous Phrases

Education is a wonderful thing. If you couldn't sign your name you'd have to pay cash. ~ Rita Mae Brown

Education is what survives when what has been learned has been forgotten. ~ B.F. Skinner

We receive three educations, one from our parents, one from our schoolmasters, and one from the world. The third contradicts all that the first two teach us. ~ Montesquieu

Nothing will kill the movies except education. ~ Will Rogers

The well-meaning people who talk about education as if it were a substance distributed by coupon in large or small quantities never exhibit any understanding of the truth that you cannot teach anybody anything that he does not want to learn. ~ George Sampson

And if the student finds that this [school subject] is not to his taste, well, that is regrettable. Most regrettable. His taste should not be consulted; it is being formed. ~ Flannery O'Connor

The aim of education is the knowledge not of fact but of values.
~ Dean Inge

Education does not mean teaching people to know what they do not know; it means teaching them to behave as they do not behave.
~ John Ruskin

In one century, we went from teaching Latin and Greek in high school to offering remedial English in college. ~ Joseph Sobran, U.S. columnist

Education is the ability to listen to almost anything without losing your temper or your self-confidence. ~ Robert Frost

Education is a progressive discovery of our own ignorance. ~ Will Durant

I have never let my schooling interfere with my education. ~ Mark Twain

Sit at the feet of the master long enough, and they'll start to smell.
~ John Sauget, *Law of Education, The New Official Rules*

Lack of education is an extraordinary handicap when one is being offensive. ~ Josephine Tey

At present we educate people only up to the point where they can earn a living and marry; then education ceases altogether, as though a complete mental outfit had been acquired. ... Vast numbers of men and women thus spend their entire lives in complete ignorance of the most important things. ~ Carl Jung

The highest result of education is tolerance. ~ Helen Keller

## Efficiency

Efficiency is intelligent laziness. ~ David Dunham

## Efforts

I have always tried to hide my efforts and wished my works to have the light joyousness of springtime which never lets anyone suspect the labours it has cost me. ~ Henri Matisse

The bitter and the sweet come from the outside, the hard from within, from one's own efforts. ~ Albert Einstein

You can't always get what you want, but if you try, sometimes you just might find you get what you need. ~ Mick Jagger and Keith Richards

There are no traffic jams when you go the extra mile. ~ Anonymous

## Egoists

One nice thing about egoists – they don't talk about other people. ~ Lucille Harper

## Egotism

Egotism is the anesthetic that dulls the pain of stupidity. ~ Frank Leahy

Egotism is the anesthetic given by a kindly nature to relieve the pain of being a damned fool. ~ Bellamy Brooks

## Elections

Do you ever get the feeling that the only reason we have elections is to find out if the polls were right? ~ Robert Orben

An elected official is one who gets 51 percent of the vote cast by 40 percent of the 60 percent of voters who registered. ~ Dan Bennett

Our elections are free, it's in the results where eventually we pay. ~ Bill Stern

## Electricity

All power corrupts but we need the electricity. ~ Anonymous

Never hire an electrician whose eyebrows are scorched. ~ Mason Wilder

## Elegance

Elegance is refusal. ~ Coco Chanel

Elegance is good taste plus a dash of daring. ~ Carmel Snow

## Eloquence

Eloquence is vehement simplicity. ~ Richard Cecil

Eloquence may set fire to reason. ~ Oliver Wendell Holmes

Of all eloquence a nickname is the most concise; of all arguments, the most unanswerable. ~ William Hazlitt

The prime purpose of eloquence is to keep other people from talking.
~ Louis Vermeil

## Elvis

If life were fair, Elvis would be alive and all the impersonators would be dead. ~ Johnny Carson

## Emotion

Nothing vivifies, and nothing kills, like the emotions. ~ Joseph Roux

## Empires

The empires of the future are empires of the mind. ~ Winston Churchill

## Encouragement

A good horse should be seldom spurred. ~ Thomas Fuller, M.D.

## Ending

Great is the art of beginning, but greater the art is of ending.
~ Henry Wadsworth Longfellow

Men perish because they cannot join the beginning with the end.
~ Alcmaeon

Better is the end of a thing than the beginning thereof. ~ The Bible

To make an end is to make a beginning. ~ T.S. Eliot

## Endurance

He who limps is still walking. ~ Stanislaw Lec

Some days are for living. Others are for getting through. ~ Malcolm Forbes

## Enemies

Speak well of your enemies – remember you made them. ~ Anonymous

A man cannot be too careful in the choice of his enemies ~ Oscar Wilde

It is your enemies who keep you straight. For real use, one active, sneering enemy is worth two ordinary friends. ~ Edgar Watson Howe

This is no time for making new enemies.
~ Voltaire, on his deathbed, being asked to renounce the devil

We often give our enemies the means for our own destruction. ~ Aesop

An enemy's gift is ruinous and no gift. ~ Sophocles

A man's worst enemy can't wish him what he thinks up for himself.
~ Yiddish proverb

We have found the enemy and it were us! ~ Pogo

Do not swallow a bait offered by the enemy. ~ Sun Tzu

The wise learn many things from their enemies. ~ Aristophanes

Our worst enemies here are not the ignorant and the simple, however cruel; our worst enemies are the intelligent and corrupt. ~ Graham Greene

I'm lonesome; they are all dying; I have hardly a warm personal enemy left. ~ James Abbott McNeill Whistler

It's an old axiom of mine: marry your enemies and behead your friends. ~ Robert N. Lee

## Energy

Energy rightly applied and directed will accomplish anything.
~ Nellie Bly

The world belongs to the energetic. ~ Ralph Waldo Emerson

## Engineering Terminology

"Customer satisfaction is assured." (We are so far behind schedule that the customer is happy to receive it.)

"All new." (Parts not interchangeable with the previous design.)

"Rugged." (Too damn heavy to lift.)

"Low maintenance." (Impossible to fix if broken.)
~ compiled by Oliver Capio of Playa Del Rey, California

## English Language

If you can describe clearly without a diagram the proper way of making this or that knot, then you are a master of the English language.
~ Hilaire Belloc

## Enjoyment

If you are going to do something wrong, at least enjoy it. ~ Leo Rosten

For most men, an ignorant enjoyment is better than an informed one; it is better to conceive the sky as a blue dome than a dark cavity: and the cloud as a golden throne than a sleety mist. ~ John Ruskin

Enjoy to the full the resources that are within thy reach. ~ Pindar

## Enlightenment

Before enlightenment: Chopping wood, Carrying water.
After enlightenment: Chopping wood, Carrying water. ~ Zen proverb

## Enough

Enough is as good as a feast. ~ John Heywood

Nothing is enough to the man for whom enough is too little. ~ Epicurus

## Entertainment Medium

There's a standard formula for success in the entertainment medium
and that is: Beat it to death if it succeeds. ~ Ernie Kovacs

## Enthusiasm

Enthusiasm is a virtue seldom met with in seasons of calm and
unruffled prosperity. ~ Thomas Chalmers

Nothing is so contagious as enthusiasm. ~ Edward Bulwer-Lytton

I prefer the errors of enthusiasm to the indifference of wisdom.
~ Anatole France

If you are not fired with enthusiasm, you'll be fired with enthusiasm.
~ Vincent Lombardi

Every production of genius must be the product of enthusiasm.
~ Benjamin Disraeli

Enthusiasm, *n.* A distemper of youth, curable by small doses of
repentance in connection with outward applications of experience.
~ Ambrose Bierce

If you can give your son or daughter only one gift, let it be enthusiasm.
~ Bruce Barton

Years wrinkle the skin, but to give up enthusiasm wrinkles the soul.
~ Samuel Ullman

## Enthusiasts

It is unfortunate, considering that enthusiasm moves the world, that so
few enthusiasts can be trusted to speak the truth.
~ Arthur Balfour

## Entrepreneur

You don't deserve to be called an entrepreneur unless you've
mortgaged your house to the business. ~ Ted Rogers, 1985

## Environment

The emergence of intelligence, I am convinced, tends to unbalance the ecology. In other words, intelligence is the great polluter. It is not until a creature begins to manage its environment that nature is thrown into disorder. ~ Clifford Simak in *Shakespeare's Planet*

All men and women, even those whose lives appear on the surface to be thoroughly conventional, invent themselves to a very great extent. Man is unique in the ways that he does not come to terms with his environment. Every other species adapts by passively responding to its environment, the place where it happens to have been born. In contrast, man is what he chooses to be. Eccentrics take that basic human prerogative of free choice and force it to the limit.
~ Dr. David Weeks and Jamie James

The environment is everything that isn't me. ~ Albert Einstein

## Envy

As rust corrupts iron, so envy corrupts men. ~ Antisthenes

The torment of envy is like a grain of sand in the eye. ~ Chinese proverb

If envy were a disease, everyone would be sick. ~ Proverb

How much better a thing it is to be envied than to be pitied.
~ Herodotus

The dullard's envy of brilliant men is always assuaged by the suspicion that they will come to a bad end. ~ Max Beerbohm

## Equality

Equality may perhaps be a right, but no power on Earth can ever turn it into a fact. ~ Honoré de Balzac

Before God we are all equally wise – and equally foolish. ~ Albert Einstein

It is better that some should be unhappy than that none should be happy, which would be the case in a general state of equality.
~ Samuel Johnson

All animals are equal, but some animals are more equal than others.
~ George Orwell

The cry of equality pulls everyone down. ~ Iris Murdoch

## Equals

The trouble with treating people as equals is that the first thing you know they may be doing the same thing to you.
~ Peter De Vries, U.S. novelist, *The Prick of Noon*

What makes equality such a difficult business is that we only want it with our superiors. ~ Henry Becque, French dramatist

## Era

An era can be said to have ended when its basic illusions are exhausted. ~ Arthur Miller

## Err

To err is human, to blame the next guy even more so. ~ Unknown

To err is dysfunctional, to forgive co-dependent. ~ Berton Averre

## Error

Every absurdity has a champion to defend it, for error is always talkative. ~ Oliver Goldsmith

All human error is impatience, a premature renunciation of method, a delusive pinning down of a delusion. ~ Franz Kafka

Things could be worse. Suppose your errors were counted and published every day, like those of a baseball player.
~ Anonymous, cited in *The Fitzhenry & Whiteside Book of Quotations*

"It is destiny!" – dark apology for every error. ~ Edward Bulwer-Lytton

The world always makes the assumption that the exposure of an error is identical with the discovery of the truth – that error and truth are simply opposite. They are nothing of the sort. What the world turns to, when it has been cured of one error, is usually simply another error, and maybe one worse than the first one. ~ H.L. Mencken

All erroneous ideas would perish of their own accord if expressed clearly. ~ Marquis de Vauvenargues

The man who can own up to his error is greater than he who merely knows how to avoid making it. ~ Cardinal de Retz

No doubt about it: Error is the rule; truth is the accident of error.
~ Georges Duhamel

The progress of rivers to the ocean is not so rapid as that of man to error. ~ Voltaire

Love truth but pardon error. ~ Voltaire

Admitting Error clears the Score
And proves you Wiser than before. ~ Arthur Guitermann

It is one thing to show a man that he is in error and another to put him in possession of the truth. ~ John Locke

One's opponent must be weaned from error by patience and sympathy. ~ Mahatma Gandhi

Life is only error, and death is knowledge. ~ Johann von Schiller

If you shut the door to all error, truth will be shut out. ~ Rabindranath Tagore

Every error under the sun seems to arise from thinking that you are right yourself because you are yourself, and other people are wrong because they are not you. ~ Thomas Hardy

## Escape

When the mouse laughs at the cat, there is a hole nearby. ~ Nigerian proverb

## Eternity

All things from eternity are of like forms and come round in a circle. ~ Marcus Aurelius

We feel and know by experience that we are eternal. ~ Baruch Spinoza

As if you could kill time without injuring eternity. ~ Henry David Thoreau

## Ethical

An ethical man is a Christian holding four aces. ~ Mark Twain

## Europe

Europe is the unfinished negative of which America is the proof. ~ Mary McCarthy

## Events

When I can't handle events, I let them handle themselves. ~ Henry Ford

Events play cat-and-mouse with our ideas. They belong to a quite different species and even when seeming to bear out our preconceptions are never quite as we expected. Foresight is a dream from which the event wakes us. ~ Paul Valéry

I claim not to have controlled events, but confess plainly that events have controlled me. ~ Abraham Lincoln

It is one thing to be moved by events; it is another thing to be mastered by them. ~ Ralph Stockman

## Evil

If evil be said of thee, and it is true, correct it: if it be a lie, laugh at it. ~ Proverb

It is a sin to believe in the evil of others – but it is seldom a mistake. ~ H.L. Mencken

There is scarcely a man sufficiently aware to know all the evil he does. ~ La Rochefoucauld

There aren't very many really evil people. But there are an awful lot of selfish ones. ~ Walter Cronkite

When choosing between two evils, I always like to try the one I've never tried before. ~ Mae West

May the forces of evil become confused on the way to your house. ~ George Carlin

The wise man avoids evil by anticipating it. ~ Publilius Syrus

We are no more responsible for the evil thoughts which pass through our minds than a scarecrow [is] for the birds which fly over the seedplot he has to guard; the sole responsibility in each case is to prevent them from settling. ~ Churton Collins, aphorisms in the *English Review*, 1914

Evil draws men together. ~ Aristotle

Most of the evils of life arise from man's being unable to sit still in a room. ~ Blaise Pascal

Yield not to evils, but attack all the more boldly. ~ Virgil

A resolution to avoid an evil is seldom framed till the evil is so far advanced as to make avoidance impossible. ~ Thomas Hardy

## Evolution

My theory of evolution is that Darwin was adopted. ~ Steven Wright

## Exaggeration

An exaggeration is a truth that has lost its temper. ~ Kahlil Gibran

To exaggerate is to weaken. ~ Jean-François de la Harpe

## Examinations

Examinations are formidable, even to the best-prepared, for the greatest fool may ask more than the wisest man can answer.
~ Charles Caleb Colton

## Example

You can preach a better sermon with your life than with your lips.
~ Oliver Goldsmith

Do not seek to follow in the footsteps of the men of old; seek what they sought. ~ Matsuo Basho

Even a useless person can serve as a bad example. ~ Unknown

Nothing is so contagious as example, and our every good or bad action inspires a similar one. ~ La Rochefoucauld

## Exasperation

The mass of men lead lives of quiet exasperation. ~ Phyllis McGinley

## Excellence

There are no speed limits on the road to excellence. ~ David W. Johnson

We measure the excellency of other men by some excellency we conceive to be in ourselves. ~ John Selden

To fight and conquer in all your battles is not supreme excellence; supreme excellence consists in breaking the enemy's resistance without fighting. ~ Sun Tzu

## Exceptions

The mark of an exceptional company is how it treats its exceptions.
~ Joe DeGeorge, Federal Express

Exceptions prove the rule – and wreck the budget. ~ Olin Miller

## Excess

Excess on occasion is exhilarating. It prevents moderation from acquiring the deadening effect of habit.
~ W. Somerset Maugham in The Summing Up

Stretch a bow to the very full,
And you will wish you had stopped in time. ~ Lao-tzu

The road of excess leads to the palace of wisdom. ~ William Blake

When water covers the head, a hundred fathoms are as one.
~ Persian proverb

If I can't have too many truffles, I'll do without truffles. ~ Colette

They are as sick that surfeit with too much as they that starve with nothing. ~ Shakespeare

Moderation is a fatal thing. Nothing succeeds like excess. ~ Oscar Wilde

## Excuses

The girl who can't dance says the band can't play. ~ Yiddish proverb

He who excuses himself accuses himself. ~ Gabriel Meurier

The longer the excuse, the less likely it's true. ~ Robert Half

## Exercise

The need for exercise is a modern superstition, invented by people who ate too much and had nothing to think about. Athletics don't make anybody either long-lived or useful.
~ George Santayana, Spanish-born philosopher

I've given up exercise. No pain, no pain. ~ Anonymous

## Exhilaration

Exhilaration is that feeling you get just after a great idea hits you and just before you realize what's wrong with it. ~ Anonymous

## Existence

Call a thing immoral or ugly, soul-destroying or a degradation of man, a peril to the peace of the world or to the well-being of future generations: As long as you have not shown it to be "uneconomic" you have not really questioned its right to exist, grow and prosper.
~ E.F. Schumacher in *Small is Beautiful*

Existence precedes and rules essence. ~ Jean-Paul Sartre

## Expansion

Executive behaviour is based on the managerial myth that future organizational expansion will resolve past institutional incompetence.
~ Doug Moseley

## Expectation

Nothing is so good as it seems beforehand.
~ George Eliot, *Silas Marner*

If you cannot catch a bird of paradise, better take a wet hen.
~ Nikita Khrushchev

Blessed is he who expects nothing, for he shall never be disappointed.
~ Alexander Pope

It's just as unpleasant to get more than you bargain for as to get less.
~ George Bernard Shaw

For people who live on expectations, to face up to their realization is something of an ordeal. ~ Elizabeth Bowen

Expect nothing. Live frugally on surprise. ~ Alice Walker

## Expenses

It's not hard to meet expenses, they're everywhere. ~ Will Rogers

## Experience

Experience is not what happens to you; it is what you do with what happens to you. ~ Aldous Huxley

Experience teaches you that the man who looks you straight in the eye, particularly if he adds a firm handshake, is hiding something.
~ Clifton Fadiman

Experience is that marvellous thing that enables you to recognize a mistake when you make it again. ~ Franklin P. Jones

We learn from experience. A man never wakes up his second baby just to see it smile. ~ Grace Williams

Experience is a good teacher, but her fees are very high. ~ W.R. Inge

The school of hard knocks is an accelerated curriculum. ~ Menander

You cannot create experience. You must undergo it. ~ Albert Camus

I was thinking that we all learn by experience, but some of us have to go to summer school. ~ Peter De Vries

Only the wearer knows where the shoe pinches. ~ English proverb

Experience teaches us only one thing at a time – and hardly that in my case. ~ Mark Twain

We should be careful to get out of an experience only the wisdom that is in it – and stop there; lest we be like the cat that sits down on a hot stove-lid. She will not sit down on a hot stove-lid again – and that is well; but also she will not sit down on a cold one anymore. ~ Mark Twain

Human beings, who are almost unique in having the ability to learn from the experience of others, are also remarkable for their apparent disinclination to do so. ~ Douglas Adams, *Last Chance to See*

Experience has two things to teach: The first is that we must correct a great deal; the second, that we must not correct too much. ~ Delacroix

Information's pretty thin stuff, unless mixed with experience.
~ Clarence Day

Experience dulls the edges of all our dogmas.
~ Sir Gilbert Murray

Experience is only half of experience. ~ Goethe

All experience is an arch to build upon. ~ Henry Adams

He who neglects to drink of the spring of experience is likely to die of thirst in the desert of ignorance. ~ Ling Po

Experience is a good school, but the fees are high. ~ Heinrich Heine

A farmer learns more from a bad harvest than a good one. ~ Anonymous

Experience is one thing you can't get for nothing. ~ Oscar Wilde

The years teach much which the days never know. ~ Ralph Waldo Emerson

When a person with money meets a person with experience, the person with the experience winds up with the money and the person with the money winds up with the experience.
~ Harvey Mackay, U.S. businessman and columnist

Men are wise in proportion, not to their experience, but to their capacity for experience. ~ George Bernard Shaw

Experience is a hard teacher because she gives the test first, the lesson afterward. ~ Vernon Law, U.S. baseball player

A smooth sea never made a skillful mariner. ~ English proverb

No one is ever old enough to know better. ~ Holbrook Jackson

A new broom sweeps clean but an old one knows the corners.
~ English saying

You've got to know when to hold 'em,
Know when to fold 'em,
Know when to walk away. - Don Schlitz

In the business world, everyone is paid in two coins: cash and experience. Take the experience first; the cash will come later.
~ Harold Geneen

## Experiments

There is no such thing as a failed experiment, only experiments with unexpected outcomes. ~ Buckminster Fuller

## Experts

An expert is a person who avoids the small errors as he sweeps on to the grand fallacy. ~ Benjamin Stolberg

When facts are few, experts are many. ~ Donald R. Gannon

Make three correct guesses consecutively and you will establish a reputation as an expert. ~ Laurence J. Peter

An expert is a man who has stopped thinking. Why should he think? He is an expert. ~ Frank Lloyd Wright

No lesson seems to be so deeply inculcated by the experience of life as that you should never trust experts. If you believe the doctors, nothing is wholesome; if you believe the theologians, nothing is innocent; if you believe the soldiers, nothing is safe. They all require to have their strong wine diluted by a very large admixture of insipid common sense.
~ Lord Salisbury

Experts are never right or wrong; they win or lose. Right and wrong are decided by proof; winning and losing are decided by who is doing the talking or talks the loudest, has the last, latest or only word, and is quoted by reporters. ~ M.A. Zeidner, *Quarterly Review of Doublespeak*

An expert is one who knows more and more about less and less.
~ Nicholas Butler

## Explanations

There is no waste of time in life like that of making explanations.
~ Benjamin Disraeli

Never explain. Your friends do not need it and your enemies will not believe you anyway. ~ Elbert Hubbard

## Expressing Oneself

Think like a wise man but express yourself like the common people.
~ William Butler Yeats

## Expression

Expression is the dress of thought. ~ Alexander Pope

## Extinction

Millennarian fervour, it is true, tends to get edged to the margins of society, because you have to be poor, dumb, defeated, exploited or otherwise down on your luck to want the world to end. But mild millennarianism … is compatible with a rational reading of the evidence. Every known species has become extinct or shown signs of potential extinctions; so humankind is unlikely to be exempt. Nothing has ever had immunity from destruction, so why should we?
~ Felipe Fernandez-Armesto, *The Spectator*

## Extremists

Extremists think "communication" means agreeing with them.
~ Leo Rosten

## Eye

The ear tends to be lazy, craves the familiar and is shocked by the unexpected; the eye, on the other hand, tends to be impatient, craves the novel and is bored by repetition. ~ W.H. Auden

What you don't see with your eyes, don't invent with your mouth.
~ Jewish proverb

Eyes are more accurate witnesses than ears. ~ Heraclitus

Truly it has been said, that to a clear eye the smallest fact is a window through which the Infinite may be seen. ~ Thomas Henry Huxley

## Face

Be it ever so homely, there's no face like one's own. ~ Anonymous

The best way to save face is to keep the lower half of it shut. ~ Unknown

There's no art to find the mind's construction in the face.
~ Shakespeare

## Facts

The facts will eventually test all our theories, and they form, after all, the only impartial jury to which we can appeal. ~ Louis Agassiz

Facts do not cease to exist because they are ignored.
~ Aldous Huxley, *Proper Studies*

In all of this world, there is nothing more dismal than a fact.
~ Jim Moran, U.S. publicist

To treat your facts with imagination is one thing, but to imagine your facts is another. ~ John Burroughs

The facts are always less than what really happened. ~ Nadine Gordimer

A fact is a simple statement that everyone believes. It is innocent, unless found guilty. A hypothesis is a novel suggestion that no one wants to believe. It is guilty, until found effective. ~ Edward Teller

Facts are stupid things. ~ Ronald Reagan

An ounce of fact is worth a ton of conjecture. ~ Anonymous

If facts do not conform to the theory, they must be disposed of.
~ N.R.F. Maier

If facts conflict with a theory, either the theory must be changed or the facts. ~ Baruch Spinoza

RICHARD W. POUND

Facts, or what a man believes to be the facts, are delightful. Get your facts first, and then you can distort them as much as you please.
~ Mark Twain

Every story has three sides, yours, mine and the facts. ~ René Fumoleau

## Failure

Not failure, but low aim, is crime. ~ James Russell Lowell

People aren't failures until they begin to blame somebody else.
~ Unknown

Failure is more frequently from want of energy than want of capital.
~ Daniel Webster

Show me a thoroughly satisfied man – and I will show you a failure.
~ Thomas Edison

Half the failures in life arise from pulling in one's horse as it is leaping.
~ Julius Hare

Generally, it is our failures that civilize us. Triumph confirms us in our habits. ~ Clive James

The only people who never fail are those who never try. ~ Ilka Chase

There is much to be said for failure. It is more interesting than success.
~ Max Beerbohm

O human race! Born to ascend on wings,
Why do you fall at such a little wind? ~ Dante

The line between failure and success is so fine that we scarcely know when we pass it; so fine that we are often on the line and do not know it. ~ Elbert Hubbard

If we don't succeed, we run the risk of failure. ~ Dan Quayle

Flops are a part of life's menu, and I've never been a girl to miss out on any of the courses. ~ Rosalind Russell

Whoever is aware of his own failing will not find fault with the failings of other men. ~ Sa'di

A person of 12 professions and 13 failures. ~ Dutch proverb

Every great improvement has come after repeated failure. Virtually nothing comes out right the first time. Failures, repeated failures, are posts on the road to achievement. ~ Charles F. Kettering

## Faith

Faith may be defined briefly as an illogical belief in the occurrence of the improbable. ~ H.L. Mencken

We walk by faith, not by sight. ~ Corinthians I

Faith is the substance of things hoped for, the evidence of things not seen. ~ Timothy IV

It is at night that faith in light is admirable. ~ Edmond Rostand

## False Friends

A false friend and a shadow attend only when the sun shines.
~ Benjamin Franklin

## False Knowledge

Beware of false knowledge; it is more dangerous than ignorance.
~ George Bernard Shaw

## False Pretenses

I do not approve of guys using false pretenses on dolls, except, of course, when nothing else will do. ~ Damon Runyon

## Falsehoods

Falsehoods not only quarrel with truth, but usually quarrel among themselves. ~ Daniel Webster

False in one thing, false in everything. ~ Legal maxim

Whatever is only almost true is quite false, and among the most dangerous of errors, because being so near the truth, it is the more likely to lead astray. ~ Henry Ward Beecher

## Fame

The fame of great men must always be estimated by the means used to acquire it. ~ La Rochefoucauld

A special fame is reserved for the beautiful and the damned, whose money, talent and fame can be forgiven because it never made them happy. These are our true folk heroes, for when a democracy bestows vast rewards on a very few, it is natural that those less blessed would seek to equalize this imbalance by choosing to admire people [such as Elvis, James Dean and Marilyn Monroe] they can also pity.
~ Elizabeth Kaye

Fame is proof that the people are gullible. ~ Ralph Waldo Emerson

One of the drawbacks of fame is that one can never escape from it.
~ Dame Nellie Melba

Now when I bore people at a party, they think it's their fault.
~ Henry Kissinger

"I am world famous," Dr. Parks said, "all over Canada."
~ Mordecai Richler in *The Incomparable Atuk*

## Familiarity

Familiarity breeds attempt. ~ Goodman Ace

The aspects of things that are most important for us are hidden because of their simplicity and familiarity. ~ Ludwig Wittgenstein

Familiarity breeds. ~ Graffito

In the human world, it seems to me that the feeling of living among growing millions of others has produced alterations in the way we address one another. More nicknames, fewer honorifics, unwarranted endearments. To try to salvage a sense of human intimacy in a quick-contact world, a certain overfamiliarity is setting in.
~ Dierdre McNamer in *Town & Country* magazine

## Famous Last Words

The cinema is little more than a fad. It's canned drama. What audiences really want to see is flesh and blood on the stage.
~ Charlie Chaplin, circa 1916

Machines are good at chess but hopeless at recognizing patterns, learning and fibbing – things a three-year-old child does every day.
~ John Naughton in *The Observer*

Who the hell wants to hear actors talk? ~ Harry M. Warner, Warner Bros., 1927

There is no likelihood that man can ever tap the power of the atom.
~ Robert Millikan, awarded Nobel Prize in Physics, 1923

Heavier than air flying machines are impossible.
~ Lord Kelvin, pres. British Royal Society, 1885

Newspapers will ultimately engross all literature – there will be nothing else published but newspapers.
~ Alphonse de Lamartine, French poet

X-rays are a hoax. ~ Lord Kelvin, pres. British Royal Society, circa 1900

Radio has no future. ~ Lord Kelvin (1824-1907), pres. British Royal Society, 1897

Television won't matter in your lifetime or mine.
~ R.S. Lambert, Canadian radio broadcaster, 1936

I think there is a world market for maybe five computers.
~ Thomas Watson, chairman IBM, 1943

There is no reason for any individual to have a computer in his home.
~ Ken Olsen, president, Digital Equipment Corp., 1977

Computers in the future may weigh only 1.5 tons. ~ *Popular Mechanics*, 1949

The horse is here to stay, but the automobile is only a novelty, a fad.
~ The president of The Michigan Savings Bank, advising Horace Rackman, lawyer to
Henry Ford, not to invest in The Ford Motor Co. Rackman ignored the advice. In 1903
he bought $5,000 worth of the stock, later unloading it for $12.5 million.

Airplanes are interesting toys, but of no military value.
~ Marshal Ferdinand Foch, French military commander, 1911

Stocks have reached what looks like a permanently high plateau.
~ Irving Fisher, professor of economics, Yale University, October 17, 1929. The stock
market crashed a week later.

We don't like their sound, and guitar music is on the way out.
~ Decca Records executive, rejecting a Beatles demo tape, 1962

640K ought to be enough for anybody. ~ Bill Gates, 1981

## Fanaticism

Fanaticism consists in redoubling your effort when you have forgotten
your aim. ~ George Santayana

## Fashion

Fashion is something that goes in one year and out the other.
~ Unknown

It is fashion's business to manipulate our memories. Fashion is in
ceaseless pursuit of things that are about to look familiar and in uneasy
flight from things that have just become a bore. Pretending frenziedly
to market enthusiasm for novelty, in fact it sells disgust for previous
modes. ~ Kennedy Fraser, *The Fashionable Mind*, 1982

I base most of my fashion taste on what doesn't itch. ~ Gilda Radner

If men can run the world, why can't they stop wearing neckties? How
intelligent is it to start the day by tying a little noose around your neck?
~ Linda Ellerbee

If high heels were so wonderful, men would be wearing them.
~ Sue Grafton

Every generation laughs at the old fashions but religiously follows the new. ~ Henry David Thoreau

## Fate

We may become the makers of our fate when we have ceased to pose as its prophets. ~ Karl Popper, Austrian-British philosopher

If fate means you lose, give him a good fight anyhow. ~ William McFee

Fate leads the willing and drags along the reluctant. ~ Seneca

Granting our wish one of Fate's saddest jokes is! ~ James Russell Lowell

Fate is not an eagle; it creeps like a rat. ~ Elizabeth Bowen

I am the master of my fate: I am the captain of my soul. ~ W.E. Henley

I do not believe in a fate that falls on men however they act, but I do believe in a fate that falls on them unless they act. ~ G.K. Chesterton

Men at some time are master of their fates:
The fault, dear Brutus, is not in our stars,
But in ourselves, that we are underlings. ~ Shakespeare, *Julius Caesar*

The glories of our blood and state are shadows, not substantial things; there is no armour against fate. Death lays his icy hand on kings.
~ James Shirley

There is no fate that cannot be surmounted by scorn. ~ Albert Camus

Human reason needs only to will more strongly than fate, and she *is* fate! ~ Thomas Mann

## Fathers

That is the thankless position of the father in the family – the provider for all, and the enemy of all. ~ August Strindberg, 1886

If a man lives without being a father, he will die without having been a human being. ~ Russian proverb

The most important thing a father can do for his children is to love their mother. ~ Theodore Hesburgh

Mothers are a biological necessity; fathers are a social invention.
~ Margaret Mead

## Faults

The greatest of faults, I should say, is to be conscious of none.
~ Thomas Carlyle

When you have faults, do not fear to abandon them. ~ Confucius

If we had no faults, we would not take so much pleasure in noticing them in others. ~ La Rochefoucauld

A man does not mind being blamed for his faults, and being punished for them, and he patiently suffers much for them; but he becomes impatient if he is required to give them up. ~ Goethe in *Maxims and Reflections*

He is lifeless that is faultless. ~ English proverb

Deal with the faults of others as gently as you deal with your own.
~ Chinese proverb

We confess to little faults only to persuade ourselves that we have no great ones. ~ La Rochefoucauld

It had only one fault. It was kind of lousy. ~ James Thurber

## Favour

The man who confers a favour would rather not be repaid in the same coin. ~ Aristotle Thesaurus

Most people return small favours, acknowledge middling ones, and repay great ones with ingratitude. ~ Benjamin Franklin

## Fear

There are few monsters who warrant the fear we have of them.
~ André Gide

Of all the passions, fear weakens judgment most. ~ Cardinal De Retz

He who is too much afraid of being duped has lost the power of being magnanimous. ~ Henri Frédéric Amiel

He who fears he shall suffer, already suffers what he fears.
~ Michel de Montaigne

To fear the worst oft cures the worse. ~ Shakespeare

Present fears are less than horrible imaginings. ~ Shakespeare

Fear makes the wolf bigger than he is. ~ German proverb

No passion so effectually robs the mind of all its powers of acting and reasoning as fear. ~ Edmund Burke

We are all dangerous till our fears grow thoughtful. ~ John Ciardi

Fear and hope are alike underneath. ~ Richard Ford

Fear is implanted in us as a preservative from evil; but its duty, like that of other passions, is not to overbear reason but to assist it.
~ Samuel Johnson

Who is more foolish, the child afraid of the dark or the man afraid of the light? ~ Maurice Freehill

Oh! How vain and vile a passion is this fear!
What base uncomely things it makes men do. ~ Ben Jonson, *Thesaurus*

Excessive fear is always powerless. ~ Aeschylus

It takes up too much time, being afraid. ~ Pierre Trudeau

When men are ruled by fear, they strive to prevent the very changes that will abate it. ~ Alan Paton

Men are not afraid of things, but of how they view them. ~ Epictetus

Just as courage imperils life, fear protects it. ~ Leonardo da Vinci

The first and greatest commandment is don't let them scare you.
~ Elmer Davis, U.S. journalist

All fear is painful, and when conduces not to safety, is painful without use. Every consideration, therefore, by which groundless terrors may be removed, adds something to human happiness. ~ Samuel Johnson

There were all kinds of things of which I was afraid at first, from grizzly bears to "mean" horses and gunfighters, but by acting as if I was not afraid I gradually ceased to be afraid.
~ Theodore Roosevelt, *An Autobiography*, 1913

Fear has the largest eyes of all. ~ Boris Pasternak

## Feelings

Better to be without logic than without feeling. ~ Charlotte Bronte

All great discoveries are made by people whose feelings run ahead of their thinking. ~ C.H. Oakhurst

## Feet

Why isn't there a special name for the tops of your feet? ~ Lily Tomlin

## Feminists

Some of us are becoming the men we wanted to marry. ~ Gloria Steinem

Our struggle today is not to have a female Einstein get appointed as an assistant professor. It is for a woman schlemiel to get as quickly promoted as a male schlemiel. ~ Bella Abzug

## Fiction

Reporting the extreme things as if they were the average things will start you on the art of fiction. ~ F. Scott Fitzgerald

The trouble with fiction is that it makes too much sense, whereas reality never makes sense. ~ Aldous Huxley

Literature is a luxury; fiction is a necessity. ~ G.K. Chesterton

The truer the facts, the better the fiction. ~ Virginia Woolf

## Fifth Ace

He said it was not always the timid fellow with four conventional aces in his hand who won the highest honours. "It is often," he said, "the fifth ace that makes all the difference between success and failure."
~ J.B. Morton, *Beachcomber*

## Fighting

It is a perplexing and unpleasant truth that when men already feel they have "something worth fighting for," they do not feel like fighting.
~ Eric Hoffer

He will win who knows when to fight and when not to fight. ~ Sun Tzu

He who fights too long against dragons becomes a dragon.
~ Friedrich Nietzsche

## Film

Film is more than the 20th-century art. It's another part of the 20th-century mind. It's the world seen from inside. ~ Don Delillo, 1982

A good film is when the price of the dinner, the theatre admission and the babysitter were worth it. ~ Alfred Hitchcock

## Fine Print

The big print giveth and the fine print taketh away. ~ Fulton J. Sheen

## Fitting In

You had better be a round peg in a square hole than a square peg in a round hole. The latter is in for life, while the first is only an indeterminate sentence. ~ Elbert Hubbard

## Flattery

It is flattering some men to endure them. ~ John Morely

What really flatters a man is that you think him worth flattering.
~ George Bernard Shaw

Flattery is all right, so long as you don't inhale. ~ Adlai Stevenson

Flattery sits in the parlour when plain dealing is kicked out of doors.
~ Thomas Fuller, M.D.

## Florida

My parents didn't want to move to Florida, but they turned 60, and that's the law. ~ Jerry Seinfeld

## Flowers

If you want to say it with flowers, a single rose says: "I'm cheap."
~ Delta Burke

Our national flower is the concrete cloverleaf. ~ Lewis Mumford

## Fly

God in his wisdom made the fly
And then forgot to tell us why. ~ Ogden Nash

## Flying

This new sport is comparable to no other. It is, in my opinion, one of the most intoxicating forms of sport, and will, I am sure, become one of the most popular. Many of us will perish before then, but that prospect will not dismay the braver spirits….It is so delicious to fly like a bird! ~ Marie Marvingt, French pioneer aviator and inventor of the ambulance airplane writing *The Sky Women* for *Collier's* magazine in 1911.

## Folk Sayings

Hard to tell from its looks how far a frog will jump.

He's got more tongue than a Mountie's boot.

I'll tow that alongside awhile, before I bring it aboard.

Heavier than a dead minister.

He's got his solar panels on the north side. ~ Bill Casselman, *Casselmania*

## Folly

The chief characteristic of folly is that it mistakes itself for wisdom.
~ Fray Luis de Leon

One man's folly is another man's wife. ~ Helen Rowland

## Food

Food is an important part of a balanced diet. ~ Fran Lebowitz

A food is not necessarily essential just because your child hates it.
~ Katharine Whitehorn

Food is the most primitive form of comfort. ~ Sheila Graham

What makes food such a tyranny for women? A man, after all, may in times of crisis, hit the bottle (or another person), but he rarely hits the fridge. ~ Joanna Trollope

We may find in the long run that tinned food is a deadlier weapon than the machine gun. ~ George Orwell

## Foolish

If fifty million people say a foolish thing, it is still a foolish thing.
~ Bertrand Russell

## Fools

The ultimate effect of shielding men from the effects of folly is to fill the world with fools. ~ Herbert Spencer

Learned fools are the greatest fools. ~ Proverb

Every man is a damn fool for at least five minutes every day; wisdom consists of not exceeding the limit. ~ Elbert Hubbard

Let us be thankful for the fools. But for them the rest of us could not succeed. ~ Mark Twain

If you can't spot the sucker in the game in the first 10 minutes, then it must be you. ~ Poker saying

He who despairs of the human condition is a coward, but he who has hope for it is a fool. ~ Albert Camus

A fool in a hurry drinks tea with a fork.
~ Title of a book of proverbs edited by Norma Gleason

There are two kinds of fools: one says "This is old, therefore it is good"; the other says, "This is new, therefore it is better."
~ W.R. Inge, also attributed to Dr. Laurence J. Peter and Molly Ivins

It's only damned fools who argue! Never Contradict. Never Explain. Never Apologize. Those are the secrets of a happy life.
~ British Admiral Fisher in a letter to *The Times of London*, Sept. 15, 1919

Suffer fools gladly. They may be right. ~ Holbrook Jackson

Everybody loves a fool, but nobody wants him for a son.
~ Malinke (West African) proverb

The haste of a fool is the slowest thing in the world. ~ Thomas Shadwell

A fool and his money are soon invited everywhere. ~ Elsie, Lady Mendl

Fools give you reasons, wise men never try. ~ Oscar Hammerstein

The greatest lesson in life is to know that fools are right sometimes.
~ Winston Churchill

Fools act on imagination without knowledge, pedants act on knowledge without imagination. ~ Alfred North Whitehead

Foolproof implies a finite number of fools. ~ Anonymous

There are more fools in the world than there are people. ~ Heinrich Heine

The fool doth think he is wise, but the wise man knows himself to be a fool. ~ Shakespeare, *As You Like It*

If the fools do not control the world, it isn't because they are not in the majority. ~ Edgar Watson Howe

The best way to convince a fool that he is wrong is to let him have his own way. ~ Josh Billings

There is no need to fasten a bell to a fool. ~ Danish proverb

Little is needed to make a wise man happy, but nothing can content a fool. ~ La Rochefoucauld

A fool sees not the same tree that a wise man sees. ~ William Blake

A knowledgeable fool is a greater fool than an ignorant one. ~ Molière

A fellow who is always declaring he is no fool usually has his suspicions. ~ Wilson Mizner

Anyone who feels at ease in the world today is a fool.
~ Robert Hitchens, 1959

Fools out of favour grudge at knaves in place. ~ Daniel Defoe

A fool and his money are soon parted. What I want to know is how they got together in the first place. ~ Cyril Fletcher

Young men think old men are fools; but old men know young men are fools. ~ George Chapman

## Football Fans

The natural state of the football fan is bitter disappointment, no matter what the score. ~ Nick Hornby, *Fever Pitch*, 1992

## Forbearance

There is, however, a limit at which forbearance ceases to be a virtue.
~ Edmund Burke

## Forbidden

Things forbidden have a secret charm. ~ Tacitus

## Force

Are you going to come quietly, or do I have to use earplugs?
~ Spike Milligan

Brute force without wisdom falls by its own weight. ~ Horace

## Forecasting

Forecasting is very difficult – especially if it's about the future.
~ Edgar Fiedler

## Foreign Aid

Foreign aid might be defined as a transfer from poor people in rich countries to rich people in poor countries. ~ Douglas Casey, 1992

## Foresight

In action, be primitive; in foresight, a strategist. ~ René Char

## Forewarning

A forewarned man is worth two. ~ Spanish proverb

Oh that a man might know
The end of this day's business ere it come! ~ Shakespeare

## Forget

If you wish to forget anything on the spot, make a note that this thing is to be remembered. ~ Edgar Allan Poe

Till you forget, we shall not twice have died. ~ John E. Nixon

We have all forgot more than we remember. ~ Thomas Fuller, M.D.

I never forget a face, but in your case I'll make an exception.
~ Groucho Marx

We learn so little and forget so much. ~ Sir John Davies

## Forgive

The stupid neither forgive nor forget; the naive forgive and forget; the wise forgive but do not forget. ~ Thomas Szasz

Those who cannot forgive others break the bridge over which they themselves must pass. ~ Confucius

There are many circumstances in life where it is possible to effect by forgiveness every object which you propose to effect by resentment.
~ Sydney Smith, in a sermon, "The Forgiveness of Injuries"

It is easier to forgive an enemy than to forgive a friend. ~ William Blake

Nobuddy ever fergits where he buried a hatchet. ~ Abe Martin

## Form

When one starts from a portrait and seeks by successive eliminations to find pure form...one inevitably ends up with an egg. ~ Pablo Picasso

## Forms

Forms are for mediocrity, and it is fortunate that mediocrity can act only according to routine. Ability takes its form unhindered. ~ Napoleon

## Fortune

It is we that are blind, not Fortune. ~ Sir Thomas Browne

He who asks fortune-tellers the future unwittingly forfeits an inner intimation of coming events that is a thousand times more exact than anything they may say. ~ Walter Benjamin in *One-Way Street*, 1925-1926

How fortune brings to earth the oversure! ~ Petrarch

Want to make a small fortune? Start with a large fortune – and then hire an advertising agency. ~ Herbert Kelleher, Southwest Airlines chairman

Fortune pays you sometimes for the intensity of her favours by the shortness of their duration. She soon tires of carrying anyone long on her shoulders. ~ Baltasar Gracian

When Fortune comes, seize her in front with a sure hand, because behind she is bald. ~ Leonardo da Vinci

We must master our good fortune, or it will master us. ~ Publilius Syrus

Let everyone witness how many different cards fortune has up her sleeve when she wants to ruin a man. ~ Benvenuto Cellini

Fortune does not change men, it unmasks them. ~ Suzanne Necker

Fortune sides with him who dares. ~ Virgil

Fortune never appears so blind as to those whom she does no good. ~ La Rochefoucauld

Fortune brings in some boats that are not steered. ~ Shakespeare

Here is a rule to remember in future, when anything tempts you to be bitter: not "This is a misfortune," but "To bear this worthily is good fortune." ~ Marcus Aurelius

## Foundations

The loftiest edifices need the deepest foundations. ~ George Santayana

## France

What kind of country puts up more resistance to Disney than they did to the Nazis? ~ Conan O'Brien, talk show host

## Fraud

There are some frauds so well conducted that it would be stupidity not to be deceived by them. ~ Charles Caleb Colton

## Free Gifts

You pay a great deal too dear for what's given freely. ~ Shakespeare

## Free Society

A free society is a place where it's safe to be unpopular. ~ Adlai Stevenson

## Free Speech

Everyone is in favour of free speech. Hardly a day passes without it being extolled, but some people's idea of it is that they are free to say what they like, but if anyone says anything back, that is an outrage. ~ Winston Churchill

### Free Trade

Free trade, one of the greatest blessings which a government can confer upon a people, is in almost every country unpopular.
~ Lord Macaulay

### Free Will

We have to believe in free will. We've got no choice. ~ Isaac Bashevis Singer

We ride through life on the beast within us. Beat the animal, but you can't make it think. ~ Luigi Pirandello

### Freedom

Freedom is a habit that must be kept alive by use. ~ F.R. Scott, 1932

If we don't believe in freedom of expression for people we despise, we don't believe in it at all. ~ Noam Chomsky, 1992

This is a free country. Folks have a right to send me letters, and I have a right not to read them. ~ William Faulkner

Freedom is what you do with what's been done to you. ~ Jean-Paul Sartre

Who dares not speak his free thoughts is a slave. ~ Euripides

You should never have your best trousers on when you go out to fight for freedom and truth. ~ Henrik Ibsen

Those who deny freedom to others deserve it not for themselves.
~ Abraham Lincoln

The freedom of the individual is tied thoroughly and completely with the sanctity of private property. ~ Stephen Roman

Aren't people absurd! They never use the freedoms they do have but demand those they don't have; they have freedom of thought, they demand freedom of speech. ~ Soren Kierkegaard

Freedom is the right to be wrong, not the right to do wrong.
~ Bits & Pieces, December 5, 1995

Is something a blow against your freedom just because it can seriously damage your wealth? ~ Jonathan Lynn and Sir Anthony Jay

On the mountains there is freedom!
The world is perfect everywhere,
Save where man comes with his torment. ~ Friedrich von Schiller

Freedom is just chaos with better lighting. ~ Alan Dean Foster

I know but one freedom, and that is the freedom of the mind.
~ Antoine de Saint-Exupéry

Freedom is always and exclusively freedom for the one who thinks differently. ~ Rosa Luxemburg

To win true freedom, you must be a slave to philosophy. ~ Epicurus

When people are free to do as they please, they usually imitate each other. ~ Eric Hoffer

## French

The French are a logical people, which is one reason the English dislike them so intensely. The other is that they own France, a country which we have always judged to be much too good for them.
~ Robert Morley, A Musing Morley, 1974

## Freudian Slip

A Freudian slip is when you say one thing but mean your mother.
~ Unknown

## Friend

The friend who understands you, creates you. ~ Romain Rolland

If you would win a man to your cause, first convince him that you are his sincere friend. ~ Abraham Lincoln

He that would lose a friend for jest deserves to die a beggar by the bargain. ~ Sir Thomas Fuller

God save me from my friends, I can protect myself from my enemies.
~ Marshal de Villars

It's the friends that you can call up at 4 a.m. that matter.
~ Marlene Dietrich

We need two kinds of acquaintances: one to complain to, while we boast to the other. ~ Logan Pearsall Smith

I hate it in friends when they come too late to help. ~ Euripides

"Stay" is a charming word in a friend's vocabulary. ~ Louisa May Alcott

Hold a true friend with both hands. ~ Nigerian proverb

A friend is a present which you give yourself. ~ Robert Louis Stevenson

A friend's eye is a good mirror. ~ Irish proverb

The best mirror is an old friend. ~ George Herbert

A true friend is the most precious of all possessions and the one we take least thought about acquiring. ~ La Rochefoucauld

I was the kid next door's imaginary friend. ~ Emo Phillips

Some men are better served by their bitter-tongued enemies than by their sweet-smiling friends; because the former often tell the truth, the latter, never. ~ Cato the Younger

It is in the thirties that we want friends. In the forties, we know they won't save us any more than love did. ~ F. Scott Fitzgerald

You can always tell a real friend: When you've made a fool of yourself he doesn't feel you've done a permanent job. ~ Laurence J. Peter

A true friend is someone who knows you better than you know yourself. ~ Matthew Cheng

He makes no friend who has never made a foe. ~ Alfred, Lord Tennyson

## Friendship

That friendship will not continue to the end which is begun for an end. ~ Francis Quarles

You cannot shake hands with a clenched fist. ~ Anonymous

Friendship is love minus sex and plus reason. Love is friendship plus sex and minus reason. ~ Mason Cooley

True friendship comes when silence between two people is comfortable. ~ Dave Tyson Gentry

Friendship is a strong and habitual inclination in two persons to promote the good and happiness of one another. ~ Eustace Budgell

Do not let a little dispute injure a great friendship. ~ Dalai Lama

## Fugitive

I feel like a fugitive from the law of averages. ~ William Mauldin

## Fun

Most of the time I don't have much fun. The rest of the time I don't have any fun at all. ~ Woody Allen

## Funerals

Why is it that we rejoice at a birth and grieve at a funeral? Is it because we are not the person involved? ~ Mark Twain

## Funny

Everything is funny as long as it is happening to somebody else.
~ Will Rogers

## Futility

Conspicuous futility is something only for the young. One cannot go on "despairing of life" into a ripe old age. ~ George Orwell

## Future

The future is no more uncertain than the present. ~ Walt Whitman

In the future everyone will be world famous for fifteen minutes.
~ Andy Warhol

The danger of the past was that men became slaves. The danger of the future is that men may become robots. ~ Erich Fromm, 1955

The best prophet of the future is the past. ~ John Sherman

It is horrible to see everything that one detested in the past coming back wearing the colours of the future. ~ Jean Rostand

I have seen the Future – and it was being repaired. ~ Mel Calman

The future is like heaven – everyone exalts it, but no one wants to go there now. ~ James Baldwin

Still round the corner there may wait, a new road, or a secret gate.
~ J.R.R. Tolkien

And all your future lies beneath your hat. ~ John Oldham

I never think of the future. It comes soon enough. ~ Albert Einstein

In a hundred years? All new people. ~ Anne Lamott

The only reason people want to be masters of the future is to change the past. ~ Milan Kundera

All of us are looking at the future with yesterday's eyes. ~ Dan Burns

If you do not think about the future, you cannot have one.
~ John Galsworthy

RICHARD W. POUND

You can never plan the future by the past. ~ Edmund Burke

The future has a way of arriving unannounced. ~ E. George Will

Future, *n*. That period of time in which our affairs prosper, our friends are true and our happiness is assured. ~ Ambrose Bierce, U.S. writer

The future will be better tomorrow. ~ Dan Quayle

One should never place one's trust in the future. It doesn't deserve it. ~ Andre Chamson

The best way to predict the future is to invent it. ~ Alan Kay

The future is hidden even from the men who make it. ~ Anatole France

The future lies ahead. ~ Mort Sahl

What happens when the future has come and gone? ~ Robert Half

To know the road ahead, ask those coming back. ~ Chinese proverb

### Gag

In the end, everything is a gag. ~ Charlie Chaplin

### Gambling

The best throw of the dice is to throw them away. ~ English proverb

### Games

No human being is innocent, but there is a class of innocent human actions called Games. ~ W.H. Auden, 1962

Man is a gaming animal. He must always be trying to get the better in something or other. ~ Charles Lamb

### Gardeners

Like a gardener, I believe that what goes down must come up.
~ Lynwood L. Giacomini

### Gardens

I have a rock garden. Last week, three of them died. ~ Richard Diran

### Gene Pool

The problem with the gene pool is, that there is no lifeguard.
~ Steven Wright, comedian

### Generalizations

All generalizations are dangerous, even this one. ~ Alexandre Dumas

Generalizations are generally wrong. ~ Mary Wortley Montagu

### Generals

It is not the job of the general to be winning. It is his job to win.
~ Nancy Banks-Smith

## Generations

We think of generations as a 20-year unit, which is about as long as it takes one batch of humans to create its successors. But to adolescents, a generation lasts about three years, as long as it takes a group of them to take over a school and start laying down the stylistic rules. ... Style is how adolescent generations mark out their territory. *This is who we are. This is who we aren't.* ... "They're all the same kid," my older son said, after glimpsing the eighth-graders during their sidewalk procession. "He's right," my younger son said. "But they're not the kid he thinks they are." ~ John Powers in the *Boston Globe* magazine

## Generosity

We'd all like a reputation for generosity and we'd all like to buy it cheap. ~ Mignon McLaughlin

## Genius

Genius does what it must; talent does what it can. ~ Unknown

Genius is patience.
Genius is only a greater aptitude for patience. ~ Compte de Buffon

Talent is what you possess; genius is what possesses you.
~ Malcolm Cowley

Sometimes men come by the name of genius in the same way that certain insects come by the name of centipede – not because they have a hundred feet, but because most people can't count above 14.
~ Georg Christoph Lichtenberg

Attention makes the genius. All learning, fancy, science and skill depend upon it. Newton traced his great discoveries to it. It builds bridges, opens new worlds, heals disease, carries on the business of the world. Without it, taste is useless and the beauties of literature unobserved.
~ Robert Willmott, 19th century English author

There was never a genius without a tincture of madness. ~ Aristotle

Talent is that which is in a man's power; genius is that in whose power a man is. ~ James Russell Lowell

Genius ... means little more than the faculty of perceiving in an unhabitual way. ~ William James

Every family should have at least three children. Then, if one is a genius, the other two can support him. ~ George Coote

Talent is a very common family trait; genius belongs rather to individuals – just as you find one giant or one dwarf in a family, but rarely a full brood of either. Talent is often to be envied, and genius very commonly to be pitied. It stands twice the chance of the other of dying in a hospital, in jail, in debt, in bad repute. It is a perpetual insult to mediocrity; its every word is a trespass against somebody's vested ideas. ~ Oliver Wendell Holmes

Genius is the ability to act wisely without precedent – the power to do the right things for the first time. ~ Elbert Hubbard

I can't tell you if genius is hereditary because heaven has granted me no offspring. ~ James Abbott McNeill Whistler

In every work of genius we recognize our rejected thoughts.
~ Ralph Waldo Emerson

## Gentleman

A gentleman takes as much trouble to discover what is right as the lesser men take to discover what will pay. ~ Confucius

This is the final test of a gentleman: his respect for those who can be of no possible service to him. ~ William Phelps

A gentleman is a man who can play the accordion but doesn't.
~ Unknown

## Gentleness

There is nothing stronger in the world than gentleness. ~ Han Suyin

## Getting Up

It was such a lovely day I thought it was a pity to get up.
~ W. Somerset Maugham

## Ghosts

you want to know / whether i believe in ghosts / of course i do not believe in them / if you had known as many of them as i have / you would not believe in them either. ~ Don Marquis in *archy and mehitabel*

## Gifts

Rich gifts wax poor when givers prove unkind. ~ Shakespeare

Some people have a knack of putting upon you gifts of no real value, to engage you to substantial gratitude. We thank them for nothing.
~ Charles Lamb

There is no benefit in the gifts of a bad man. ~ Euripides

## Giving

Blessed are those who can give without remembering, and take without forgetting. ~ Princess Elizabeth Asquith Bibesco, English-born Romanian poet and writer

The manner of giving is worth more than the gift.
~ Pierre Corneille, French dramatist

It is one of the most beautiful compensations of life that no man can sincerely try to help another without helping himself. ~ John P. Webster

… and in the end it was said of him in the balance of life and in the sum of small and all things, he gave more than he took. ~ William Milton

There is sublime thieving in all giving. Someone gives us all he has and we are his. ~ Eric Hoffer

One can know nothing of giving aught that is worthy to give unless he also knows how to take. ~ Havelock Ellis

Nothing that I am able to give to you do I find worthy of you, and only in this way do I discover that I am a poor man. And so I give to you the only thing that I possess – myself. ~ Aeschines to Socrates, his teacher, who was receiving presents from his students

One must be poor to know the luxury of giving. ~ George Eliot

## Glory

Glory is fleeting, but obscurity is forever. ~ Napoleon Bonaparte

Our greatest glory is not in never failing, but rising every time we fall.
~ Confucius

## Gluttony

Gluttony is not a secret vice. ~ Orson Welles

I'm not a glutton, I'm an explorer of food. ~ Erma Bombeck

Gluttony kills more than the sword. ~ George Herbert

## Goals

People are not lazy. They simply have impotent goals – goals that do not inspire them. ~ Anthony Robbins

The soul that has no established aim loses itself. ~ Michel de Montaigne

It is not enough to take steps which may some day lead to a goal; each step must itself be a goal and a step likewise. ~ Goethe

## God

In the nineteenth century the problem was that God is dead; in the twentieth century the problem is that man is dead. ~ Erich Fromm

God helps those who get up early. ~ Spanish proverb

God gives the nuts, but He does not crack them. ~ Proverb

God is on the side not of the heavy battalions, but of the best shots. ~ Voltaire

God is a comedian playing to an audience too afraid to laugh. ~ Voltaire

God heard the embattled nations sing and shout
"Gott strafe England!" and "God save the King!"
God this God that and God the other thing
"Good God," said God, "I've got my work cut out." ~ J.C. Squire in 1914

God will pardon me. It's his business. ~ Heinrich Heine

Many people believe that they are attracted by God or nature, when they are only repelled by man. ~ W.R. Inge

You can't imagine the extra work I had when I was a god.
~ Hirohito, Emperor of Japan, during a London visit

If triangles had a God, He'd have three sides. ~ Yiddish proverb

When I told the people of Northern Ireland that I was an atheist, a woman in the audience stood up and said, "Yes, but is it the God of the Catholics or the God of the Protestants in whom you don't believe?"
~ Quentin Crisp

If God wanted us to fly, He would have given us tickets. ~ Mel Brooks

If you talk to God, you are praying; if God talks to you, you have schizophrenia. ~ Thomas Szasz

The problem is that God gives men a brain and a penis, and only enough blood to run one at a time. ~ Robin Williams

God is subtle but he is not malicious. ~ Albert Einstein

God looks at the clean hands, not the full ones. ~ Publilius Syrus

God is love, but get it in writing. ~ Gypsy Rose Lee

God hath chosen the foolish things of the world to confound the wise.
~ *The Bible*

## Gods

Ask the gods nothing excessive. ~ Aeschylus

The gods delight in an odd number. ~ Pliny the Elder

## Going

If you don't know where you're going, you will wind up somewhere else.
~ Yogi Berra

## Gold

All that glisters is not gold. ~ Shakespeare, *The Merchant of Venice*

## Golden Age

There are two golden ages: the mythical one in the past and the mythical one in the future. While it is naive to believe in the former, it is now a sign of sophistication to believe in the latter. ~ Anthony Daniels

## Golden Rule

The golden rule is that there are no golden rules. ~ George Bernard Shaw

## Golf

Man blames fate for other accidents, but feels personally responsible when he makes a hole-in-one. ~ *Horizons* magazine, cited in "Peter's Quotations"

If you watch a game, it's fun. If you play it, it's recreation.
If you work at it, it's golf. ~ Bob Hope, 1958

## Good

Have I done the world good, or have I added a menace?
~ Guglielmo Marconi

It is absurd to divide people into good and bad. People are charming or tedious. ~ Oscar Wilde

Confidence in the goodness of another is proof of one's goodness.
~ Michel de Montaigne

If merely "feeling good" could decide, drunkenness would be the supremely valid human experience. ~ William James

Good is not good where better is expected. ~ Thomas Fuller, M.D.

Do good by stealth, and blush to find it fame. ~ Alexander Pope

On the whole, human beings want to be good – but not too good and not quite all the time. ~ George Orwell

The meaning of good and bad, of better and worse, is simply helping or hurting. ~ Ralph Waldo Emerson

It used to be a good hotel, but that proves nothing –
I used to be a good boy. ~ Mark Twain

Every man is guilty of all the good he did not do. ~ Voltaire

Do you wish people to believe good of you? Don't speak. ~ Blaise Pascal

To be good is noble, but to teach others how to be good is nobler – and less trouble. ~ Mark Twain

There is an idea abroad among moral people that they should make their neighbours good. One person I have to make good: myself.
~ Robert Louis Stevenson

## Good Company

Nine-tenths of the people were created so you would want to be with the other tenth. ~ Horace Walpole

## Good Deed

No good deed goes unpunished. ~ Clare Booth Luce

One good deed is better than three days of fasting at a shrine.
~ Japanese saying

## Good Example

Really, if the lower orders don't set us a good example, what on earth is the use of them? ~ Oscar Wilde, *The Importance of Being Earnest*

Doing a good turn will not make you dizzy. ~ Anonymous

Few things are harder to put up with than the annoyance of a good example. ~ Mark Twain

## Good Fortune

Good or bad fortune usually comes to those who have more of the one than the other. ~ La Rochefoucauld

I make the most of all that comes,
And the least of all that goes. ~ Sara Teasdale

## Good Intentions

The road of good intentions is paved with hell. ~ Spencer Ante

## Good Life

The good life, as I conceive it, is a happy life. I do not mean that if you are good you will be happy – I mean that if you are happy you will be good. ~ Bertrand Russell

## Good Listener

A good listener is a good talker with a sore throat. ~ Katharine Whitehorn

## Good Looks

She got her looks from her father. He's a plastic surgeon. ~ Groucho Marx

## Good Men

Good men need no recommendation and bad men, it wouldn't help.
~ Jewish proverb

## Good Old Days

In every age, "the good old days" were a myth. No one ever thought they were good at the time. For every age has consisted of crises that seemed intolerable to the people who lived through them.
~ Brooks Atkinson

## Good Taste

Good taste is the worst vice ever invented. ~ Dame Edith Sitwell

It is a common error to think of bad taste as sterile. Rather, it is good taste, and good taste alone, that possesses the power to sterilize and is always the first handicap to any creative functioning. One has only to consider the good taste of the French: It has encouraged them not to do anything. ~ Salvador Dali

## Good Turn

One good turn gets most of the blanket. ~ Anonymous

## Gossip

Wolfgang Pauli, the quantum physics pioneer, once said of a colleague's appallingly off-base theory: "It's not even wrong." That's the time zone we're in here. ~ Phil (Mr. Sharon Stone) Bronstein, exec. ed. *San Francisco Examiner* on the accuracy of some newspaper stories about him and his beautiful wife.

Who gossips to you will gossip of you. ~ Turkish proverb

No one gossips about other people's secret vices. ~ Bertrand Russell

## Gourmet

A gourmet can tell from the flavour whether a woodcock's leg is the one on which the bird was accustomed to roost. ~ Lucius Beebe

## Government

I don't make jokes. I just watch the government and report the facts. ~ Will Rogers

No man's life, liberty, or property are safe while the legislature is in session. ~ Mark Twain, 1866

It is dangerous to be right when the government is wrong. ~ Voltaire

In general, the art of government consists in taking as much money as possible from one party of citizens to give to the other. ~ Voltaire

Government is the great fiction, through which everybody endeavours to live at the expense of everybody else. ~ Frederic Bastiat

Passion and prejudice govern the world; only under the name of reason. ~ John Wesley

It's getting harder and harder to support the government in the manner to which it has become accustomed. ~ Unknown

Government's view of the economy could be summed up in a few short phrases: If it moves, tax it. If it keeps moving, regulate it. And if it stops moving, subsidize it. ~ Ronald Reagan, 1986

If you want government to intervene domestically, you're a liberal.
If you want government to intervene overseas, you're a conservative.
If you want government to intervene everywhere, you're a moderate.
If you don't want government to intervene anywhere, you're an extremist. ~ Joseph Sobran, 1995

It is every citizen's duty to support his government – but not necessarily in the style to which it has become accustomed.
~ "Canadian Tax Highlights," June 1994

That government is the strongest in which every man feels himself a part. ~ Thomas Jefferson

Government by the people is possible, but highly improbable.
~ J. William Fulbright

Governments last as long as the under-taxed can defend themselves against the over-taxed. ~ Bernard Berenson

Those that think must govern those that toil. ~ Oliver Goldsmith

All government – indeed every human benefit and enjoyment, every virtue and every prudent act – is founded on compromise and barter. ~ Edmund Burke

Thought control is a copyright of totalitarianism, and we have no claim to it. It is not the function of our government to keep the citizen from falling into error, it is the function of the citizen to keep the government from falling into error. ~ Robert H. Jackson

An event has happened, upon which it is difficult to speak, and impossible to remain silent. ~ Edmund Burke

Government is a contrivance of human wisdom to provide for human wants. Men have a right that these wants should be provided for by this wisdom. ~ Edmund Burke

Government must be responsive to the needs and dreams of its people. ~ Mary Ellen Withrow

Whenever you have an efficient government, you have a dictatorship. ~ Harry Truman

Every country has the government it deserves. ~ Josephe de Maistre

A government which robs Peter to pay Paul can always depend on the support of Paul. ~ George Bernard Shaw

Giving money and power to government is like giving whiskey and car keys to teenage boys. ~ P.J. O'Rourke

The government must be the trustee for the little man, because no one else will be. The powerful can usually help themselves – and frequently do. ~ Adlai Stevenson

Since the beginning of time, governments have been mainly engaged in kicking people around. The astonishing acvhievement of modern times in the Western world is that the citizens should do the kicking. ~ Adlai Stevenson

Government cannot be stronger or more tough-minded than its people. It cannot be more inflexibly committed to the task than they. It cannot be wiser than the people. ~ Adlai Stevenson

Government is too big and important to be left to the politicians.
~ Chester Bowles

## Gratitude

Gratitude is the heart's memory. ~ French proverb

Blessed is he who expects no gratitude, for he will not be disappointed.
~ W.C. Bennett

Gratitude appears to be a state of mind. It is linked in part to a state of wonder, something that we often associate with childhood. And wonder is about looking beyond what is right in front of us. That's what we do when we teach kids to say "please" and "thank you." We want them to develop a sense of empathy and begin to think, "What was involved in what that person did for me?" or "What will that person actually have to do to carry out what I just asked for?"
~ Maurice Elias in *The Plain Dealer*, Cleveland

## Grave

The only difference between a rut and a grave is the depth. ~ Old saying

## Great

To do great things is difficult, but to command great things is more difficult. ~ Friedrich Nietzsche

He only is a great man who can neglect the applause of the multitude and enjoy himself independent of its favour. ~ Joseph Addison

Few great men could pass Personnel. ~ Paul Goodman

All great deeds and all great thoughts have a ridiculous beginning.
~ Albert Camus

They're only truly great who are truly good. ~ George Chapman

## Great Minds

Great minds have purposes; little minds have wishes. Little minds are subdued by misfortunes; great minds rise above them. ~ Washington Irving

The defects of great men are the consolation of dunces. ~ Isaac D'Israeli

## Great Organizations

It is the willingness of people to give of themselves over and above the demands of the job that distinguishes the great from the merely adequate organization. ~ Peter Drucker

I have never found that pay and pay alone would either bring together or hold good people. I think it was the game itself.
~ Harvey C. Firestone, founder of Firestone Tire & Rubber Company

## Greatness

It is the nature of all greatness not to be exact. ~ Edmund Burke

We feel that we are greater than we know. ~ William Wordsworth

## Greed

We are all born brave, trusting and greedy, and most of us remain greedy. ~ Mignon McLaughlin

## Greeks

I fear Greeks, even when they bring gifts. ~ Virgil

## Grief

All things grow with time, except grief. ~ Yiddish proverb

Happiness is beneficial for the body, but it is grief that develops the powers of the mind. ~ Marcel Proust

Memory nourishes the heart, and grief abates. ~ Marcel Proust

## Gross National Product

The gross national product does not allow for the health of our children, the quality of their education or the joy of their play. It does not include the beauty of our poetry or the strength of our marriages, the intelligence of our public debate or the integrity of our public officials. It measures neither our wit nor our courage, neither our wisdom nor our learning, neither our compassion nor our devotion to our country. It measures everything, in short, except that which makes life worthwhile. ~ Robert Kennedy

## Grow

Why stay we on the earth unless to grow? ~ Robert Browning

## Growing Up

You grow up the day you have your first laugh – at yourself.
~ Ethel Barrymore

## Guards

But who is to guard the guards themselves? ~ Juvenal

## Guidance

Only human beings guide their behaviour by a knowledge of what happened before they were born and a preconception of what may happen after they are dead; thus only humans find their way by a light that illuminates more than the patch of ground they stand on.
~ Peter and Jean Medawar, *The Life Science*, 1977

## Guilt

In former days, everyone found the assumption of innocence so easy; today we find fatally easy the assumption of guilt.
~ Amanda Cross, *Poetic Justice*, 1970

It is only too easy to compel a sensitive human being to feel guilty about anything. ~ Morton Irving Seinden

## Guilty

The guilty think all talk is of themselves. ~ Geoffrey Chaucer

Every man is guilty of all the good he didn't do. ~ Voltaire

There may be responsible persons, but there are no guilty ones.
~ Albert Camus

## Gun

You can get much farther with a kind word and a gun than you can with a kind word alone. ~ Al Capone

## Guts

The guts uphold the heart. ~ Thomas Fuller, M.D.

## Gym membership

Business has always been about trust. For this reason, the conduct of business has always needed a mechanism by which to estimate the trustworthiness of a prospective employee, partner or client. ... [Business has achieved it] by enforcing the rules of physical fitness. Gym membership today fills the same role as church membership more than a century ago. It is a testament of character.
~ Ronald Dworkin in *The Baltimore Sun*

## Habit

A nail is driven out by another nail; habit is overcome by habit.
~ Erasmus

Habit is stronger than reason. ~ George Santayana

Infinite toil would not enable you to sweep away a mist; but by ascending a little, you may often overlook it altogether. So it is with our moral improvement; we wrestle fiercely with a vicious habit, which would have no hold on us if we ascended into a higher moral atmosphere. ~ Sir Arthur Helps

A man's habit clings
And he will wear tomorrow what today he wears. ~ Edna St. Vincent Millay

Unles we extensively program our behaviour, we waste tremendous amounts of information-processing capacity on trivia. Watch a committee break for lunch and then return to the same room: almost invariably its members seek out the same seats they occupied earlier. … Choosing the same seat spares us the need to survey and evaluate other possibilities. ~ Alvin Toffler

Nothing so needs reforming as other people's habits. ~ Mark Twain

Man like every other animal is by nature indolent. If nothing spurs him on, then he will hardly think, and will behave from habit like an automaton. ~ Albert Einstein

Habit, *n*. A shackle for the free. ~ Ambrose Bierce

The chains of habit are too weak to be felt until they are too strong to be broken. ~ Samuel Johnson

To fall into a habit is to begin to cease to be. ~ Miguel de Unamuno

Habit will reconcile us to everything but change. ~ Charles Caleb Colton

### Hallowe'en

[Hallowe'en] is a fine American tradition of teaching our children to beg door-to-door dressed as mass murderers and co-dependent women. The planning takes weeks, but it's worth it just to see how lively a four-year-old can get after mainstreaming Milk Duds for three hours.
~ Cathy Crimmons, U.S. author

### Hang

We must all hang together, or assuredly we shall all hang separately.
~ Benjamin Franklin, at the signing of the Declaration of Independence, 1776

Never saw off the branch you are on, unless you are being hanged from it. ~ Stanislaw Lec

### Hangover

You pay for the liquor, the hangover is free. ~ Graffito

### Happen

Nothing, like something, happens anywhere. ~ Philip Larkin

### Happiness

All happiness depends on a leisurely breakfast. ~ John Gunther

We act as though comfort and luxury were the chief requirements of life, when all that we need to make us really happy is something to be enthusiastic about. ~ Charles Kingsley

When I was young, I used to think that wealth and power would bring me happiness. I was right. ~ Gahan Wilson

There is only one way to achieve happiness on this terrestrial ball And that is either to have a clear conscience or none at all.
~ Ogden Nash

Happy is the man to whom God gives with sparing hand what is sufficient for his needs. ~ Horace

Before we set our hearts too much upon anything, let us examine how happy they are, who already possess it. ~ La Rochefoucauld

If we only wanted to be happy, it would be easy; but we want to be happier than other people, and that is always difficult, since we think them happier than they are. ~ Montesquieu

Knowledge of what is possible is the beginning of happiness.
~ George Santayana

One is never either as happy or as unhappy as one imagines.
~ La Rochefoucauld

In vain do they talk of happiness who never subdued an impulse in obedience to a principle. ... He who never sacrificed a present to a future good, or a personal to a general one, can speak of happiness only as the blind speak of colour. ~ Horace Mann

If happiness in self-content is placed,
The wise are wretched, and fools only blessed. ~ William Congreve

Happiness is composed of misfortunes avoided. ~ Alphonse Karr

The really happy person is one who can enjoy the scenery when on a detour. ~ Unknown

Happiness is not a station you arrive at, but a manner of travelling.
~ Margaret Lee Runbeck

There is only one way to happiness and that is to cease worrying about things which are beyond the power of our will. ~ Epictetus

This planet has – or rather had – a problem, which was this: most of the people living on it were unhappy for pretty much of the time. Many solutions were suggested for this problem, but most of these were largely concerned with the movement of small green pieces of paper, which is odd because on the whole it wasn't the small green pieces of paper that were unhappy. ~ Douglas Adams, *The Hitchhiker's Guide to the Galaxy*

Philosophical happiness is to want little; civil or vulgar happiness is to want much and enjoy much. ~ Edmund Burke

To marvel at nothing is just about the one and only thing, Numicius, that can make a man happy and keep him that way. ~ Horace

There is in all of us an impediment to perfect happiness, namely, weariness of what we possess and a desire for what we have not.
~ Madame de Rieux, French author, circa 1757

Every time I talk to a savant I feel quite sure that happiness is no longer a possibility. Yet when I talk with my gardener, I'm convinced of the opposite. ~ Bertrand Russell

One of the keys to happiness is a bad memory. ~ Rita Mae Brown

Happiness does not reside in strength or money; it lies in rightness and many-sidedness. ~ Democritus

Happiness is a wine of rarest vintage, and seems insipid to a vulgar taste. ~ Logan Pearsall Smith

Happiness, *n.* An agreeable sensation arising from contemplating the misery of another. ~ Ambrose Bierce

Pleasure comes with the fulfilment of desire – getting what you want and wanting what you get. Happiness comes with the fulfilment of the person. And much of our moral confusion comes from the fact that we no longer know what happiness is, nor how to obtain it.
~ Roger Scruton, *The Good Life*, 1998

Happiness is no laughing matter. ~ Richard Whately

Ask yourself whether you are happy, and you will cease to be so.
~ John Stuart Mill

Happiness is not good for work. ~ Charles Darwin

Success is getting what you want, and happiness is wanting what you get. ~ Dave Gardner

## Hardship

Maybe one day we will be glad to remember even these hardships.
~ Virgil

## Harm

No people do such harm as those who go about doing good.
~ Bishop Mandell Creighton

## Harmlessness

Let harmlessness be the keynote of your life. ~ Alice Bailey

## Haste

One of the most pernicious effects of haste is obscurity.
~ Samuel Johnson

One of the great disadvantages of hurry is that it takes such a long time. ~ G.K. Chesterton

Too swift arrives as tardy as too slow. ~ Shakespeare

Whatever is produced in haste goes hastily to waste. ~ Sa'di

Haste in every business brings failures. ~ Herodotus

# Hate

Hate is not the opposite of love, apathy is. ~ Rollo May

Take care that no one hates you justly. ~ Publilius Syrus

The love of wicked men converts to fear,
That fear to hate, and hate turns one or both
To worthy danger and deserved death. ~ Shakespeare, *King Richard* II

# Headlines

Some people make headlines while others make history.
~ Philip Elmer-De Witt

# Healing

Healing is a matter of time, but it is sometimes a matter of opportunity.
~ Hippocrates

# Health

Only do always in health what you have often promised to do when
you are sick. ~ Advice of Sigismund, Holy Roman Emperor, on achieving happiness.

A cloudy day or a little sunshine have as great an influence on many
constitutions as the most real blessings or misfortunes. ~ Joseph Addison

Quit worrying about your health. It will go away. ~ Robert Orben

Preserving health by too severe a rule is a worrisome malady.
~ La Rochefoucauld

What use is a good head if the legs won't carry it? ~ Yiddish proverb

Health consists of having the same diseases as one's neighbours.
~ Quentin Crisp

# Health Care

If you think health care is expensive now, wait until you see what it
costs when it's free. ~ P.J. O'Rourke

# Hear

People don't hear what you say, but interpret what you say.
~ Graham McNally

# Heart

Measure men around the heart. ~ English proverb

The thing that eats the heart is mostly heart. ~ Stanley Kunitz

Don't worry about your heart, it will last you all of your life.
~ Dr. Albert Bach

## Heaven/Hell

I don't like to commit myself about heaven and hell – you see, I have friends in both places. ~ Mark Twain

Heaven is the place the donkey at last catches up with the carrot.
~ Anonymous

Maybe this world is another planet's Hell. ~ Aldous Huxley

Hell has three gates: lust, anger and greed. ~ Bhagavadgita

Where am I going and why am I in this handbasket? ~ Bumper Sticker

To different minds, the same world is a hell, and a heaven.
~ Ralph Waldo Emerson

In heaven, all the interesting people are missing. ~ Friedrich Nietzsche

## Helpfulness

It was as helpful as throwing a drowning man both ends of the rope.
~ Bugs Baer

It is hideous and coarse to assume that we can do something for others – and it is vile not to endeavour to do it. ~ Edward Dahlberg

It is one of the beautiful compensations of this life that no one can sincerely try to help another without helping himself.
~ Charles Dudley Warner

## Helping Hand

We are all here on earth to help others; what on earth the others are here for I don't know. ~ W.H. Auden

See me safe up, and for my coming down, let me shift for myself.
~ Thomas More, on ascending the scaffold

## Hero

To become a hero, one must give an order to oneself. ~ Simone Weil

Heroes are very human, most of them; very easily touched by praise.
~ Max Beerbohm

A hero is a man who does what he can. ~ Romain Rolland

The greatest obstacle to being heroic is the doubt whether one may not be going to prove one's self a fool. The truest heroism is to resist the doubt. ~ Nathaniel Hawthorne

Everyone is necessarily the hero of his own life story. ~ John Barth

Every hero becomes a bore at last. ~ Ralph Waldo Emerson

## Hesitation

He who hesitates is sometimes saved. ~ James Thurber

He who hesitates is probably right. ~ Graffito

We often wait too long to do what must be done today, in a world that gives us only one day at a time, without any assurance of tomorrow. ~ A reading from the *Mahzor*, a prayer book used on Yom Kippur

It's all right to hesitate if you then go ahead. ~ Bertolt Brecht

He who hesitates is a damn fool. ~ Mae West

Never put off doing something useful for fear of evil that may never arrive. ~ James Watson, Nobel Prize in Medicine, 1962

## Hidden

There it was, hidden in alphabetical order. ~ Rita Holt

## Hierarchy

The probability of, and resulting cost of, incompetence increases in direct proportion to the size of the hierarchy. ~ Chris Gundlach

The inevitable result of improved and enlarged communication between different levels in a hierarchy is a vastly increased area of misunderstanding. ~ Thomas L. Martin, Jr.

## Hindsight

After the ship has sunk everyone knows how she might have been saved. ~ Italian proverb

Hindsight is an exact science. ~ Anonymous

## Historians

Historians have been drug dealers to the addicts of national self-affirmation. ~ E. J. Hobsbawm

## History

History is the record of an encounter between character and circumstances. ~ Donald Creighton, 1972

History would be an excellent thing if only it were true. ~ Leo Tolstoy

History is a collection of agreed upon lies. ~ Voltaire

A historian is a prophet in reverse. ~ Friedrich von Schlegel

Human blunders usually do more to shape human history than human wickedness. ~ A.J.P. Taylor

God cannot alter the past, but historians can. ~ Samuel Butler

History repeats itself. Historians repeat each other. ~ Philip Guedalla

It takes a great deal of history to produce a little literature.
~ Henry James

It is not history that makes judgments, but judgments that make history. ~ Gaetan Picon

Our ignorance of history makes us libel our own times. People have always been like this. ~ Gustave Flaubert

There is properly no history, only biography. ~ Ralph Waldo Emerson, 1841

All history is the record of man's signal failure to thwart his destiny...
~ Henry Miller

Universal history is the history of a few metaphors. ~ Jorge Luis Borges

History says, if it pleases, Excuse me, I beg your pardon, it will never happen again if I can help it. ~ Carl Sandburg

The only lesson history has taught us is that man has not yet learned anything from history. ~ Anonymous

Like most of those who study history, [Napoleon III] learned from the mistakes of the past how to make new ones. ~ A.J.P. Taylor

A generation which ignores history has no past and no future.
~ Robert Heinlein

History is indeed little more than the register of the crimes, follies and misfortunes of mankind. ~ Edward Gibbon

News is the first rough draft of history. ~ Benjamin Bradlee

History will be kind to me for I intend to write it. ~ Winston Churchill

One of the lessons of history is that nothing is often a good thing to do and always a clever thing to say. ~ Will Durant

We learn from history that we do not learn from history. ~ Georg Hegel

History is a vast early-warning system. ~ Norman Cousins

History is more or less bunk. ~ Henry Ford

History is the essence of innumerable biographies. ~ Thomas Carlyle

Anybody can make history. Only a great man can write it. ~ Oscar Wilde

A wise man does not try to hurry history. ~ Adlai Stevenson

The world's history is the world's judgment. ~ Friedrich von Schiller

History gets thicker as it approaches recent times. ~ A.J.P. Taylor

Happy the people whose annals are blank in history books.
~ Montesquieu

The history of every country begins in the heart of a man or a woman.
~ Willa Cather

The unhistorical are usually, without knowing it, enslaved to a fairly recent past. ~ C.S. Lewis

## Holiday

A perpetual holiday is a good working definition of hell.
~ George Bernard Shaw

## Hollywood

You can take all the sincerity in Hollywood, place it in the navel of a fruit fly and have room left over for three caraway seeds and a producer's heart. ~ Fred Allen

However flawed and occasionally inaccurate Hollywood's history of the world may have been, there is this to be said for it, that it was certainly better fun than the real thing.
~ George MacDonald Fraser in *The Hollywood History of the World*

Hollywood is a great place if you're an orange. ~ Fred Allen

Strip away the phony tinsel of Hollywood and you find the real tinsel underneath. ~ Oscar Levant

## Home

A house is a home when it shelters the body and comforts the soul.
~ Phillip Moffitt, 1984

Home is not where you live but where they understand you.
~ Christian Morgenstern

It is the personality of the mistress that the home expresses. Men are forever guests in our homes, no matter how much happiness they may find there. ~ Elsie de Wolfe in *The House in Good Taste*, 1920

To be happy at home is the ultimate aim of all ambition; the end to which every enterprise and labour tends, and of which every desire prompts the prosecution. ~ Samuel Johnson

## Honesty

Honesty is something you can't wear out. ~ Waylon Jennings

There's one way to find out if a man is honest – ask him. If he says, "Yes," you know he is a crook. ~ Groucho Marx

Honesty is the best image. ~ Tom Wilson

Honesty is the best policy; but he who is governed by that maxim is not an honest man. ~ Richard Whately

## Honour

Show me the man you honour and I will know what kind of man you are, for it shows me what your ideal of manhood is, and what kind of man you long to be. ~ Thomas Carlyle

What is honoured in a country will prosper there. ~ Plato

Many shall be restored that are now fallen and many
Shall fall that now are in honour. ~ Horace, *Ars Poetica*

But if it be a sin to covet honour,
I am the most offending soul alive. ~ Shakespeare, *King Henry* V

There could be no honour in a sure success, but much might be wrested from a sure defeat. ~ T.E. Lawrence

## Hope

Not to hope for things to last forever, is what the year teaches and even the hour which snatches a nice day away. ~ Horace

Hope is a good breakfast, but it is a bad supper. ~ Francis Bacon

It's good to hope; it's the waiting that spoils it. ~ Yiddish proverb

Hope deceives more men than cunning. ~ Marquis de Vauvenargues

Never give out while there is hope; but hope not beyond reason, for that shows more desire than judgment. ~ William Penn

If you do not hope, you will not find what is beyond your hopes.
~ St. Clement of Alexandria

He that lives in hope danceth without music. ~ George Herbert

Hope is the feeling you have that the feeling you have isn't permanent.
~ Jean Kerr

We must rediscover the distinction between hope and expectation.
~ Ivan Illich

# Hospitality

Never mistake endurance for hospitality. ~ Anonymous

# House

A house is a machine for loving in. ~ Craig McGregor

# Housekeeping

Keeping house is as unpleasant and filthy as coal mining, and the pay's a lot worse. ~ P.J. O'Rourke in *The Bachelor Home Companion*, 1987

Housework can't kill you, but why take a chance? ~ Phyllis Diller

I personally am inclined to approach [housework] the way governments treat dissent: ignore it until it revolts. ~ Barbara Kingsolver, *The Household Zen*

# Human

The human race has improved everything except the human race.
~ Adlai Stevenson

The essence of being human is that one does not seek perfection.
~ George Orwell

# Human Nature

Human nature is not of itself vicious. ~ Tom Paine

Most human beings have an almost infinite capacity for taking things for granted. ~ Aldous Huxley

The human race, to which so many of my readers belong, has been playing at children's games from the beginning, and will probably do it until the end, which is a nuisance for the few people who grow up. ~ G.K. Chesterton

It is part of human nature to hate the man you have hurt. ~ Tacitus

Civilized ages inherit the human nature which was victorious in barbarous ages, and that nature is, in many respects, not at all suited to civilized circumstances. ~ Walter Bagehot

## Human Rights

There is only one basic human right, the right to do as you damn well please. And with it comes the only basic human duty, the duty to take the consequences. ~ P.J. O'Rourke, 1993

## Humanity

Humanity is just a work in progress. ~ Tennessee Williams

We must all learn to be guests of each other. ~ George Steiner

## Humiliation

We all have these places where shy humiliations gambol on sunny afternoons. ~ W.H. Auden

## Humility

Become humble as the market goes your way. ~ Bernard Baruch

## Humour

Nothing in man is more serious than his sense of humour; it is the sign that he wants all the truth. ~ Mark Van Doren

All my humour is based upon destruction and despair. If the whole world were tranquil, without disease and violence, I'd be standing in the breadline right in back of J. Edgar Hoover. ~ Lenny Bruce

The wit makes fun of other persons; the satirist makes fun of the world; the humorist makes fun of himself, but in so doing, he identifies himself with people. ~ James Thurber

I'm learning the difference between humour and comedy, between the laugh that lasts and the one that evaporates as soon as it hits air. Humour is giving, and comedy is taking away. Humour is companionable, comedy cold. Humour is character, comedy personality. ~ Roger Rosenblatt

Nowadays if you're funny at anyone's expense they run to the UN and say, "I must have an ombudsman to protect me." ~ Robertson Davies, 1991

Every survival kit should include a sense of humour. ~ Frank Baer

Humour is the best way of dealing with complete and utter nonsense … Because we are mad, we are prone to making absurd conclusions regardless of the evidence. The only true wisdom in life is [coping with] complete and utter confusion. ~ John (Johnny Rotten) Lydon

One doesn't have a sense of humour. It has you. ~ Larry Gelbart

A good half of the humour of the late Mark Twain consisted of admitting frankly the possession of vices and weaknesses that all of us have and few of us care to acknowledge. Practically all the sagacity of George Bernard Shaw consists of bellowing vociferously what everyone knows. ~ H.L. Mencken

## Humour Books

Relax: You May Have Only a Few Minutes Left, by Loretta LaRoche

Stressed is Desserts Spelled Backwards, by Brian Seaward

I'm Alive and the Doctor's Dead, by Sue Buchanan

301 Ways to Have Fun at Work, by Dave Hemsath and Leslie Yerkes

Fun? But We're Married, by Lois and Joel Davitz

## Hunch

A hunch is creativity trying to tell you something. ~ Unknown

## Hunger

The belly overreaches the head. ~ French proverb

Hunger is the best sauce in the world. ~ Miguel de Cervantes

## Hurry

We can outrun the wind and the storm, but we cannot outrun the demon of Hurry. ~ John Burroughs

Whoever is in a hurry shows that the thing he is about to do is too big for him. ~ Lord Chesterfield

Hurry, hurry has no blessing. ~ Swahili proverb

## Hypochondria

The best cure for hypochondria is to forget about your own body and get interested in someone else's
~ Goodman Ace, U.S. radio and TV writer

## Hypocrisy

Hypocrisy is the necessary burden of villainy. ~ Albert Camus

No man is a hypocrite in his pleasures. ~ Samuel Johnson

## Hysteria

My quiet exterior used to be a mask for hysteria. After seven years of analysis, it just became a habit. ~ Gene Wilder

## Ice

Everybody in life gets the same amount of ice. The rich get it in the summer and the poor in the winter. ~ Message found on the typewriter of *New York Morning Telegram* sports writer Bat Masterson, formerly a Dodge City lawman and latterly a Wild West icon, after he suffered a fatal heart attack.

## Iconoclast

In the whole range of human occupations, is it possible to imagine a poorer thing to be than an iconoclast? It is the lowest of all the unskilled trades. ~ G.K. Chesterton

## Ideas

Serious people have few ideas. People with ideas are seldom serious. ~ Paul Valéry, French poet/essayist

She never lets ideas interrupt the easy flow of her conversation. ~ Jean Webster, U.S. writer in *Daddy-Long-Legs*

A powerful idea communicates some of its strength to him who challenges it. ~ Marcel Proust

A fixed idea ends in madness or heroism. ~ Victor Hugo

Not to engage in the pursuit of ideas is to live like ants instead of men. ~ Mortimer J. Adler

Let us remind ourselves that last year's fresh idea is today's cliché. ~ Austen Briggs, U.S. commercial artist

An idea isn't responsible for the people who believe in it. ~ Don Marquis

A man with a new idea is a crank until the idea succeeds. ~ Mark Twain

If at first the idea is not absurd, there is no hope for it. ~ Albert Einstein

Between the idea and the reality falls the shadow. ~ T.S. Eliot

Launching a breakthrough idea is like shooting skeet. People's needs change, so you must aim well ahead of the target to hit it.
~ Raymond Kurzweil

Man's mind, stretched to a new idea, never goes back to its original dimensions. ~ Oliver Wendell Holmes, Jr.

Lack of money is no obstacle. Lack of ideas is an obstacle. ~ Ken Hakuta

The stock of ideas which mankind has to work with is very limited, like the alphabet, and can at best have an air of freshness given it by new arrangements and combinations, or by application to new times and circumstances. ~ James Russell Lowell

We must change our ideas when they have served their purpose.
~ Claude Bernard

Men become susceptible to ideas, not by discussion and argument, but by seeing them personified and by loving the person who so embodies them. ~ Lewis Mumford

No idea is so antiquated that it was not once modern. No idea is so modern that it will not some day be antiquated.
~ Ellen Glasgow in 1936

An invasion of armies can be resisted, but not an idea whose time has come. ~ Victor Hugo

To die for an idea is to place a pretty high price upon conjecture.
~ Anatole France

I pressed down on the mental accelerator. The old lemon throbbed fiercely. I got an idea. ~ P.G. Wodehouse

Many ideas grow better when transplanted into another mind than in the one where they sprang up. ~ Oliver Wendell Holmes

Everything you see and touch was once an invisible idea until someone chose to bring it into being. Any powerful idea is absolutely fascinating and absolutely useless until we choose to use it. ~ Richard Bach

Nothing is more dangerous than an idea, when it's the only one we have. ~ Emile-Auguste Chartier

Every time a man puts a new idea across, he finds 10 men who thought of it before he did – but they only thought of it. ~ Anonymous

In our society, the simplest person is involved with ideas. Every person we meet in the course of our daily life, no matter how unlettered he may be, is groping with sentences toward a sense of his life and his position in it; and he has what almost always goes with an impulse to ideology, a good deal of animus and anger.
~ Lionel Trilling, *The Liberal Imagination*, 1950

When ideas fail, words come in very handy. ~ Goethe

## Ideals

Ideals are very often formed in the effort to escape from the hard task of dealing with facts. ~ William Sumner

## Idealism

Idealism increases in direct proportion to one's distance from the problem. ~ John Galsworthy

Idealism is the noble toga that political gentlemen drape over their will to power. ~ Aldous Huxley

The idealist walks on his toes, the materialist on his talons.
~ Malcolm de Chazal in *Sens Plastique*

## Idealists

An idealist is one who, on noticing that a rose smells better than a cabbage, concludes that it will also make better soup. ~ H.L. Mencken

An idealist is a person who helps others be prosperous. ~ Henry Ford

## Identity

How can we know the dancer from the dance? ~ William Butler Yeats

## Idleness

Too much idleness, I have observed, fills up a man's time much more completely, and leaves him less his own master, than any sort of employment whatsoever. ~ Edmund Burke

Do not allow idleness to deceive you; for while you give him today he steals tomorrow from you. ~ Alfred Crowquill

Any fool can be fussy and rid himself of energy all over the place, but a man has to have something in him before he can settle down to do nothing. ~ J.B. Priestly

Nothing is so intolerable to a man as being fully at rest, without passion, without business, without entertainment, without care. It is then that he recognizes that he is empty, insufficient, dependent, ineffectual. ~ Blaise Pascal

It is impossible to enjoy idling thoroughly unless one has plenty of work to do. ~ Jerome K. Jerome

We would all be idle if we could. ~ Samuel Johnson

## Ignorance

He that knows little often repeats it. ~ Thomas Fuller, M.D.

If ignorance is bliss, 'Tis folly to be wise. ~ Thomas Gray

A man is never astonished that he doesn't know what another does, but he is surprised at the gross ignorance of the other in not knowing what he does. ~ Thomas Chandler Haliburton

Ignorance alone makes monsters and bugbears; our actual acquaintances are very commonplace people. ~ William Hazlitt

There is nothing more frightening than active ignorance. ~ Goethe

The ignorant man always adores what he cannot understand.
~ Cesare Lombroso

Most ignorance is vincible ignorance. We don't know because we don't want to know. ~ Aldous Huxley

I know of no disease of the soul but ignorance. ~ Ben Jonson

If ignorance is bliss, why aren't more people happy?
~ Leonard Rossiter, British actor

Better to be ignorant of a matter than half know it. ~ Publilius Syrus

When ignorance gets started, it knows no bounds. ~ Will Rogers

Everybody is ignorant, only on different subjects. ~ Will Rogers

The trouble ain't that people are ignorant; it's that they know so much that ain't so. ~ Josh Billings

I do not approve of anything that tampers with natural ignorance. Ignorance is like a delicate exotic fruit. Touch it and the bloom is gone.
~ Oscar Wilde in *The Importance of Being Earnest*

I am not ashamed to admit that I am ignorant of what I do not know.
~ Cicero

Genuine ignorance is ... profitable because it is likely to be accompanied by humility, curiosity, and open-mindedness; whereas ability to repeat catch-phrases, cant terms, familiar propositions, gives the conceit of learning and coats the mind with varnish waterproof to new ideas. ~ John Dewey

To be ignorant of one's ignorance is the malady of the ignorant.
~ Bronson Alcott

## Ill

She was dangerously ill, now she's dangerously well. ~ Anonymous

If a man thinks about his physical or moral state, he usually discovers that he is ill. ~ Goethe

## Illiteracy

There is that indescribable freshness and unconsciousness about an illiterate person that humbles and mocks the power of the noblest expressive genius. ~ Walt Whitman

According to the United Nations' latest count, of the approximately 3,000 languages spoken in the world today, only some 78 have a literature. Of those 78, a scant five or six enjoy a truly international audience. Literates make up a very small minority of the world's population, but they make their force felt out of all proportion to their number. ~ Barry Sanders in A Is For Ox

## Illness

Illness is the most heeded of doctors: To kindness and wisdom we make promises only; pain we obey. ~ Marcel Proust

It's no fun being sick when you don't feel well. ~ Olga Shoaff

Illness is the night-side of life, a more onerous citizenship.
~ Susan Sontag

## Illusion

Illusion is the first of all pleasures. ~ Oscar Wilde

The most dangerous of our calculations are those we call illusions.
~ Georges Bernanos

It is respectable to have no illusions, and safe and profitable and dull.
~ Joseph Conrad

## Imagination

Imagination is the beginning of creation. You imagine what you desire, you will what you imagine and at last you create what you will.
~ George Bernard Shaw

Imagination and fiction make up more than three-quarters of our real life. ~ Simone Weil, French writer

Imagination is one of the last remaining legal means you have to gain an unfair advantage over your competition.
~ Pat Fallon, of the Minneapolis advertising firm Fallon McElligott Rice

Where there is no imagination there is no horror.
~ Sir Arthur Conan Doyle, 1888

Castles in the air – they're so easy to take refuge in. So easy to build, too. ~ Henrik Ibsen

Imagination is more important than knowledge. Knowledge is limited. Imagination circles the world ~ Albert Einstein

Imagination is the highest kite one can fly. ~ Lauren Bacall

Imagination grows by exercise and contrary to common belief is more powerful in the mature than in the young. ~ W. Somerset Maugham

There are no days in life so memorable as those which vibrated to some stroke of the imagination. ~ Ralph Waldo Emerson

The most imaginative people are the most credulous, for to them everything is possible. ~ Alexander Chase

Fantasies are more than substitutes for unpleasant realities, they are also dress rehearsals. All acts performed in the world begin in the imagination. ~ Barbara Grizzuti Harrison

Imagination is the mad boarder. ~ Nicolas Malebranche

I have imagination, and nothing that is real is alien to me.
~ George Santayana

Everything you can imagine is real. ~ Pablo Picasso

Imagination is the one weapon in the war against reality.
~ Jules de Gaultier

It is the spirit of the age to believe that any fact, no matter how suspect, is superior to any imaginative exercise, no matter how true.
~ Gore Vidal

RICHARD W. POUND

Imagination, *n*. A warehouse of facts, with poet and liar in joint ownership. ~ Ambrose Bierce

The hardest thing to imagine is yourself. ~ David Wevill

I like to have a thing suggested rather than told in full. When every detail is given, the mind rests satisfied and the imagination loses the desire to use its own wings. ~ Thomas Bailey Aldrich

## Imbeciles

When a finger points to the moon the imbecile looks at the finger.
~ Chinese proverb

## Imitation

We forfeit three-quarters of our lives to be like other people.
~ Arthur Schopenhauer

## Immaturity

The mark of the immature man is that he wants to die nobly for a cause, while the mark of the mature man is that he wants to live humbly for one. ~ Wilhelm Stekel

## Immortality

Millions long for immortality who do not know what to do with themselves on a rainy Sunday afternoon. ~ Susan Ertz

If all else fails, immortality can always be assured by spectacular error.
~ John Kenneth Galbraith

The only thing wrong with immortality is that it tends to go on forever.
~ Herb Caen

The nearest approach to immortality on earth is a government bureau.
~ James Byrnes

## Impartiality

There are only two ways to be quite unprejudiced and impartial. One is to be completely ignorant. The other is to be completely indifferent. Bias and prejudice are attitudes to be kept in mind, not attitudes to be avoided. ~ Charles P. Curtis

## Impatience

Successful salespeople, authors, executives, and workers of every sort need patience. The great liability of youth is not inexperience but impatience. ~ William Feather

## Imperfection

A good garden may have some weeds. ~ Thomas Fuller, M.D.

We're all somewhat courageous and we're all considerably cowardly.
We're all imperfect and life is simply a perpetual, unending struggle
against those imperfections. ~ Sidney Poitier

## Importance

It is well to remember that the entire population of the universe, with
one trifling exception, is composed of others. ~ Andrew Holmes, cited in
Fitzhenry & Whiteside Book of Quotations

It is completely unimportant. That is why it is so interesting.
~ Agatha Christie

If it is not worth doing, it is not worth doing well. ~ Donald O. Hebb

At any given time there are more important people in the world than
important jobs to contain them. ~ Bunk Carter

## Impossible

Few things are of themselves impossible, and we lack the application to
make them a success rather than the means. ~ La Rochefoucauld

If an elderly but distinguished scientist says that something is possible
he is almost certainly right, but if he says that it is impossible he is very
probably wrong. ~ Arthur C. Clarke

It's kind of fun to do the impossible. ~ Walt Disney

Probable impossibilities are to be preferred to improbable possibilities.
~ Aristotle

## Impressions

The world is for thousands a freak show; the images flicker past and
vanish; the impressions remain flat and unconnected in the soul.
~ Goethe, 1776

## Improbable

Man can believe the impossible, but man can never believe the
improbable. ~ Oscar Wilde

## Improvement

There's only one corner of the universe you can be certain of improving
and that's your own self. ~ Aldous Huxley

None will improve your lot
If you yourselves do not. ~ Bertolt Brecht

If a way to the Better there be, it exacts a full look at the worst.
~ Thomas Hardy

## Improvise

In the long history of humankind (and animalkind, too) those who
learned to collaborate and improvise most effectively have prevailed.
~ Charles Darwin

## Inaccuracy

A little inaccuracy sometimes saves tons of explanations.
~ Saki (H.H. Munro)

## Income

If your outgo exceeds your income, your upkeep will be your downfall.
~ Anonymous

## Income Tax

The hardest thing in the world to understand is income tax.
~ Albert Einstein (attributed)

The only thing that hurts more than paying an income tax is not having
to pay an income tax. ~ Lord Thomas Dewar

Income tax has made more liars out of the American people than golf
has. ~ Will Rogers

In filling out an income tax return, let an accountant instead of your
conscience be your guide. ~ Will Rogers

## Incommunicable

I distrust the incommunicable: it is the source of all violence.
~ Jean-Paul Sartre

## Inconstancy

Nothing that is not a real crime makes a man appear so contemptible
and little in the eyes of the world as inconstancy, especially when it
regards religion or party. ~ Joseph Addison

## Independence

Let all your views in life be directed to a solid, however moderate,
independence; without it, no man can be happy, nor even honest.
~ Junius

### Indifference

The worst sin toward our fellow creatures is not to hate them, but to be indifferent to them; that's the essence of inhumanity.
~ George Bernard Shaw

### Indignation (Moral)

Moral indignation is jealousy with a halo. ~ H.G. Wells

A good indignation makes an excellent speech. ~ Ralph Waldo Emerson

### Individualism

Individualism is rather like innocence; there must be something unconscious about it. ~ Louis Kronenberger

### Indolence

Though you may have known clever men who were indolent, you never knew a great man who was so; and when I hear a young man spoken of as giving promise of great genius, the first question I ask about him always is: Does he work? ~ John Ruskin

### Industry

Life without industry is guilt, and industry without art is brutality.
~ John Ruskin

### Inequality

The worst form of inequality is to try to make unequal things equal.
~ Aristotle

### Inevitability

There is no good in arguing with the inevitable. The only good argument available with an east wind is to put on your overcoat.
~ James Russell Lowell

Science fiction writers foresee the inevitable, and although problems and catastrophes may be inevitable, solutions are not. ~ Isaac Asimov

### Inferiority

Nobody can make you feel inferior without your consent.
~ Eleanor Roosevelt

### Infinitude

All finite things reveal infinitude. ~ Theodore Roethke

If you wish to advance into the infinite, explore the finite in all directions. ~ Goethe

## Inflation

It's kind of like duck hunting. You aim ahead of the duck, not at the duck. The same is true of inflation. You have to act in advance.
~ Sung Won Sohn, economist, of Norwest Corp.

One of the benefits of inflation is that kids can no longer get sick on a nickel's worth of candy. ~ *Journeyman Barber* magazine

## Information

Information is the currency of democracy. ~ Ralph Nader

We all get heavier as we get older because there is more information in our heads. ~ Vlade Divac

## Informed

It is better to be un-informed than ill-informed. ~ Keith Duckworth

## Ingratitude

People who bite the hand that feeds them usually lick the boot that kicks them. ~ Eric Hoffer

## Inheritance

Say not you know another entirely, till you have divided an inheritance with him. ~ Johann Kaspar Lavater

## Inhumanity

In the nineteenth century, inhumanity meant cruelty; in the twentieth century it means schizoid self-alienation. The danger of the past was that men became slaves. The danger of the future is that men may become robots. ~ Erich Fromm, *The Sane Society*, 1955

## Initiative

It is much easier to ask for forgiveness than for permission. ~ Unknown

You miss 100 percent of the shots you never take. ~ Wayne Gretzky

Everything comes to him who hustles while he waits. ~ Thomas A. Edison

We often get in quicker by the back door than by the front.
~ Napoleon Bonaparte

## Innocence

It's innocence when it charms us, ignorance when it doesn't.
~ Mignon McLaughlin

The truly innocent are those who not only are guiltless themselves, but who think others are. ~ Josh Billings

What is our innocence, what is our guilt? All are naked, none is safe.
~ Marianne Moore

## Innovation

Innovation is the central issue in economic prosperity.
~ Michael Porter, Harvard Bus. School

Just as energy is the basis of life itself, and ideas the source of innovation, so is innovation the vital spark of all human change, improvement and progress. ~ Theodore Levitt

Instead of pouring knowledge into people's heads, we need to help them grind a new set of eyeglasses so that we can see the world in a new way. ~ J.S. Brown

## Insanity

Insanity is hereditary; you can get it from your children. ~ Sam Levenson

## Insight

Nothing is more terrible than activity without insight. ~ Thomas Carlyle

A moment's insight is sometimes worth a life's experience.
~ Oliver Wendell Holmes, Jr.

## Insistence

One who is too insistent on his own views finds few to agree with him.
~ Lao-tzu, *Tao-te ching*

## Insomnia

The best cure for insomnia is to get a lot of sleep. ~ W.C. Fields

## Inspiration

Keep your fears to yourself but share your inspiration.
~ Robert Louis Stevenson

So-called "inspiration" is no more than an extreme example of a process which constantly goes on in the minds of all of us.
~ Anthony Storr

176                                                            RICHARD W. POUND

## Instant Gratification

Instant gratification takes too long. ~ Carrie Fisher

## Instincts

A few strong instincts, and a few plain rules. ~ William Wordsworth

Be a good animal, true to your instincts. ~ D.H. Lawrence

## Instructions

When all else fails, read instructions. ~ Graffito

## Insult

The only gracious way to accept an insult is to ignore it; if you can't ignore it, top it; if you can't top it, laugh at it; if you can't laugh at it, it's probably deserved. ~ Russell Lynes

An injury is much sooner forgotten than an insult. ~ Lord Chesterfield

## Insurance

What can't be cured, must be insured. ~ Oliver Herford

## Intellect

The highest intellects, like the tops of mountains, are the first to catch and to reflect the dawn. ~ Thomas Macaulay

## Intellectual

Definition of an intellectual: someone who can listen to Rossini's "William Tell" Overture without thinking of the Lone Ranger. ~ Unknown

An intellectual is not only a person for whom books are essential but one for whom an idea, however elementary, absorbs and orders his life. ~ André Malraux, *The Walnut Trees of Altenburg*

An intellectual is "a man who writes his own speeches." ~ C. Wright Mills, U.S. sociologist

The terrifying thing about modern intellectuals everywhere is that they are always changing idols. ~ Charles Simic, poet

An intellectual is a man who takes more words than necessary to tell more than he knows. ~ Dwight Eisenhower

An intellectual is a man who does not know how to park a bike. ~ Spiro T. Agnew

An intellectual is someone whose mind watches itself. ~ Albert Camus

As Marshall McLuhan [put it]: "Moral indignation is a technique used to endow the idiot with dignity." Precisely which intellectuals of the 20th century were or were not idiots is a debatable point, but it is hard to argue with the definition I once heard a French diplomat offer at a dinner party: "An intellectual is a person knowledgeable in one field who speaks out only in others." ~ Tom Wolfe

Intellectual passion dries out sensuality. ~ Leonardo da Vinci

There is a Northwest passage to the intellectual World. ~ Laurence Stern

## Intelligence

Respond intelligently even to unintelligent treatment.
~ Lao-tzu, *Tao-te ching*

He who knows much about others may be learned, but he who understands himself is more intelligent. He who controls others may be powerful, but he who has mastered himself is mightier still.
~ Lao-tzu, *Tao-te ching*

One can live in the shadow of an idea without grasping it.
~ Elizabeth Bowen

A man is not necessarily intelligent because he has plenty of ideas, any more than he is a good general because he has plenty of soldiers.
~ Sébastien Chamfort

No man is smart, except by comparison with others who know less; the smartest man who ever lived has reason to be ashamed of himself.
~ Edgar Watson Howe

Intelligence is what you use when you don't know what to do.
~ Jean Piaget (attributed)

What a distressing contrast there is between the radiant intelligence of the child and the feeble mentality of the average adult. ~ Sigmund Freud

Intelligence is not all that important in the exercise of power and is often, in point of fact, useless. Just as a leader doesn't need intelligence, a man in my job doesn't need too much of it either.
~ Henry Kissinger

Intelligence is almost useless to someone who has no other quality.
~ Alexis Carrel, *Man the Unknown*

Artificial intelligence is no match for artificial stupidity. ~ Unknown

Intelligence is not to make no mistakes
But quickly to see how to make them good. ~ Bertolt Brecht

It has yet to be proven that intelligence has any survival value.
~ Arthur C. Clarke

Nothing so gives the illusion of intelligence as personal association
with large sums of money. ~ John Kenneth Galbraith

Intelligence is quickness to apprehend, as distinct from ability, which is
capacity to act wisely on the thing apprehended. ~ Alfred North Whitehead

There is no such thing as an underestimate of average intelligence.
~ Henry Adams

Military intelligence is a contradiction in terms. ~ Groucho Marx

## Intelligent

There are some men who are so intelligent that you wonder whether
anything can still interest them. ~ Maurice Martin du Gard, 1944

## Interesting

Nothing is interesting if you're not interested. ~ Anne Lindbergh

## Interests

We have no eternal allies, we have no perpetual enemies. Our interests
are eternal and perpetual, and those interests it is our duty to follow.
~ Viscount Henry John Temple Palmerston

## Internal World

We contain an internal world which is just as active and complicated as
the one we live in. It is an interior of which we are largely unaware, and
one to which we have no personal access. We cannot be tourists in our
own insides. ~ Dr. Jonathan Miller, The Body in Question

## International

How horrible, fantastic, incredible it is that we should be digging
trenches and trying on gas masks here because of a quarrel in a
faraway country between people of whom we know nothing.
~ Neville Chamberlain, radio broadcast September 27, 1938, re Czechoslovakia

## Interpretation

Interpretation is the revenge of the intellect upon art. ~ Susan Sontag

### Intrigue

There are masked words abroad, I say, which nobody understands.
~ John Ruskin

### Intuition

Often you just have to rely on your intuition. ~ Bill Gates

The intuitive mind is a sacred gift, and the rational mind is a faithful servant. We have created a society that honours the servant and has forgotten the gift. ~ Albert Einstein

### Inventions

I just invent, then wait until man comes around to needing what I've invented. ~ R. Buckminster Fuller, 1964

Everything that can be invented has been invented.
~ Charles H. Duell, Dir. U.S. Patent Office, 1899

There ought to be a monument to the man who invented neon lights....There's a boy who really made something out of nothing.
~ Raymond Chandler in *The Little Sister*

Getting caught is the mother of invention. ~ Robert Byrne

If you took away everything in the world that had to be invented, there'd be nothing left except a lot of people getting rained on.
~ Tom Stoppard

### Inventors

Only an inventor knows how to borrow. ~ Ralph Waldo Emerson

### Investments

Never invest money in anything that eats or needs repainting.
~ Billy Rose

He has spent all his life letting down empty buckets into empty wells; and he is frittering away his age in trying to draw them up again.
~ Sydney Smith, 1885

You must lose a fly to catch a trout. ~ George Herbert

Sometimes your best investments are the ones you don't make.
~ Donald Trump

### Irish

We in coming days may be still the indomitable Irishy.
~ William Butler Yeats

I am troubled, I'm dissatisfied, I'm Irish. ~ Marianne Moore

### Irony

Irony may be a universal device but it is also a divisive and unstable one. ~ Alexander Star

### Irresistible

Only that which does not teach, which does not cry out, which does not condescend, which does not explain, is irresistible.
~ William Butler Yeats

## "Jacketspeak"

Provocative and enlightening = querulous and crabby

Compelling = no big words

Breathtaking and compelling = hackneyed and no big words

Definitive = beware: footnotes

Sprawling = unedited

Controversial = inadequately researched

Monumental = see "sprawling"

A groundbreaking achievement = deserves to be interred

Daring = smutty

A daring breakthrough = smutty and degenerate

Engaging = aimed at Barbie Doll collectors

Enchanting = warning: may induce insulin shock
~ from *Globe & Mail*, Charles Macli

## January

January, month of empty pockets!...Let us endure this evil month, anxious as a theatrical producer's forehead. ~ Colette

## Jaundice

All looks yellow to a jaundiced eye. ~ Alexander Pope

## Jest

A jest often decides matters of importance more effectually and happily than seriousness. ~ Horace

RICHARD W. POUND

## Jewellery

Never wear artistic jewellery; it ruins a woman's reputation. ~ Colette

## Job

A job is death without the dignity. ~ Brendan Behan

Look for a tough wedge for a tough log. ~ Publilius Syrus

All paid jobs absorb and degrade the mind. ~ Aristotle

Oh, you hate your job? Why didn't you say so? There's a support group for that. It's called EVERYBODY and they meet at the bar. ~ Drew Carey

In an undeveloped country, when you are absent, your job is taken away from you; in a developed country, a new one is piled on you.
~ Charles Issawi

## Jogging

The only reason I would take up jogging is so I could hear heavy breathing again. ~ Erma Bombeck

## Jokes

Behind every joke there is a deep cultural grievance. You cannot have a joke without a grievance. ~ Marshall McLuhan, 1977

A difference of taste in jokes is a great strain on the affections.
~ George Eliot, *Daniel Deronda*

Many a folly, which all the serious preaching in the world could not cure, has been driven from the stage of living realities by a joke.
~ William Fleet, 1852

At bottom, the world isn't a joke. We only joke about it to avoid an issue with someone, to let someone know that we know he's there with his questions; to disarm him by seeming to have heard and done justice to his side of the standing argument. ~ Robert Frost

The problem with political jokes is they get elected. ~ Henry Cate VII

## Journalism

...there is much to be said in favour of modern journalism. By giving us the opinions of the uneducated, it keeps us in touch with the ignorance of the community. ~ Oscar Wilde

### Journalists

Most journalists are restless voyeurs who see the warts on the world, the imperfections in people and places...gloom is their game, the spectacle their passion, normality their nemesis. ~ Gay Talese, 1969

### Joys

Great joys, like griefs, are silent. ~ Shackerley Marmion

### Judge

Judge: a law student who marks his own papers. ~ H.L. Mencken

### Judgment

We should not fear the strategies of our enemies – only the possible mistakes in our own judgment. ~ Unknown

Snap judgments often snap back. ~ Anonymous

You can't depend on your judgment when your imagination is out of focus. ~ Mark Twain

Good judgment comes from experience, and experience comes from bad judgment. ~ Barry LePatner

Judgment comes from experience, and great judgment comes from bad experience. ~ Saying, *Quotationary*

Obviously, a man's judgment cannot be better than the information on which he has based it. ~ Arthur Hays Sulzberger

Sir Roger told them, with the air of a man who would not give his judgement rashly, that much might be said on both sides. ~ Joseph Addison

Don't judge a man until you have walked two moons in his moccasins. ~ American Indian proverb

Every man ought to be a judge of pictures, and every man is so who has not been connoisseured out of his senses. ~ William Blake

Knowledge is the treasure, but judgment the treasurer of a wise man. ~ William Penn

Rightness of judgment is bitterness to the heart. ~ Euripides

Most people have ears, but few have judgment. ~ Lord Chesterfield

At 20 years of age, the will reigns; at 30, the wit; and at 40, the judgment. ~ Benjamin Franklin

Everyone complains of his memory, but no one complains of his judgment. ~ La Rochefoucauld

If you are pained by external things, it is not they that disturb you, but your own judgment of them. And it is in your power to wipe out that judgment now. ~ Marcus Aurelius

## Judgment (Bad)

Men of ill-judgment oft ignore the good that lies within their hands, till they have lost it. ~ Sophocles

## Judgment (Last)

I shall tell you a great secret, my friend. Do not wait for the last judgment; it takes place every day. ~ Albert Camus

## Judgment (Rush to)

But now all these and all things else hear the trumpet, and must rush to judgment. ~ Ralph Waldo Emerson

## Justice

Justice is too good for some people and not good enough for the rest.
~ Norman Douglas, Scottish novelist

Injustice all around is justice. ~ Persian proverb

I have a secret passion for mercy...but justice is what keeps happening to people. ~ Ross Macdonald

Justice is the insurance we have on our lives and property, and obedience is the premium we pay for it. ~ William Penn

Wrong must not win by technicalities. ~ Aeschylus

The price of justice is eternal publicity. ~ Arnold Bennett

Let justice be done, though the world perish. ~ Emperor Ferdinand I

## Justification

The end cannot justify the means, for the simple and obvious reason that the means employed determine the nature of the ends produced.
~ Aldous Huxley in *Ends and Means*

### Kafka

You don't actually have to be intelligent if you can just create the impression. This can usually be accomplished by a reference to Kafka. Even if you never read any of his – or her – works. ~ Bob Newhart

### Karate

Karate is a form of martial arts in which people who have had years and years of training can, using only their hands and feet, make some of the worst movies in the history of the world. ~ Dave Barry

### Kill

How many times do I have to kill before I get a name in the paper or some national attention?
~ a Kansas serial killer, complaining by letter to police, circa 1993.

### Kindness

Forget injuries, never forget kindnesses. ~ Chinese proverb

Be kind to unkind people – they need it the most. ~ Anonymous

In this world, you must be a bit too kind in order to be kind.
~ Pierre Marivaux

Always be a little kinder than necessary. ~ James M. Barrie

### Kinship

Kinship is healing; we are physicians to each other.
~ Oliver Sacks, *Awakenings*, 1973

### Knowledge

A wise question is half of knowledge. ~ Francis Bacon

The mind is the man, and knowledge mind; the man is but what he knoweth. ~ Francis Bacon

Nobody knows anything until he is fifty. ~ F.H. Underhill, 1976

When a man's knowledge is not in order, the more of it he has, the greater will be his confusion. ~ Herbert Spencer

Nobody knows enough, but many know too much.
~ Marie von Ebner-Eschenbach, Austrian novelist

The gift of fantasy has meant more to me than my talent for absorbing positive knowledge. ~ Albert Einstein

If I had only known, I would have been a locksmith. ~ Albert Einstein

The knowledge that you can have is inexhaustible, and what is inexhaustible is benevolent. The knowledge that you cannot have is of the riddles of birth and death, of our future destiny and the purposes of God. Here there is no knowledge, but illusions that restrict freedom and limit hope. Accept the mystery behind knowledge: It is not darkness, but shadow. ~ Northrop Frye

The more I read, the more I meditate; and the more I acquire, the more I am able to affirm that I know nothing. ~ Voltaire

Knowledge is said to be power; and it is power in the same sense that wood is fuel. Wood on fire is fuel. Knowledge on fire is power.
~ Henry MacKenzie, Scottish novelist

We know accurately only when we know little; with knowledge doubt increases. ~ Goethe

Be avaricious of time; do not give any moment without receiving it in value; only allow the hours to go from you with as much regret as you give your gold; do not allow a single day to pass without increasing the treasure of your knowledge and virtue. ~ Nicholas Le Tourneux

I do not know which makes a man more conservative – to know nothing but the present or nothing but the past. ~ John Maynard Keynes

In order that knowledge be properly digested, it must have been swallowed with a good appetite. ~ Anatole France

I prefer tongue-tied knowledge to ignorant loquacity. ~ Cicero

Knowledge is power, if you know it about the right person.
~ Ethel Mumford

In expanding the field of knowledge, we but increase the horizon of ignorance. ~ Henry Miller

What can give us surer knowledge than our senses? With what else can we better distinguish the true from the false? ~ Lucretius

Some drink at the fountain of knowledge. Others just gargle.
~ Anonymous

Every step by which men add to their knowledge and skills is a step also by which they can control other men. ~ Max Lerner

I hold myself indebted to any one from whose enlightened understanding another ray of knowledge communicates to mine. Really, to inform the mind is to correct and enlarge the heart. ~ Junius

What one knows is, in youth, of little moment;
they know enough who know how to learn. ~ Henry Brooks Adams

Knowledge is of two kinds: we know a subject ourselves, or we know where we can find information on it. ~ Samuel Johnson

Knowledge is the true organ of sight, not the eyes. ~ Panchatantra

It is better to know nothing than to know everything by halves.
~ Friedrich Nietzsche

We owe almost all our knowledge not to those who have agreed, but to those who have differed. ~ Charles Caleb Colton

If a little knowledge is dangerous, where is the man who has so much as to be out of danger? ~ Thomas Henry Huxley

Since we cannot be universal and know all that is to be known of everything, we ought to know a little about everything. ~ Blaise Pascal

Know thyself. ~ Oracle, Delphi

'Tis not knowing much, but what is useful, that makes a wise man.
~ Thomas Fuller, M.D.

As we acquire more knowledge, things do not become more comprehensible, but more mysterious. ~ Albert Schweitzer

It is better to know nothing than to know what ain't so. ~ Josh Billings

The more you know the less the better. ~ Billy Connolly

The fox knows many things – the hedgehog one big one. ~ Archilochus

## Labels

One of the unpardonable sins, in the eyes of most people, is for a man to go about unlabelled. The world regards such a person as the police do an unmuzzled dog, not under proper control. ~ Thomas Henry Huxley

## Labour

I pity the man who wants a coat so cheap that the man or woman who produces the cloth shall starve in the process. ~ Benjamin Harrison

Labour is the superior of capital and deserves much the higher consideration. ~ Abraham Lincoln

## Lady

The attributes of a great lady may still be found in the four S's: Sincerity, Simplicity, Sympathy, Serenity. ~ Emily Post

## Language

If language is not correct, then what is said is not what is meant; if what is said is not what is meant, then what ought to be done remains undone. ~ Confucius

Language, particularly language in public, is very serious business because the way people talk is an indication of the way they are, how they feel, where they put the limits, where their culture is. If measuring offensive language in American culture tells us anything, it is that something elemental has changed since mid-century, leaving us awash in a four-letter-word frenzy. ~ Charles Madigan, *Chicago Tribune*

Language most shews a man: Speak, that I may see thee. ~ Ben Jonson

Language is the amber in which a thousand precious thoughts have been safely embedded and preserved. ~ Richard Trench

I wonder what language truck drivers are using, now that everyone is using theirs? ~ Beryl Pfizer

Man invented language to satisfy his deep need to complain.
~ Lily Tomlin

Since the concepts people live by are derived only from perceptions and from language and since the perceptions are received and interpreted only in light of earlier concepts, man comes pretty close to living in a house that language built. ~ Russell R.W. Smith

As the Latin languages are not composed of two diverse elements, as English is of Latin and German, so the Latin mind does not have two spheres of sentiment, one vulgar and the other sublime. All changes are variations on a single key, which is the key of intelligence.
~ George Santayana

Language exerts a hidden power, like a moon on the tides.
~ Rita Mae Brown

England and America are two countries divided by a common language.
~ George Bernard Shaw

In language, the ignorant have prescribed laws to the learned.
~ Richard Duppa

The limits of my language mean the limits of my world.
~ Ludwig Wittgenstein

## Laughter

Strange, when you come to think of it, that of all the countless folk who have lived before our time on this planet, not one is known in history or in legend as having died of laughter. ~ Sir Max Beerbohm

Among those whom I like, I can find no common denominator, but among those whom I love, I can; all of them make me laugh.
~ W.H. Auden, 1962

There are some things that are so serious you have to laugh at them.
~ Niels Bohr

The world should laugh more. But after having eaten. ~ Cantinflas

Laugh when you can. Everything has its time. ~ Voltaire

He who laughs last has not heard the bad news. ~ Bertolt Brecht

Laughter is the shortest distance between two people. ~ Victor Borge

In this life, he laughs longest who laughs last. ~ John Masefield

The most wasted of all days is one without laughter. ~ e.e. cummings

It's an odd job, making decent people laugh. ~ Molière

## Laurels

Nothing is harder on your laurels than resting on them. ~ Anonymous

## Law

Laws are like cobwebs that entangle the weak, but are broken by the strong. ~ Solon

The reason of the law is the law. ~ Walter Scott

The law often allows what honour forbids. ~ Jacques Saurin

Law is the backbone which keeps man erect. ~ S.C. Yuter

The law must be stable, but it must not stand still. ~ Roscoe Pound

To be completely free one must be a slave to a set of laws. ~ Cicero

Laws, like houses, lean on one another. ~ Edmund Burke

The law, in its majestic equality, forbids the rich as well as the poor to sleep under bridges and to steal bread. ~ Anatole France

Laws were made to be broken. ~ Christopher North

Law is order; and good law is good order. ~ Aristotle

## Lawyers

There is no law without lawyers. ~ Roscoe Pound

Whatever else their contributions may be to our society, lawyers could be an important source of protein. ~ *Globe & Mail*, April 1992

Lawyers know that truth is a kind of seeming, a subtle blend of what is demonstrable and what cannot be disproved. ~ John le Carré

They have no lawyers in Utopia for they consider them as a sort of people whose profession it is to disguise matters.
~ Sir Thomas More, *Utopia*, 1516

A businessman who had just returned from a consultation with his attorney recounted his experience to a friend.

"But why pay all that money to a lawyer?" his friend asked. "Didn't you see all those books in his office? The answer to your problem was right there!"

"Yes," the businessman replied, "but the lawyer knows what page it's on!" ~ Unknown

No brilliance is needed in the law. Nothing but common sense and relatively clean finger nails. ~ John Mortimer, 1971

As your attorney, it is my duty to inform you that it is not important that you understand what I'm doing or why you're paying me so much money. What's important is that you continue to do so.
~ Hunter S. Thompson's Samoan attorney

## Lawsuit

Lawsuit: a machine which you go into as a pig and come out as a sausage. ~ Ambrose Bierce

## Laziness

Failure is not our only punishment for laziness: There is also the success of others. ~ Jules Renard

We make a mistake if we believe that only the violent passions like ambition and love can subdue the others. Laziness, for all her languor, is nevertheless often mistress; she permeates every aim and action in life and imperceptibly eats away and destroys passions and virtues alike. ~ La Rochefoucauld

## Leader

As long as I am your leader I am going to tell you when you are wrong and I will congratulate you when you are right. ~ Nelson Mandela, ANC leader, 1993, admonishing a crowd that demanded that he take a more militant stand against white South Africans after a bloody spate of violence left more than 140 people dead in previous week

The successful person, in any field, takes time out to confer with himself or herself. Real leaders use solitude to put the pieces of a problem together, to work out solutions, and to plan.
~ Dr. David Schwartz, author of The Magic of Self Direction

A born leader of men is somebody who is afraid to go anywhere by himself. ~ Clifford Hanley, Scottish Quotations

Leaders are people who do the right thing: managers are people who do things right. Both roles are crucial, but they differ profoundly. I often observe people in top positions doing the wrong thing well.
~ Warren Bennis, *Why Leaders Can't Lead*, 1989

O ye who lead, take heed!
Blindness we may forgive, but baseness we will smite.
~ William Vaughn Moody

## Leadership

Anyone can hold the helm when the sea is calm. ~ Publilius Syrus

In calm water, every ship has a good captain. ~ German proverb

To have his path made clear for him is the aspiration of every human being in our beclouded and tempestuous existence. ~ Joseph Conrad

Every leader starts by first leading himself. ~ Norman Bethune

Too bad all the people who know how to run the country are busy driving taxi cabs and cutting hair. ~ George Burns

When the eagles are silent, the parrots begin to jabber.
~ Winston Churchill

## Learn

You live and learn. At any rate, you live. ~ Douglas Adams

## Learning

Learning is a treasure which follows its owner everywhere.
~ Chinese proverb

The only things worth learning are the things you learn after you know it all. ~ Harry S. Truman

Learning is not child's play; we cannot learn without pain. ~ Aristotle

Learning is not compulsory; neither is survival. ~ W. Edwards Deming

Some people will never learn anything, for this reason: Because they understand everything too soon. ~ Alexander Pope

The brighter you are, the more you have to learn. ~ Don Herold

You have learnt something. That always feels at first as if you had lost something. ~ George Bernard Shaw

It is better to be able neither to read nor write than to be able to do nothing else. ~ William Hazlitt, *On the Ignorance of the Learned*

Learn as much by writing as by reading. ~ Lord Acton

When the student is ready, the lesson appears. ~ Gene Oliver

Much learning does not teach understanding. ~ Heraclitus

Things take indeed a wondrous turn
When learned men do stoop to learn. ~ Bertolt Brecht

A learned man is an idler who kills time with study. ~ George Bernard Shaw

A little learning is a dangerous thing;
Drink deep, or taste not the Pierian Spring. ~ Alexander Pope

The wisest mind has something yet to learn. ~ George Santayana

## Legislators

When buying and selling are controlled by legislation, the first things to be bought and sold are legislators. ~ Unknown

## Leisure

People who know how to employ themselves always find leisure moments, while those who do nothing are forever in a hurry.
~ Marie-Jeanne Roland, French political leader

It is in the improvident use of our leisure, I suspect, that the greatest wastes of American life occur. ~ Robert Park, sociologist

The future will belong not only to the educated man, but to the man who is educated to use his leisure wisely. ~ C.K. Brightbill

Your job today tells me nothing of your future – your use of your leisure today tells me just what your tomorrow will be.
~ Robert Jackson, U.S. Supreme Court justice

## Less

Less is more. ~ Robert Browning

## Lessons

When you lose, do not lose the lesson. ~ Dalai Lama

## Let

A Zen master once asked an audience of Westerners what they thought was the most important word in the English language. After giving his listeners the chance to think about such favourite words as love, truth, failure and so on, he said, "No, it's a three letter word; it's the word 'let.' Let it be. Let it happen." ~ W. Timothy Gallwey, *The Inner Game of Tennis*

## Liars

The liar's punishment is not in the least that he is not believed but that he cannot believe anyone else. ~ George Bernard Shaw

He led a double life. Did that make him a liar? He did not feel a liar. He was a man of two truths. ~ Iris Murdoch, *The Sacred and Profane Love Machine*

The most mischievous liars are those who keep sliding on the edge of truth. ~ Julius and Augustus Hare

## Liberal

We who are liberal and progressive know that the poor are our equals in every sense except that of being equal to us.
~ Lionel Trilling, *The Liberal Imagination*

A liberal is someone who feels a great debt to his fellow man, which debt he proposes to pay off with your money. ~ G. Gordon Liddy

## Liberty

Liberty is the right of doing whatever the laws permit.
~ Montesquieu, *De l'esprit des lois*

They that give up essential liberty to obtain a little temporary safety deserve neither liberty nor safety. ~ Benjamin Franklin

Liberty, too, must be limited to be possessed. ~ Edmund Burke

In my youth I stressed freedom, and in my old age I stress order.
I have made the great discovery that liberty is a product of order.
~ Will Durant, American historian

Liberty too can corrupt, and absolute liberty can corrupt absolutely.
~ Gertrude Himmelfarb

Liberty doesn't work as well in practice as it does in speeches.
~ Will Rogers

I prefer liberty to chains of diamonds. ~ Lady Mary Wortley Montagu

The liberty of the individual must be thus far limited: he must not make himself a nuisance to other people. ~ John Stuart Mill

Eternal vigilance is the price of liberty. ~ Thomas Jefferson

Liberty is a beloved discipline. ~ George Caspar Homans

O Liberty! what crimes are committed in thy name. ~ Mme Rolland

Liberty is being free from the things we don't like in order to be slaves of the things we do like. ~ Ernest Benn

## Libraries

A library, to modify the famous metaphor of Socrates, should be the delivery room for the birth of ideas – a place where history comes to life. ~ Norman Cousins

My library was dukedom large enough. ~ Shakespeare

If you file your waste-paper basket for 50 years, you have a public library. ~ Tony Benn

## Lies

A lie which is half a truth is ever the blackest of lies.
~ Alfred, Lord Tennyson

Never chase a lie. Let it alone and it will run itself to death.
~ Lyman Beecher

I do not mind lying, but I hate inaccuracy. ~ Samuel Butler, *Notebooks*, 1912

A lie has always a certain amount of weight with those who wish to believe it. ~ E.W. Rice

If a lie is repeated often enough all the dumb jackasses in the world not only get to believe it, they even swear by it. ~ Billy Boy Franklin

A lie told often enough becomes the truth. ~ Lenin

Repetition does not transform a lie into truth. ~ Franklin Delano Roosevelt

A lie can be halfway around the world before the truth has got its boots on. ~ James Callaghan

We lie loudest when we lie to ourselves. ~ Eric Hoffer

In human relations kindness and lies are worth 1,000 truths.
~ Graham Greene

There are three kinds of lies – lies, damned lies and statistics.
~ Mark Twain

Whoever would lie usefully, should lie seldom. ~ Lord Hervey

The cruelest lies are often told in silence. ~ Robert Louis Stevenson

There is no greater lie than a truth misunderstood. ~ William James

Pretending that you believe a liar is also a lie. ~ Arthur Schnitzler

## Life

My theory is to enjoy life, but the practice is against it. ~ Charles Lamb

We are always complaining that our days are few, and acting as though there would be no end of them. ~ Seneca

Life is divided into the horrible and the miserable. ~ Woody Allen

Life is like a game of cards. The hand that is dealt you represents determinism; the way you play it is free will. ~ Jawaharlal Nehru

Life is a tragedy full of joy. ~ Bernard Malamud

Life is short, the art long, opportunity fleeting, experience treacherous, judgment difficult. ~ Hippocrates

Life is like riding a bicycle. You don't fall off unless you stop pedalling.
~ Claude Pepper

Henceforth I shall accept what I am and what I am not. With my limitations and my gifts, I shall go on using life as long as I am in this world and afterwards. Not to use life – that alone is death. ~ George Sand

Life is too short to be little. ~ Benjamin Disraeli

Life is one long process of getting tired. ~ Samuel Butler

We do not know what to do with this short life, yet we yearn for another that will be eternal. ~ Anatole France

Life is strange. Every so often a good man wins. ~ Frank Dane

Life is like playing a violin solo in public and learning the instrument as one goes on. ~ Samuel Butler, 1895

One must live the way one thinks or end up thinking the way one has lived. ~ Paul Bourget, French novelist/critic

To die and not be lost is the real blessing of a long life. ~ Lao-tzu

There are two things to aim at in life: first, to get what you want; and, after that, to enjoy it. Only the wisest of mankind achieve the second. ~ Logan Pearsall Smith

I'm not going to starve to death just so I can live a little longer. ~ Irene Peter

Life is hard. After all, it kills you. ~ Katharine Hepburn

How long do you have to live before the odds of getting to your next birthday are worse than 50:50? The answer is encouraging – 104. ~ Norris McWhirter, founder/editor of the *Guinness Book of Records*

There are two ways to slide easily through life: to believe everything or to doubt everything: both ways save us from thinking. ~ Alfred Korzybski

There is an ambush everywhere from the army of accidents; therefore the rider of life runs with loosened reins. ~ Hafiz, Persian poet

You have a choice of two things in life: remembering and hoping. ~ Paul Villeneuve

Life does not consist mainly – or even largely – of facts and happenings. It consists mainly of the storm of thoughts that is forever blowing through one's head. ~ Mark Twain

Life is either a daring adventure or nothing. ~ Helen Keller

Life is a succession of lessons enforced by immediate reward, or, oftener, by immediate chastisement. ~ Ernest Dimnet

We arrive at the various stages of life quite as novices. ~ La Rochefoucauld

The best part of our lives we pass in counting on what is to come. ~ William Hazlitt

Few people make all of life's journey on a green light. ~ Dr. Ernest A. Fitzgerald

Somehow life doesn't always pay off to those who are most insistent. ~ Max Lerner

Life is too short for traffic. ~ Dan Bellack

The world is so constructed that if you wish to enjoy its pleasures, you must also endure its pains. Whether you like it or not, you cannot have one without the other. ~ Brahmananda, Hindu philosopher

If you look at life one way, there is always cause for alarm.
~ Elizabeth Bowen

Life for the European is a career; for the American, it is a hazard.
~ Mary McCarthy

The art of living is more like wrestling than dancing. ~ Marcus Aurelius

Life is not a spectator sport. ~ Anonymous

Life, I fancy, would very often be insupportable, but for the luxury of self-compassion. ~ George Gissing

I finally figured out the only reason to be alive is to enjoy it.
~ Rita Mae Brown

Life is change. Growth is optional. Choose wisely. ~ Karen Kaiser Clark

Not only is life a bitch, it has puppies. ~ Adrienne E. Gusoff

Life is made up of two phases. In the first you try to make a name for yourself and in the second you try to keep it.
~ Bits & Pieces, December 5, 1995

I think the purpose of life is to be happy, to be useful, to be responsible, to be honourable, to be compassionate. It is, above all, to matter; to count, to stand for something, to have made a difference that you lived at all. ~ Leo Rosten, American author and humorist

Life is made up of constant calls to action, and we seldom have time for more than hastily contrived answers. ~ Learned Hand

Life's under no obligation to give us what we expect. ~ Margaret Mitchell

Live your life so that if someone says "Be yourself," it's good advice.
~ Robert Orwen

If I were to begin life again, I should want it as it was. I would only open my eyes a little more. ~ Jules Renard

The difficulty in life is the choice. ~ George Moore

The great secret of life is to learn lessons, not to teach them.
~ Thomas Chandler Haliburton

Life is short, art long, opportunity fleeting, experience treacherous, judgment difficult. ~ Hippocrates

It's life, Jim ... but not as we know it. ~ Mr. Spock, Star Trek

What a rotten writer of detective stories life is. ~ Nathan Leopold

Life flows on within you and without you. ~ George Harrison, Beatle

Try to arrange your life in such a way that you can afford to be disinterested. It is the most expensive of all luxuries, and the one best worth having. ~ W.R. Inge

Life may have no meaning. Or, even worse, it may have a meaning of which I disapprove. ~ Ashley Brilliant

That's the secret to life – replace one worry with another.
~ Charles Schulz

By his very success in inventing labour-saving devices, modern man has manufactured an abyss of boredom that only the privileged classes in earlier civilizations have ever fathomed.
~ Lewis Mumford in *The Conduct of Life*, 1951

Life is made up of marble and mud. ~ Nathaniel Hawthorne

Life is a copiously branching bush, continually pruned by the grim reaper of extinction, not a ladder of predictable progress.
~ Stephen Jay Gould

Organic life, we are told, has developed gradually from the protozoon to the philosopher, and this development, we are assured, is indubitably an advance. Unfortunately, it is the philosopher, not the protozoon, who gives us this assurance. ~ Bertrand Russell

It is only knowing how little life has in store for us that we are able to look upon the bright side and avoid disappointment. ~ Ellen Glasgow

Life is a great bundle of little things. ~ Oliver Wendell Holmes

Life is a gamble at terrible odds – if it was a bet, you wouldn't take it.
~ Tom Stoppard

Life after 50: Your back goes out more than you do. ~ Rex Guinn

You make a living by what you get. You make a life by what you give.
~ Winston Churchill

Life is not a spectacle or a feast; it is a predicament. ~ George Santayana

We live in a rainbow of Chaos. ~ Paul Cezanne

The fullness of life is in the hazards of life. ~ Edith Hamilton

If you don't run your own life, somebody else will. ~ John Atkinson

It takes a lifetime to know what to do with life. ~ Juliette Greco

An imaginative man is apt to see, in his life, the story of his life; and is thereby led to conduct himself in his life in such a manner as to make a good story of it rather than a good life.
~ Sir Henry Taylor in *The Statesman*, 1836

No one achieves a house by blueprints alone, no matter how accurate or detailed. A time comes when one must take up hammer and nails. In building a house, the making of blueprints may be delegated to an architect, the construction to a carpenter. In building the house of one's life or in its remodelling, one may delegate nothing.
~ Allen Wheelis, *How People Change*, 1973

Life is a long lesson in humility. ~ James M. Barrie

I'd always assumed I was the central character in my own story, but now it occurred to me I might in fact be only a minor character in someone else's. ~ Russell Hoban in *Turtle Diary*

I don't want the cheese; I just want out of the trap. ~ Graffito

Life is not a static thing. The only people who do not change their minds are incompetents in asylums, who can't, and those in cemeteries. ~ Everett M. Dirksen

My grandfather always said that living is like licking honey off a thorn.
~ Louis Adamic

Life is very singularly made to surprise us (when it does not utterly appall us). ~ Rainer Maria Rilke

We live our lives, forever taking leave. ~ Rainer Maria Rilke

One must choose in life between boredom and torment. ~ Mme de Stael

In life, as in chess, one's own pawns block one's way. A man's very wealth, ease, leisure, children, books, which should help him to win, more often checkmate him. ~ Charles Buxton

Life depends on awkward people. ~ Margaret Thatcher

Life is a zoo in a jungle. ~ Peter De Vries

Though we seem grieved at the shortness of life in general, we are wishing every period of it at an end. ~ Joseph Addison

Life is uncertain. Eat dessert first. ~ Ernestine Ulmer

We are always getting to live, but never living. ~ Ralph Waldo Emerson

Life is a succession of lessons which must be lived to be understood.
~ Ralph Waldo Emerson

The true meaning of life is to plant trees, under whose shade you do
not expect to sit. ~ Nelson Henderson

The tragedy of life is not that man loses but that he almost wins.
~ Heywood Broun

Flops are part of life's menu, and I've never been a girl to miss out on
any of the courses. ~ Rosalind Russell

Life is something to do when you can't get to sleep. ~ Fran Lebowitz

The life which is unexamined is not worth living. ~ Plato

All that matters is love and work. ~ Sigmund Freud

To be able to enjoy one's past life is to live twice.
~ Martial (Marcus Valerius Martialis)

In three words I can sum up everything I've learned about life:
it goes on. ~ Robert Frost

Life would be tolerable but for its amusements.
~ Sir George Cornewall Lewis

I long ago came to the conclusion that all life is 6 to 5 against.
~ Damon Runyon

Life is made up of sobs, sniffles and smiles, with sniffles predominating.
~ O. Henry, *Gift of the Magi*

Human life begins on the other side of despair. ~ Jean-Paul Sartre

The goal of life is living in agreement with nature. ~ Zeno

The essential of life is statistical improbability on a colossal scale.
~ Richard Dawkins

Life is what happens when you're making other plans. ~ John Lennon

Life isn't fair. It's just fairer than death, that's all. ~ William Goldman

Oh, isn't life a terrible thing, thank God? ~ Dylan Thomas

Man is born to live, not to prepare for life. ~ Boris Pasternak

To beautify life is to give it an object. ~ José Martí

Life is like an onion: you peel it off one layer at a time and sometimes you weep. ~ Carl Sandburg

Don't take life too seriously – you will never get out of it alive. ~ Elbert Hubbard

Life isn't meant to be easy. It's hard to take being on the top – or on the bottom. ~ Richard Nixon

## Life Expectancy

It is astonishing to realize that the human species survived hundreds of thousands of years, more than 99 per cent of its time on the planet, with a life expectancy of only 18 years. ~ Leonard Hayflick

## Life (Mysteries of)

When we remember that we are all mad, the mysteries disappear and life stands explained. ~ Mark Twain

## Light

There are two ways of spreading light: to be the candle or the mirror that reflects it. ~ Edith Wharton, U.S novelist/critic in *Artemis to Actaeon*

## Lighthouses

Lighthouses don't go running all over an island looking for boats to save; they just stand there shining. ~ Anne Lamott

## Lightning

It is the mountaintop that the lightning strikes. ~ Horace

## Like

Some people will like me and some won't. So I might as well be myself, and then at least I'll know that the people who like me, like *me*. ~ Hugh Prather

## Limits

Between the ages of 20 and 40, we are engaged in the process of discovering who we are, which involves learning the difference between accidental limitations, which it is our duty to outgrow, and the necessary limitations of our nature which we cannot trespass with impunity. ~ W.H. Auden

Every man takes the limits of his own field of vision for the limits of the world. ~ Arthur Schopenhauer

## Lions

It's better to be a lion for a day than a sheep all your life. ~ Sister Kenny

## Listen

To listen is an effort, and just to hear is no merit. A duck hears also.
~ Igor Stravinsky, 1957

Give us the grace to listen well. ~ John Keble

He hears but half who hears one party only. ~ Aeschylus

No one really listens to anyone else, and if you try it for a while you'll
see why. ~ Mignon McLaughlin

If you tell people what they want to hear, they'll listen to what you have
to say. ~ Louis Morgante, Toronto stockbroker

The reason why we have two ears and only one mouth is that we may
listen the more and talk the less. ~ Zeno of Citium

From listening comes wisdom, and from speaking, repentance.
~ Italian proverb

The hearing ear is always found close to the speaking tongue.
~ Ralph Waldo Emerson

A good listener is a silent flatterer. ~ Bits & Pieces, December 7, 1995

He listens well who takes notes. ~ Dante

No one ever listened himself out of a job. ~ Calvin Coolidge

## Literacy

The ratio of literacy to illiteracy is constant, but nowadays the illiterates
can read and write. ~ Alberto Moravia

## Literature

Literature is the art of writing something that will be read twice;
journalism what will be grasped at once. ~ Cyril Connolly

Literature is news that stays news. ~ Ezra Pound

If a nation's literature declines, the nation atrophies and decays.
~ Ezra Pound, 1934

The end of doubt is the beginning of prose. ~ Petrarch

Woe to that nation whose literature is cut short by intrusion of force.
~ Alexander Solzhenitsyn, 1974

Nearly all literature, in one sense, is made up of guidebooks.
~ Herman Melville

## Liver

Your liver is the size and weight of a small chicken. It receives 25 per cent of the blood your heart pumps – more than two litres a minute. Without it, you'd be unable to digest a meal, and your cholesterol reading would go through the roof. And yet your liver grabs none of the recognition it deserves – until something goes wrong.
~ Men's Health magazine

## Loan

I just need enough to tide me over till I need more. ~ Bill Hoest

## Logic

Logic is like the sword – those who appeal to it shall perish by it.
~ Samuel Butler

Logic is the art of making truth prevail. ~ Jean de la Bruyère

No mistake is more common and more fatuous than appealing to logic in cases which are beyond her jurisdiction. ~ Samuel Butler

## Loneliness

If you're lonely while you're alone, you're in bad company.
~ Jean-Paul Sartre

Loneliness is the poverty of self; solitude is the richness of self.
~ May Sarton

## Looking Back

Don't look back. Something may be gaining on you. ~ Leroy (Satchel) Paige

## Lose

No man can lose what he never had. ~ Izaak Walton

## Loser

If there was a contest to find the world's biggest loser, I'd win – unless there was a prize. ~ Stan Bowles, retired British soccer star

There are two kinds of losers: (1) the good loser, and (2) those who can't act. ~ Laurence J. Peter

He turned being a big loser into a perfect triumph. ~ Gore Vidal

## Losing

Men hate to lose. I once beat my husband at tennis six-love six-love. I came right out and asked him, "Are we ever going to have sex again?" He said, "Yes, but not with each other." ~ Rita Rudner, U.S. humorist

Sometimes it is too late to win. But it's never too late to lose.
~ Tom Watson

The art of losing isn't hard to master. ~ Elizabeth Bishop

It is better to lose the saddle than the horse. ~ Italian proverb

## Loss

There are occasions when it is undoubtedly better to incur loss than to make gain. ~ Plautus

## Lost

A lost thing could I never find. ~ Hilaire Belloc

## Lost Souls

The real lost souls don't wear their hair long and play guitars. They have crew cuts, trained minds, sign on for research in biological warfare, and don't give their parents a moment's worry.
~ J.B. Priestly

## Lovable

To be loved, be lovable. ~ Ovid

## Love

The love that dare not speak its name has become the neurosis that does not know when to shut up. ~ *Time* magazine, 1964

The art of love ... is largely the art of persistence. ~ Dr. Albert Ellis

When someone says, "It's better to have loved and lost than never to have loved at all," keep in mind you're talking to a loser. Try to find someone who's never loved at all and get their side of the story.
~ Rich Hall, *Self-Help for the Bleak*

Love: an ocean of emotions entirely surrounded by expenses.
~ Thomas R. Dewar

Whatever else is unsure in this stinking dunghill of a world a mother's love is not. ~ James Joyce, 1916

A man when he is making up to anybody can be cordial and gallant and full of little attentions and altogether charming. But when a man is really in love he can't help looking like a sheep. ~ Agatha Christie

Love does not consist in gazing at each other, but in looking together in the same direction. ~ Antoine de Saint-Exupéry

Of course there is such a thing as love or there wouldn't be so many divorces. ~ Ed Howe

Civilized people cannot fully satisfy their sexual instinct without love. ~ Bertrand Russell

Four be things I'd been better without:
Love, curiosity, freckles and doubt. ~ Dorothy Parker

There's nothing worth the wear of winning but laughter and the love of friends. ~ Hilaire Belloc

Love conquers all things except poverty and toothache. ~ Mae West

Love is the only disease that makes you feel better. ~ Sam Shepard

What will survive of us is love. ~ Philip Larkin

Love never dies of starvation, but often of indigestion. ~ Ninon de Lenclos

Love is what we call the situation which occurs when two people who are sexually compatible discover that they can also tolerate each other in various other circumstances. ~ Marc Mailhuerd, French writer

The first duty of love is to listen. ~ Paul Tillich

I was taught when I was young that if people would only love one another, all would be well with the world. This seemed simple and very nice; but I found when I tried to put it in practice not only that other people were seldom lovable, but that I was not very lovable myself. ~ George Bernard Shaw

I believe that love produces a certain flowering of the whole personality which nothing else can achieve. ~ Ivan Turgenev, Russian writer

We are shaped and fashioned by what we love. ~ Goethe

The way to love anything is to realize that it might be lost. ~ G.K. Chesterton

Love makes your soul crawl out from its hiding place. ~ Zora Neale Hurston

A crowd is not company, and faces are but a gallery of pictures, and talk is but a tinkling cymbal, where there is no love.
~ Francis Bacon

Love is what happens to a man and woman who don't know each other. ~ W. Somerset Maugham

Love ... is the extremely difficult realization that something other than oneself is real. ~ Iris Murdoch

Love is the triumph of imagination over intelligence. ~ H.L. Mencken

Sometimes I wish I could fall in love. Then at least you know who your opponent is. ~ Peter Ustinov

Where they love they do not desire and where they desire they do not love. ~ Sigmund Freud

I was in love with loving. ~ St. Augustine

Love doesn't just sit there, like a stone, it has to be made, like bread; remade all the time, made new. ~ Ursula LeGuin

True love comes quietly, without banner or flashing lights. ~ Erich Segal

Love is like any other luxury. You have no right to it unless you can afford it. ~ Anthony Trollope

Real love is like a pilgrimage. It happens when there is no strategy, but it is very rare because most people are strategists. ~ Anita Brookner

Love set you going like a fat gold watch. ~ Sylvia Plath

Love is space and time made perceptible to the heart. ~ Marcel Proust

## Loyalty

You can buy people's time; you can buy their physical presence at a given place; you can even buy a measured number of their skilled muscular motions per hour. But you cannot buy enthusiasm...you cannot buy loyalty...you cannot buy the devotion of hearts, minds, or souls. You must earn these. ~ Clarence Francis

Fidelity bought with money can be overcome by money. ~ Seneca

## Luck

I am a great believer in luck, and I find the harder I work, the more I have of it. ~ Stephen Leacock

The only sure thing about luck is that it will change. ~ Wilson Mizner

Some folk want their luck buttered. ~ Thomas Hardy

It is a great piece of skill to know how to guide your luck even while you're waiting for it. ~ Baltasar Gracian

When luck joins the game, cleverness scores double. ~ Yiddish proverb

The protected man doesn't need luck; therefore, it seldom visits him.
~ Alan Harrington

Shallow men believe in luck... Strong men believe in cause and effect.
~ Ralph Waldo Emerson

Care and diligence bring luck. ~ Thomas Fuller, M.D.

Not a man alive
Has so much luck that he can play with it. ~ William Butler Yeats

It will generally be found that men who are constantly lamenting their ill-luck, are only reaping the consequences of their own neglect, mismanagement and improvidence, or want of application.
~ Samuel Smiles

Of course I don't believe in it. But I understand that it brings you luck whether you believe in it or not. ~ Niels Bohr, Danish nuclear physicist, explaining why he had hung a horseshoe on the wall

Never have anything to do with an unlucky place or an unlucky man. I have seen many clever men, very clever men, who had no shoes to their feet. I never act with them. Their advice sounds very well, but they cannot get on themselves; and if they cannot do good to themselves, how can they do good to me? ~ Mayer Rothschild

Luck never made a man wise. ~ Seneca

Some people are so fond of ill luck that they run halfway to meet it.
~ Douglas Jerrold

Do not reveal your thoughts to everyone, lest you drive away your good luck. ~ Apocrypha

Luck is being ready. ~ Brian Eno

True luck consists not in holding the best of cards at the table;
Luckiest he who knows just when to rise and go home. ~ John Milton Hay

We must believe in luck. For how else can we explain the success of those we don't like? ~ Eric Satie, French composer

If there is such a thing as luck, then I must be the most unlucky fellow in the world. I've never once made a lucky strike in all my life. When I get after something that I need, I start finding everything in the world that I don't need – one damn thing after another, and then comes number one hundred, and that – at the very last – turns out to be just what I had been looking for. ~ Thomas Alva Edison

Some luck lies in not getting what you thought you wanted, but getting what you have. ~ Garrison Keillor

Born under a bad sign I been down since I began to crawl. If it wasn't for bad luck, I wouldn't have no luck at all. ~ Booker T. Jones and William Bell

Once you're lucky, you don't have to work for other people. You make them work for you. ~ Dan Totheroh, Stephen Vincent Benet, William Dieterle

## Lust

Anybody who repudiates the lust for life because he is caught in the lust for ideals has not advanced in the most fundamental sense.
~ Eugen Herrigel

## Luxuries

Give us the luxuries of life and we will dispense with the necessities.
~ J.L. Motley

Every luxury must be paid for, and everything is a luxury, starting with being in the world. ~ Cesare Pavese

## Lying

I do not mind lying, but I hate inaccuracy. ~ Samuel Butler

Lord, Lord, how this world is given to lying. ~ Shakespeare

Lying is like trying to hide in a fog. If you move about, you are in danger of bumping your head against the truth. And as soon as the fog blows away you are gone, anyhow. ~ William Hazlitt

## Machines

Man is a slow, sloppy and brilliant thinker; the machine is fast, accurate and stupid. ~ William M. Kelly

One machine can do the work of 50 ordinary men. No machine can do the work of one extraordinary man. ~ Elbert Hubbard

## Mad

There is less harm to be suffered in being mad among madmen than in being sane all by oneself. ~ Denis Diderot

The only difference between me and a madman is that I am not mad.
~ Salvador Dali

We are all born mad. Some remain so. ~ Samuel Beckett

Most men are within a finger's breadth of being mad. ~ Diogenes the Cynic

Everyone is more or less mad on one point. ~ Rudyard Kipling

## Magazines

Magazines all too frequently lead to books and should be regarded by the prudent as the heavy petting of literature. ~ Fran Lebowitz

## Majority

We go by the major vote, and if the majority are insane, the sane must go to the hospital. ~ Horace Mann

When you get too big a majority, you're immediately in trouble.
~ Sam Rayburn

## Males

There is, of course, no reason for the existence of the male sex except that one sometimes needs help with moving the piano.
~ Rebecca West, author and journalist

## Man

Man is a social animal who dislikes his fellow men.
~ Eugene Delacroix, French painter

Man is a two-legged animal without feathers. ~ Plato

Man is the only creature that consumes without producing.
~ George Orwell

Men are cruel, but man is kind. ~ Rabindranath Tagore

But we were born of risen apes, not fallen angels, and the apes were armed killers besides … The miracle of man is not how far he has sunk but how magnificently he has risen. We are known among the stars by our poems, not our corpses. ~ Robert Audrey

Mankind is not a tribe of animals to which we owe compassion. Mankind is a club to which we owe our subscription. ~ G.K. Chesterton

Maybe in order to understand mankind, we have to look at the word itself. Basically, it's made up of two words: "mank" and "ind." What do these words mean? It's a mystery, and that's why so is mankind.
~ Jack Handey

The intellect of man is forced to choose
Perfection of the life or of the work. ~ William Butler Yeats

The greatest nuisance to mankind is man. ~ Samuel Butler

The man who is master of his passions is Reason's slave. ~ Cyril Connolly

A man who is master of himself can end a sorrow as easily as he can invent a pleasure. ~ Oscar Wilde

I believe that our Heavenly Father invented man because he was disappointed in the monkey. ~ Mark Twain

Man is the creature made at the end of the week's work when God was tired. ~ Mark Twain

Man is a gaming animal. He must be always trying to get the better in something or other. ~ Charles Lamb

Man is an intellectual animal and, therefore, an everlasting contradiction to himself. His senses centre in himself, his ideas reach to the ends of the universe; so that he is torn in pieces between the two, without a possibility of its ever being otherwise.
~ William Hazlitt, 1823

To be a man is to feel that one's own stone contributes to building the edifice of the world. ~ Antione de Saint-Exupéry

Man is by nature a political animal. ~ Aristotle

Man is the only animal that blushes. Or needs to. ~ Mark Twain

Man will only become better when you make him see what he is like.
~ Anton Chekhov

The ultimate measure of a man is not where he stands in moments of comfort and convenience, but where he stands at times of challenge and controversy. ~ Martin Luther King, Jr.

Man must be invented each day. ~ Jean-Paul Sartre

## Management

So much of what we call management consists in making it difficult for people to work. ~ Peter Drucker, U.S. management expert

The secret of managing is to keep the five guys who hate you away from the guys who are undecided. ~ Casey Stengel

You don't manage people; you manage things. You lead people.
~ Admiral Grace Hooper

It is possible that people need to believe that they are unamnaged if they are to be managed effectively. ~ John Kenneth Galbraith

The myth of management is that it exists. ~ Robert Heller

## Mañana

Mañana is often the busiest day of the week. ~ Spanish proverb

Tomorrow is often the busiest day of the year. ~ Spanish proverb

## Manhood

Years ago, manhood was an opportunity for achievement, and now it is a problem to be overcome. ~ Garrison Keillor

## Manners

The only substitute for good manners is fast reflexes. ~ Steven Wright

## Market

There are two fools in every market: one asks too little, one asks too much. ~ Russian proverb

## Marriage

The fellow who waits to get married until he has enough money isn't really in love. ~ Kin Hubbard

Marriage is like a cage; one sees the birds outside desperate to get in, and the birds on the inside desperate to get out. ~ Michel de Montaigne

Even if we take matrimony at its lowest, even if we regard it as no more than a sort of friendship that is recognized by the police...marriage is a step so grave and decisive that it attracts light-headed, variable men by its very awfulness. ~ Robert Louis Stevenson

So that is marriage, Lily thought, a man and a woman looking at a girl throwing a ball. ~ Virginia Woolf in *To the Lighthouse*

Both my marriages were failures! Number one departed and number two stayed. ~ Gustav Mahler, in a Swiss radio interview

As a general thing, people marry most happily with their own kind. The trouble lies in the fact that people usually marry at an age when they do not really know what their own kind is. ~ Robertson Davies

Marriage is a lot like the army; everyone complains, but you'd be surprised at the large number that re-enlist. ~ James Garner

The most happy marriage I can picture or imagine to myself would be the union of a deaf man to a blind woman. ~ Samuel Taylor Coleridge

I think – therefore I'm single. ~ Lizz Winstead

I have yet to hear a man ask for advice on how to combine marriage and a career. ~ Gloria Steinem

I never married because there was no need. I have three pets at home which answer the same purpose as a husband. I have a dog which growls every morning, a parrot which swears all afternoon and a cat that comes home late at night. ~ Marie Corelli

He tricked me into marrying him. He told me he was pregnant.
~ Carol Leifer

All marriages are mixed marriages. ~ Chantal Saperstein

There's only one way to have a happy marriage and as soon as I learn what it is I'll get married again. ~ Clint Eastwood

In a happy marriage, it is the wife who provides the climate, the husband the landscape. ~ Gerald Brennan

Instead of getting married again, I'm going to find a woman I don't like and just give her a house. ~ Lewis Grizzard

All the unhappy marriages come from the husband having brains.
~ P.G. Wodehouse

Marriage has many pains, but celibacy has no pleasures.
~ Samuel Johnson

All marriages are happy. It's the living together afterward that causes all the trouble. ~ Raymond Hull

I married beneath me, all women do. ~ Nancy Astor

The critical period in matrimony is breakfast time. ~ A.P. Herbert

Staying married may have long-term benefits. You can elicit much more sympathy from friends over a bad marriage than you ever can from a good divorce. ~ P.J. O'Rourke

## Martini

The proper union of gin and vermouth is a great and sudden glory; it is one of the happiest marriages on earth and one of the shortest-lived.
~ Bernard De Voto

## Martyrs

There have been quite as many martyrs for bad causes as good ones.
~ Martin Van Loon

## Masses

First you take their faces from 'em by calling 'em the masses, and then you accuse 'em of not having any faces. ~ J.B. Priestly

The masses have never thirsted after truth. They turn aside from evidence that is not to their taste, preferring to deify error, if error seduce[s] them. Whoever can supply them with illusions is easily their master; whoever attempts to destroy their illusions is always their victim. ~ Gustave Le Bon, *The Crowd: A Study of the Popular Mind*

Leave this hypocritical prating about the masses. Masses are rude, lame, unmade, pernicious in their demands and influence, and need not be flattered but to be schooled. I wish not to concede anything to them, but to tame, drill, divide and break them up, and draw individuals out of them. ~ Ralph Waldo Emerson

The quality of ideas seems to play a minor role in mass-movement leadership. What counts is the arrogant gesture, the complete disregard of the opinion of others, the single-handed defiance of the world. ~ Eric Hoffer

## Materialism

The cure for "Materialism" is to have enough for everybody and to spare. When people are sure of having what they need they cease to think about it. ~ Henry Ford

## Mathematics

Moriarty: "How are you at mathematics?"
Harry Secombe: "I speak it like a native." ~ Spike Milligan in *The Goon Show*

If a man's wit be wandering, let him study the mathematics. ~ Francis Bacon

I don't believe in mathematics. ~ Albert Einstein

All the mathematical sciences are founded on relations between physical laws and laws of numbers. ~ James Clerk Maxwell

## Matter

What is Matter? Never mind. What is Mind? No matter. ~ *Punch*, 1855

## Maturity

Maturity is the capacity to endure uncertainty. ~ John Finley

Maturity is only a short break in adolescence. ~ Jules Feiffer

He that has seen both sides of 50 has lived to little purpose if he has no other views of the world than he had when he was young. ~ William Cowper

A mark of maturity seems to be the range and extent of one's feeling of self-involvement in abstract ideals. ~ Gordon Wallport

The immature mind hops from one thing to another; the mature mind seeks to follow through. ~ Harry Overstreet

The nobler and more perfect a thing is, the later and slower it is in arriving at maturity. ~ Arthur Schopenhauer

## Maxim

It is more trouble to make a maxim than it is to do right. ~ Mark Twain

## Mean

To the mean, all becomes mean. ~ Friedrich Nietzsche

## Means

When we deliberate it is about means and not ends. ~ Aristotle

Take care of the means and the end will take care of itself.
~ Mahatma Gandhi

## Media

The media's power is frail. Without the people's support, it can be shut off with the ease of turning a light switch. ~ Corazón C. Aquino, 1986

Nobody's interested in sweetness and light. ~ Hedda Hopper

## Medicine

Formerly, when religion was strong and science weak, men mistook magic for medicine; now, when science is strong and religion weak, men mistake medicine for magic. ~ Thomas Szasz

## Mediocrity

Only a mediocre person is always at his best. ~ Laurence J. Peter

Only the mediocre are always at their best. ~ Jean Giraudoux

It's more than magnificent – it's mediocre. ~ Sam Goldwyn

## Meditation

My son has taken up meditation – at least it's better than sitting doing nothing. ~ Max Kauffmann

## Members

When she saw the sign "Members Only," she thought of him.
~ Spike Milligan in *Puckoon*

## Memorandum

A memorandum is written not to inform the reader but to protect the writer. ~ Dean Acheson

## Memory

How is it that our memory is good enough to retain the least triviality that happens to us, and yet not good enough to recollect how often we have told it to the same person?
~ La Rochefoucald, French epigramatist

How feeble are Man's efforts against the unyielding forces of nature – until the struggle is recounted for the grandchildren. ~ Jeanette Kubin

As we grow older our memory of past events grows better and better, whether they happened or not. ~ Mark Twain

Memory is the thing you forget with. ~ Alexander Chase

We do not remember days; we remember moments. ~ Cesare Pavese

It's a poor sort of memory that only works backwards. ~ Lewis Carroll

You never know when you're making a memory. ~ Rickie Lee Jones

My memory is so bad that many times I forget my own name!
~ Miguel de Cervantes

Memory is what tells a man that his wife's birthday was yesterday.
~ Mario Rocco

A great memory does not make a philosopher, any more than a dictionary can be called a grammar. ~ John Henry Newman

Life without memory is no life at all. ... our memory is our coherence, our reason, our feeling, even our action. Without it, we are nothing.
~ Luis Buñuel

Our memories are independent of our wills. It is not so easy to forget.
~ Richard Sheridan

Intelligence may be the pride – the towering distinction of man; emotion gives colour and force to his actions; but memory is the bastion of his being. Without memory, there is no personal identity, there is no continuity to the days of his life. Memory provides the raw material for designs both great and small. Thus governed and enriched by memory, all the enterprises of man go forward.
~ D. Ewen Cameron, British Journal of Psychiatry, 1963

The palest ink is better than the best memory. ~ Chinese proverb

Memory feeds imagination. ~ Amy Tan

A good memory constitutes about 70 per cent of what commonly passes for genius. ~ Hesketh Pearson

## Men

There are men I could spend eternity with. But not this life.
~ Kathleen Norris, U.S. poet, *The Middle of the World*, 1981

Men need women. Most single men don't even live like people. They live like bears with furniture. ~ Rita Rudner, U.S. humorist

I know this – a man got to do what he got to do.
~ John Steinbeck, in *The Grapes of Wrath*

Some men are so selfish that they read a book or go to a concert for their own sinister pleasure, instead of doing it to improve social conditions, as the good citizen does when drinking cocktails or playing bridge. ~ Jacques Barzun

Men build bridges and throw railroads across deserts, and yet they contend successfully that the job of sewing on a button is beyond them. Accordingly, they don't have to sew buttons. ~ Heywood Broun

Thank God, men cannot as yet fly, and lay waste the sky as well as the Earth. ~ Henry David Thoreau

Men, like nails, lose their usefulness when they lose direction and begin to bend. ~ Walter Savage Landor

Men are so romantic, don't you think? They look for a perfect partner when what they should be looking for is perfect love. ~ Fay Weldon

It's not the men in my life that count; it's the life in my men. ~ Mae West

If the world were a logical place, men would ride side saddle.
~ Rita Mae Brown

## Mercy

Nothing emboldens sin so much as mercy. ~ Shakespeare

## Merit

Heaven goes by favour. If it went by merit, you would stay out and your dog would go in. ~ Mark Twain

Charms strike the sight, but merit wins the soul. ~ Alexander Pope

## Messes

It's not the tragedies that kill us, it's the messes. ~ Dorothy Parker

## Metaphors

Since finding out what something is is largely a matter of discovering what it is like, the most impressive contribution to the growth of intelligibility has been made by the application of suggestive metaphors. ~ Jonathan Miller

The metaphor is probably the most fertile power possessed by men. ~ José Ortega y Gasset

## Metaphysics

Metaphysics is the finding of bad reasons for what we believe upon instinct. ~ F.H. Bradley in *Appearance and Reality*, 1893

## Microsoft

*News Release January 4, 1999, Redmond, Washington*

Bill Gates, Chairman and CEO of Microsoft Corporation, announced today that the latest version of their Windows operating system, Windows 2000, would be delayed until the second quarter of 1901. No reason was given. ~ Internet

## Middle Age

Middle age is when you're sitting home on Saturday night and the telephone rings and you hope it isn't for you.
~ Ogden Nash , U.S. poet

Middle age is when your age starts to show around the middle.
~ Bob Hope

Middle age: the time when a man is always thinking that in a week or two he will feel just as good as ever. ~ Don Marquis

## Million

I feel like a million tonight – but one at a time. ~ Mae West

## Millionaires

I'm opposed to millionaires, but it would be dangerous to offer me the position. ~ Mark Twain

## Mind

The pendulum of the mind oscillates between sense and nonsense, not between right and wrong. ~ Carl Jung

His mind was an intricate, multigeared machine, or perhaps some little animal with skittery paws. ~ Anne Tyler, U.S. novelist, *Searching for Caleb*, 1975

Some open minds should be closed for repairs. ~ Toledo Blade

Our minds are lazier than our bodies. ~ La Rochefoucauld

All sorts of bodily diseases are caused by half-used minds.
~ George Bernard Shaw

The mind is not a vessel to be filled but a fire to be kindled. ~ Plutarch

Where there is an open mind, there will always be a frontier.
~ Charles F. Kettering

The only man who can change his mind is a man who has got one.
~ Edward Noyes Westcott

The flesh endures the storms of the present alone; the mind, those of
the past and future as well as the present. ~ Epicurus

A closed mind saves time. ~ E.O. Phillips

Great minds have purposes, little minds have wishes. ~ Washington Irving

Great minds discuss ideas; average minds discuss events; small minds
discuss people. ~ Eleanor Roosevelt

I have not lost my mind – it's backed up on disk somewhere. ~ Unknown

The eyes are not responsible when the mind does the seeing.
~ Publilius Syrus

I believe in an open mind, but not so open that your brains fall out.
~ Arthur Hays Sulzberger

## Ministers

I don't mind how much my ministers talk – as long as they do
what I say. ~ Margaret Thatcher

## Minority

The minority is always right. ~ Henrik Ibsen

Minorities … are almost always in the right. ~ Sydney Smith

## Miracles

The Age of Miracles is forever here! ~ Thomas Carlyle

It was a miracle of rare device. ~ Samuel Taylor Coleridge

## Mirrors

All mirrors are magical mirrors; never can we see our faces in them.
~ Logan Pearsall Smith

## Misbehave

I don't say we all ought to misbehave, but we ought to look as if we could. ~ Orson Welles

## Mischief

Physicists and astronomers see their own implications in the world being round, but to me it means that only one-third of the world is asleep at any given time and the other two-thirds is up to something.
~ Dean Rusk, U.S. Secretary of State, 1964

## Misers

If the prodigal quits life in debt to others, the miser quits it still deeper in debt to himself. ~ Charles Caleb Colton

The miser and the pig are of no use until dead. ~ French proverb

Water will not slip through the miser's grasp. ~ Malay proverb

## Misery

Extreme hopes are born of extreme misery. ~ Bertrand Russell

## Misfortune

Some people think that all the world should share their misfortunes, though they do not share in the sufferings of anyone else. ~ A. Poincelot

To be brave in misfortune is to be worthy of manhood; to be wise in misfortune is to conquer fate. ~ Agnes Repplier

If all misfortunes were laid in one common heap whence everyone must take an equal portion, most people would be contented to take their own and depart. ~ Socrates

The greatest misfortune of all is not to be able to bear misfortune.
~ Bias, Greek sage

## Misquotation

I improve on misquotation. ~ Cary Grant

## Missouri

I am from Missouri. You have got to show me. ~ Willard Vandiver

## Mistakes

If you don't profit from your investment mistakes, someone else will.
~ Yale Hirsch

It is a capital mistake to theorize before one has data. ~ Sherlock Holmes

To stumble twice against the same stone is a proverbial disgrace.
~ Cicero

Who thinks it is just to be judged by a single error?
~ Beryl Markham, English writer/aviator

There is nothing wrong with making mistakes. Just don't respond with
encores. ~ Anonymous

The greatest mistake you can make in life is to be continually fearing
you will make one. ~ Elbert Hubbard

Don't make the wrong mistakes. ~ Yogi Berra

Mistakes live in the neighbourhood of truth and therefore delude us.
~ Rabindranath Tagore

We must learn from the mistakes of others. You can't possibly live long
enough to make them all yourself. ~ Sam Levenson

The habitually punctual make all their mistakes right on time.
~ Laurence J. Peter

Don't look where you fell, but where you slipped. ~ Proverb

Every great mistake has a halfway moment, a split second when it can
be recalled and perhaps remedied. ~ Pearl Buck

Half of our mistakes in life arise from feeling where we ought to think,
and thinking where we ought to feel. ~ John Churton Collins

When you realize you have made a mistake, take immediate steps to
correct it. ~ Dalai Lama

I make mistakes: I'll be the second to admit it. ~ Jean Kerr

We never make mistakes. ~ Alexander Solzhenitsyn

When I make a mistake, it's a beaut! ~ Fiorello H. La Guardia

## Mixed Metaphors

While I write this letter, I have a pistol in one hand and a sword in the other.

All along the untrodden paths of the future, I can see the footprints of an unseen hand.

The only thing to prevent what's past is to put a stop to it before it happens.

Mr. Speaker, I smell a rat. I see him forming in the air and darkening the sky. Let us nip him in the bud. ~ Boyle Roche, 18th century Irish politician

## Moderation

Moderation is good but boring. ~ Anonymous

## Modesty

Modesty is the only sure bait when you angle for praise.
~ Lord Chesterfield

Modesty is a vastly overrated virtue. ~ John Kenneth Galbraith

I'm very modest. I tend to hide my light under a peck. ~ Ken Mullen

The only worse thing than false modesty is no modesty at all.
~ Joseph Epstein

With people of only moderate ability, modesty is mere honesty; but with those who possess great talent, it is hypocrisy. ~ Arthur Schopenhauer

## Money

If all the rich men in the world divided up their money amongst themselves, there wouldn't be enough to go around. ~ Jules Bertillon

If money is your hope for independence you will never have it.
The only real security that a man can have in this world is a reserve of knowledge, experience and ability. ~ Henry Ford

Money is better than poverty, if only for financial reasons. Not that it can buy happiness. Take the case of the ant and the grasshopper: The grasshopper played all summer, while the ant worked and saved. When winter came, the grasshopper had nothing, but the ant complained of chest pains. ~ Woody Allen

Money is how people with no talent keep score.
~ Anonymous, cited in Glibquips: Funny Words by Funny Women

Money may buy the husk of many things, but not the kernel. It brings you food, but not appetite, medicine but not health, acquaintances but not friends, servants but not faithfulness, days of joy but not peace or happiness. ~ Henrik Ibsen

We're really all of us bottomly broke. I haven't had time to work in weeks. ~ Jack Kerouac, *On The Road*

Money doesn't always buy happiness. People with $10-million are no happier than people with $9-million. ~ Hobart Brown

When a man says money can do anything, that settles it; he hasn't any. ~ Ed Howe

Lack of money is the root of all evil. ~ George Bernard Shaw

Among the things that money can't buy is what it used to. ~ Max Kauffmann

Whoever said money doesn't buy happiness didn't know where to shop. ~ Anonymous

He without benefit of scruples
His fun and money soon quadruples. ~ Ogden Nash

Money and success don't change people; they merely amplify what is there. ~ Will Smith

Money, it turned out, was exactly like sex, you thought of nothing else if you didn't have it and thought of other things if you did.
~ James Baldwin, American writer

When it is a question of money, everybody is of the same religion.
~ Voltaire

If money could talk, it would say goodbye. ~ Elbert Hubbard

How did the fool get all that money in the first place? ~ Robert Byrne

Plenty of people despise money, but few know how to give it away.
~ La Rochefoucauld

To be clever enough to get all that money, one must be stupid enough to want it. ~ G.K. Chesterton

With money in your pocket, you are wise and you are handsome and you sing well too. ~ Yiddish proverb

Do you think money grows on trees? ~ Dad

Money often costs too much. ~ Ralph Waldo Emerson

Money always implies the promise of magic, but the effect is much magnified when, as now, people have lost faith in everything else.
~ Lewis Lapham

## Monsters

He who fights with monsters might take care lest he thereby become a monster. And if you gaze long into an abyss, the abyss gazes also into you. ~ Friedrich Nietzsche

## Montreal

Some say that no one ever leaves Montreal. ~ Leonard Cohen

## Monuments

Those only deserve a monument who do not heed one. ~ William Hazlitt

## Morals

If your morals make you dreary, depend on it, they are wrong.
~ Robert Louis Stevenson

We spend much more time tending to the quality of our emotional lives than to the quality of our moral lives. Many people are prepared to shake up their lives in a mad bid for "emotional happiness," but few will disturb their moral suppositions. When was the last time you asked yourself hard questions about your values?
~ Joshua Halberstam in *Everyday Ethics*

Eats first, morals after. ~ Bertolt Brecht in *The Threepenny Opera*

In matters of prudence, last thoughts are best; in matters of morality, first thoughts. ~ Robert Hall

From the point of view of morals, life seems to be divided into two periods. In the first, we indulge; in the second, we preach. ~ Will Durant

The higher the buildings, the lower the morals. ~ Noel Coward

Everything has got a moral, if you can only find it. ~ Lewis Carroll

One becomes moral as soon as one is unhappy. ~ Marcel Proust

Never let your morals get in the way of doing what's right. ~ Isaac Asimov

What is moral is what you feel good after. ~ Ernest Hemingway

The art of acting morally is behaving as if everything we do matters.
~ Gloria Steinem

## Morning

Never glad confident morning again! ~ Robert Browning

## Mortality

Old and young, we are all on our last cruise. ~ Robert Louis Stevenson

We are all here for a spell; get all the good laughs you can. ~ Will Rogers

## Mothers

Mother is far too clever to understand anything she does not like.
~ Arnold Bennett

I was on a corner [in Los Angeles] the other day when a wild-looking sort of gypsy-looking lady with a dark veil over her face grabbed me right on Ventura Boulevard and said, "Karen Haber! You're never going to find happiness and no one is ever going to marry you." I said, "Mom, leave me alone." ~ Karen Haber, U.S. comedian, cited in *Glibquips* by Roz Warren

In the eyes of its mother, every beetle is a gazelle. ~ Moroccan proverb

In our society, mothers take the place elsewhere occupied by the Fates, the System, Negroes, Communism or Reactionary Imperialist Plots; mothers go on getting blamed until they're 80, but shouldn't take it personally. ~ Katharine Whitehorn

Begin, baby boy, to recognize your mother with a smile. ~ Virgil

## Motion Pictures

Pictures are for entertainment, messages should be delivered by Western Union. ~ Samuel Goldwyn

There is only one thing that can kill the movies, and that is education.
~ Will Rogers

We didn't need dialogue in those days. We had faces then!
~ Gloria Swanson in *Sunset Boulevard*

## Mousetrap

In baiting a mousetrap with cheese, always leave room for the mouse.
~ Saki (H.H. Munro)

## Mouth

A closed mouth gathers no feet. ~ American saying

## Move

When you see a good move, wait, look for a better one.
~ Rudolph Spielmann

## Murphy's Law

Murphy's Law fails only when you try to demonstrate it. ~ Anonymous

## Music

Without music life would be a mistake. ~ Friedrich Nietzsche

A musician must make music, an artist must paint, a poet must write, if he is to be ultimately at peace with himself. ~ Abraham Maslow

Too many pieces [of classical music] finish too long after the end.
~ Igor Stravinsky

Wagner's music is better than it sounds. ~ Bill Nye, U.S. journalist

There is something about music that keeps its distance even at the moment that it engulfs us. It is at the same time outside and away from us and inside and part of us. ~ Aaron Copland, 1952

After silence, that which comes nearest to expressing the inexpressible is music. ~ Aldous Huxley

In music one must think with the heart and feel with the brain.
~ George Szell

I'll play it first and tell you what it is later. ~ Miles Davis

The flute is not an instrument which has a good moral effect. It is too exciting. ~ Aristotle

A good ear for music and a taste for music are two very different things which are often confounded; and so is comprehending and enjoying every object of sense and sentiment. ~ Lord Greville, English poet

Van Gogh became a painter because he had no ear for music.
~ Nikki Harris

The trouble with a lot of songs you hear nowadays is that someone forgot to put them to music. ~ Sammy Kahn

RICHARD W. POUND

Music is a language by whose means messages are elaborated. That such messages can be understood by the many but sent out only by few, and that [music] alone among all the languages unites the contradictory character of being at once intelligible and untranslatable – these facts make the creator of music a being like the gods.
~ Claude Levi-Strauss, French anthropologist

Music is a means of rapid transportation. ~ John Cage

Music is spiritual. The music business is not. ~ Van Morrison

All art constantly aspires towards the condition of music. ~ Walter Pater

What music is more enchanting than the voices of young people, when you can't hear what they say? ~ Logan Pearsall Smith

Only sick music makes money today. ~ Friedrich Nietzsche

When you are about 35 years old, something terrible always happens to music. ~ Steve Race

One good thing about music, when it hits you feel no pain. ~ Bob Marley

## Mystery

No object is mysterious. The mystery is in your eye. ~ Elizabeth Bowen

## Myths

Myths which are believed in tend to come true. ~ George Orwell, 1944

Are we the ones who think up myths or is it myths who think us up?
~ Carlo Ginzburg, *Clues, Myths and Emblems*

## Nagging

Nagging is the repetition of unpalatable truths. ~ Baroness Edith Summerskill

## Names

Names are but noise and smoke,
Obscuring heavenly light. ~ Goethe

## Nationalism

Nationalism is an infantile disease, it is the measles of mankind.
~ Albert Einstein

## Nations

If people behaved the way nations do, they would all be put in straightjackets. ~ Tennessee Williams

A nation without the means of reform is without the means of survival.
~ Edmund Burke

The great nations have always acted like gangsters, and the small nations like prostitutes. ~ Stanley Kubrick, *Guardian*, June 5, 1963

A nation is a society united by delusions about its ancestry.
~ W.R. Inge

There are truths that can kill a nation. ~ Jean Giraudoux

## Nature

Let us permit nature to have her way; she understands her business better than we do. ~ Michel de Montaigne

Nature is not human-hearted. ~ Lao-tzu

Accuse not Nature, she hath done her part;
Do thou but thine. ~ John Milton

[In a state of nature] No arts; no letters; no society; and which is worst of all, continual fear and danger of violent death; and the life of man, solitary, poor, nasty, brutish and short. ~ Thomas Hobbes

It is unfair to blame man too fiercely for being pugnacious; he learned the habit from Nature. ~ Christopher Morley

In the eyes of Nature, we are just another species in trouble.
~ Lionel Tiger and Robin Fox

Nature's laws affirm instead of prohibit. If you violate her laws you are your own prosecuting attorney, judge, jury and hangman.
~ Luther Burbank

Like all compulsory legislation, that of Nature is harsh and wasteful in its operation. Ignorance is visited as sharply as willful disobedience – incapacity meets with the same punishment as crime. Nature's discipline is not even a word and a blow, and the blow first; but the blow without the word. It is left up to you to find out why your ears are boxed. ~ Thomas Henry Huxley

All things are artificial, for nature is the art of God. ~ Sir Thomas Browne

## Necessity

Necessity is the plea for every infringement of human freedom. It is the argument of tyrants; it is the creed of slaves. ~ William Pitt

Our necessities are few but our wants are endless. ~ Anonymous

Necessity relieves us from the embarrassment of choice.
~ Marquis de Vauvenargues

Where necessity speaks, it demands. ~ Russian proverb

Necessity is not an established fact, but an interpretation.
~ Friedrich Nietzsche

Are these things then necessities?
Then let us meet them like necessities... ~ Shakespeare, *King Henry IV, Part 2*

I don't think necessity is the mother of invention. Invention, in my opinion, arises directly from idleness, possibly also from laziness. To save oneself trouble. ~ Agatha Christie

## Neighbour

Love thy neighbour as yourself, but choose your neighbourhood.
~ Louise Beal

### Neurosis

A neurosis is a secret you don't know you're keeping. ~ Kenneth Tynan

### Neurotics

I prefer neurotic people. I like to hear rumblings beneath the surface.
~ Stephen Sondheim, 1973

### Neutrality

The hottest places in hell are reserved for those who, in time of great
moral crisis, maintain their neutrality. ~ Dante

### New

What is valuable is not new, and what is new is not valuable.
~ Daniel Webster

There is no subject so old that something new cannot be said about it.
~ Fyodor Dostoevsky

New things are made familiar, and famliar things are made new.
~ Samuel Johnson

### New York

As only New Yorkers know, if you can get through the twilight, you'll live
through the night. ~ Dorothy Parker, 1964

Traffic signals in New York are just rough guidelines. ~ David Letterman

### Newspapers

Let me make the newspapers, and I care not what is preached in the
pulpit or enacted in Congress. ~ Wendell Phillips

My brother cuts the time it takes to read a newspaper by skipping
everything in the future tense; and it's amazing what he doesn't miss.
~ Katharine Whitehorn, *Never-Never Land*

Newspaper editors are men who separate the wheat from the chaff and
then print the chaff. ~ Adlai Stevenson

### News Value

To have news value is to have a tin can tied to one's tail. ~ T.E. Lawrence

### Nice Guys

Nice guys finish last, but we get to sleep in. ~ Evan Davis

### Nightmare

Have you noticed ... there is never any third act in a nightmare? They bring you to a climax of terror and then they leave you there. They are the work of poor dramatists. ~ Max Beerbohm

### Nobody

I am a nobody. Nobody is perfect, therefore I am perfect.
~ from the Internet

### Nonconformity

Nonconformity is an empty goal, and rebellion against prevailing opinion simply because it is prevailing should be no more praised than acquiescence to it. Indeed, it is often a mask for cowardice, and few are more pathetic than those who flaunt outer differences to expiate their inner surrender. ~ William Whyte, *The Organization Man*

### Nonsense

The importance of nonsense can hardly be overstated. The more clearly we experience something as "nonsense," the more clearly we are experiencing the boundaries of our own self-imposed cognitive structures. "Nonsense" is that which does not fit into the pre-arranged patterns we have superimposed on reality...Nonsense is nonsense only when we have not yet formed the point of view from which it makes sense. ~ *The Dancing Wu Li Masters: An Overview of the New Physics*

To attack a man for talking nonsense is like finding your mortal enemy drowning in a swamp and jumping in after him with a knife.
~ Sir Karl Popper

Nonsense and beauty have close connections. ~ E.M. Forster

### Normal

The trouble with being normal is it always gets worse. ~ Bruce Cockburn

Nobody realizes that some people expend tremendous energy merely to be normal. ~ Albert Camus

The only normal people are the ones you don't know very well.
~ Joe Ancis

### Nose

A great nose indicates a great man – genial, courteous, intellectual, virile, courageous. ~ Edmond Rostand

A nose that can see is worth two that sniff. ~ Eugene Ionesco

## Nosiness

Enquire not what boils in another's pot. ~ Thomas Fuller, M.D.

## Nostalgia

Nostalgia isn't what it used to be. ~ Peter De Vries

Nostalgia is a seductive liar. ~ George Ball

## Nothing

I used to believe that anything was better than nothing. Now I know that sometimes nothing is better. ~ Glenda Jackson

Nothing is often a good thing to do, and almost always a clever thing to say. ~ Will Durant

Of those who say nothing, few are silent. ~ Thomas Neill

When one does nothing, one believes oneself to be responsible for everything. ~ Jean-Paul Sartre

Nothing, like something, happens anywhere. ~ Philip Larkin

## Nothingness

Nothingness haunts being. ~ Jean-Paul Sartre

## Novelty

Novelty has charms that our minds can hardly withstand. The most valuable things, if they have for a long while appeared among us, do not make any impression as they are good, but give us a distaste as they are old. But when the influence of this fantastical humour is over, the same men or things will come to be admired again by a happy return of our good taste. ~ William Makepiece Thackeray

## Numbers

I have often admired the mystical way of Pythagoras, and the secret way of numbers. ~ Sir Thomas Browne

## Obfuscation

Our disputants put me in mind of the skuttle fish, that when he is unable to extricate himself, blackens all the water about him, till he becomes invisible. ~ Joseph Addison

## Obituaries (with a Sting)

He was liked, even loved, by all his neighbours. Many of their children looked upon him as a father, not without cause.

She spent all of her time involved in the lives of others. Now she has time for herself. Praise the Lord.

A self-made millionaire through stock-market investments, much to his credit he handled the investments of others.

It was an untimely death; but his books reveal that here was a man who must surely have had much more to say.

His commitment to atheism was total. He believed that there is no heaven or hell and strove unselfishly to share this belief with everyone at every opportunity. Wherever he is now, nothing is too good for him.

In authoring his own epitaph, "The paths of glory lead but to the grave," the professor reminded us one last time of his dedication to originality.

In memory of our neighbour's dog, who faithfully fertilized our lawn every day.

His race run, he leaves a grateful world.

The departed gang boss, who died in his bed aged 85, will be sadly missed by his early associates.

A lifelong participant in the country's political process, he will be remembered by those who knew him for what he was.

Farewell to Eileen Ann Stagger, whose devotion to John Barleycorn in later years caused Molson's to reach a high of $38 and whose passing will necessitate downsizing of the brewery industry in the Southwestern Ontario region.

A pillar of the community passed away suddenly last Monday. A devoted father, a faithful husband, a rare lover.

Widely respected for his innovative approach to justice, the judge will always be fondly remembered by his many friends at the Repeat Offenders association.

After a long career in banking, he developed a sudden interest in travel. His wife of 30 years remained in Canada, but he was accompanied by his new secretary, Fifi Latour, to Brazil, where he died yesterday.

With the demise of our most active stockbroker, we cannot begin to calculate the loss to our firm and clients. We know many in the investment community will share our grief.

The unorthodox teacher had a profound influence on his students, most of whom cannot praise him eloquently enough. A remedial literacy class will be established in his memory.

He was a sports celebrity viewed by many as an unqualified success. In honouring him posthumously, our only regret is that it was not possible to do so sooner.

The lobbyist was well-known to some MPs for his generosity and persuasiveness, and to many others for his ability to simultaneously practise those two virtues.

He had great plans for his success, and only his untimely demise at the age of 80 prevented him from making his mark on the world.

After a visit to Elmer's friendly barber shop on Main Street, his customers always left feeling they had been clipped.

While his willingness to run for public office was admired by those who knew him, this trait was particularly appreciated by the candidates running against him.

~ Compiled from the Globe & Mail

## Obscure

The obscure we see eventually, the completely apparent takes a little longer. ~ Edward R. Murrow

## Obscurity

Obscurity is the refuge of incompetence. ~ Robert A. Heinlein

## Observation

In the fields of observation, chance favours only the mind that is prepared. ~ Louis Pasteur

You can observe a lot just by watching. ~ Yogi Berra

One must always tell what one sees.
Above all, which is more difficult, one must always see what one sees.
~ Charles Peguy, French writer

Many eyes go through the meadow, but few see the flowers in it.
~ Ralph Waldo Emerson

All of us are watchers – of television, of time clocks, of traffic on the freeway – but few are observers. Everyone is looking, not many are seeing. ~ Peter Leschak

Seeing through is rarely seeing into. ~ Elizabeth Bibesco

When it's dark enough, you can see the stars. ~ Charles Beard

To observations which ourselves we make,
We grow more partial for th' observer's sake. ~ Alexander Pope

Things seen are mightier than things heard. ~ Alfred, Lord Tennyson

## Obstacles

Obstacles cannot crush me. Every obstacle yields to stern resolve. He who is fixed on a star does not change his mind. ~ Leonardo da Vinci

If there are obstacles, the shortest line between two points may be the crooked line. ~ Bertolt Brecht

## Obstinacy

Obstinacy's ne'er so stiff
As when t'is in a wrong belief ~ Samuel Butler

No man is good for anything who has not some particle of obstinacy to use upon occasion. ~ Henry Ward Beecher

I regret many follies which sprang from my obstinacy; but without that trait I would not have reached my goal. ~ Carl Jung

## Obvious

Familiar things happen, and mankind does not bother about them. It requires a very unusual mind to undertake the analysis of the obvious. ~ Alfred North Whitehead

He can see a louse as far away as China but is unconscious of an elephant on his nose. ~ Malay proverb

Ours is one of those times when it is the duty of an intelligent man to repeat the obvious. ~ George Orwell

## Occult

Some kids do get fascinated with the occult, and some of them will pull out a Ouija board or try to hold an awkward seance at some point. But what keeps them from becoming full-fledged witches or warlocks is that they quickly find out that none of the stuff actually works. ~ Bill Ferguson, in *Western*.

## Offend

Never offend people with style when you can offend them with substance. ~ Sam Brown

## Old

I love everything that's old: old friends, old times, old manners, old books, old wines. ~ Oliver Goldsmith

When your friends begin to flatter you on how young you look, it's a sure sign you're getting old. ~ Mark Twain

## Olympic Games

Pythagoras used to say life resembles the Olympic Games; a few men strain their muscles to carry off a prize; others bring trinkets to sell to the crowd for a profit; and some are there who seek no further advantage than to look at the show and see how and why everything is done. They are spectators of other men's lives in order to better judge and manage their own. ~ Michel de Montaigne

## Olympic Honour

And I now close in recalling to you one of the old Olympic Torch games. Each contestant started in the race with a lighted torch in his hand, and the winner was the youth – not the one who arrived first at the goal – but he who first reached the goal with the torch still burning brightly.

The beauty and symmetry of this restriction as touching life I leave to every man to apply and to take to his own discerning heart. To-day, as in that far-off time, the real winner is not the man who first arrives, whom the world so shallowly regards as first in the race, in terms of wealth, station, garish honours or other false standards of success.

Many a man has thus arrived apparently triumphant, but with his torch extinguished in irredeemable gloom; the torch of health, the torch of honour, the torch of domestic bliss or of parental joy. The true winner, the real winner, is he who pressed earnestly, even passionately to the goal; who has safely guarded the sacred flame, and who has held high to the end of the torch of health, the torch of honour, the torch of true fellowship, the torch of precious friends of his hour and day, the torch of everything that enriches life, and, what an encouraging thought, that in such a race every contestant may, if he so strives, win some prize. ~ Address of the Chief Justice of Ontario, delivered at a Dinner tendered to the Rt. Hon. Sir William Mulock, K.C.M.G., by the Ontario members of the Canadian Bar Association on the occasion of his 90th birthday. 12 *Can. Bar Review* (1934) at pp. 40-41.

## Opinion

When any opinion leads to absurdity, it is certainly false; but it is not certain that an opinion is false because it is of dangerous consequence. ~ David Hume

I agree with no man's opinion. I have some of my own.
~ Ivan Turgenev, in *Fathers and Sons*

The more unpopular an opinion is, the more necessary that he who holds it be somewhat punctilious in his observance of conventionalities generally. ~ Samuel Butler

Too often we...enjoy the comfort of opinion without the discomfort of thought. ~ John F. Kennedy

When the facts change I change my opinion. What do you do?
~ John Maynard Keynes, in response to a critic who accused him of contradicting himself

With effervescing opinions, as with the not yet forgotten champagne, the quickest way to let them go flat is to let them get exposed to the air. ~ Oliver Wendell Holmes, Jr.

My opinions may have changed, but not the fact that I am right.
~ Ashley Brilliant

If there is an opinion, facts will be found to support it. ~ Judy Sproles

There are a great many opinions in this world, and a good half of them are professed by people who have never been in trouble. ~ Mavis Gallant

Those who most obstinately oppose the most widely held opinions more often do so because of pride than lack of intelligence. They find the best places in the right set already taken, and they do not want back seats. ~ La Rochefoucauld

We credit scarcely any persons with good sense except those who are of our opinion. ~ La Rochefoucauld

Some men are just as sure of the truth of their opinions as are others of what they know. ~ Aristotle

Men get opinions as boys learn to spell,
By reiteration chiefly. ~ Elizabeth Barrett Browning, *Thesaurus*

People are usually more firmly convinced that their opinions are precious than they are true. ~ George Santayana

A man can brave opinion, a woman must submit to it. ~ Mme de Stael

One must judge men not by their opinions but by what their opinions have made of them. ~ Georg Christoph Lichtenberg

Don't quote me as saying that we will or we should increase our external aid. That would be my opinion if I had an opinion, but as a member of my government, I don't have an opinion.
~ Paul Martin, Canadian External Affairs Minister

## Opinions (New)

New opinions are always suspected, and usually opposed, without any other reason but because they are not already common. ~ John Locke

Opinions have vested interests, just as men have. ~ Samuel Butler

If in the last few years you haven't discarded a major opinion or acquired a new one, check your pulse – you may be dead.
~ Gelett Burgess

The more opinions you have, the less you see. ~ Wim Wenders

Express a mean opinion of yourself occasionally; it will show your friends that you know how to tell the truth. ~ Ed Howe

Every new opinion, at its starting, is precisely in a minority of one. ~ Thomas Carlyle

## Opportunity

There is no security on this Earth, there is only opportunity. ~ Douglas MacArthur

The opportunity that God sends does not wake up him who is asleep. ~ Senegalese proverb

Opportunities multiply as they are seized. ~ Sun Tzu

Make the most of all that comes and the least of all that goes. ~ Sara Teasdale

There is a tide in the affairs of men,
Which, taken at the flood, leads on to fortune; ...
On such a full sea are we now afloat,
And we must take the current when it serves,
Or lose our ventures. ~ Shakespeare, *Julius Caesar*

Opportunity is the greatest bawd. ~ Benjamin Franklin

For all sad words of tongue or pen, the saddest are these:
"It might have been!" ~ John Greenleaf Whittier

A man must make his opportunity, as oft as find it. ~ Sir Francis Bacon

## Opposites

Every sweet hath its sour; every evil its good. ~ Ralph Waldo Emerson

Every positive value has its price in negative terms. ...
Einstein leads to Hiroshima. ~ Pablo Picasso

## Oppression

He who allows oppression shares the crime. ~ Erasmus Darwin

## Optimism

I am not a pessimist; to perceive evil where it exists is, in my opinion, a form of optimism. ~ Roberto Rossellini

I find nothing more depressing than optimism. ~ Paul Fussell

Optimism is a kind of heart stimulant – the digitalis of failure.
~ Elbert Hubbard

The place where optimism most flourishes is the lunatic asylum.
~ Havelock Ellis

## Optimist

An optimist is a guy that never has much experience and a pessimist is a person who has had to listen to too many optimists.
~ Don Marquis, U.S. journalist

The optimist proclaims that we live in the best of all possible worlds, the pessimist fears this is true. ~ James Branch Cabell, 1958

An optimist is a fellow who believes what's going to be, will be postponed. ~ Kin Hubbard

An optimist is a guy who has never had much experience. ~ Don Marquis

An optimist is simply a pessimist with no job experience. ~ Anonymous

An optimist is someone who thinks the future is uncertain. ~ Anonymous

An optimist may see a light where there is one, but why must the pessimist always run to blow it out? ~ Michel de Saint-Pierre

## Orchestra

I'm not interested in having an orchestra sound like itself. I want it to sound like the composer. ~ Leonard Bernstein, 1985

There are two golden rules for an orchestra: start together and finish together. The public doesn't give a damn what goes on between.
~ Sir Thomas Beecham, conductor

## Order

Order is for idiots; genius can handle chaos. ~ Anonymous

First thing first, but not necessarily in that order. ~ Dr. Who

Order marches with weighty and measured strides; disorder is always in a hurry. ~ Napoleon Bonaparte

## Organizations

It is the willingness of people to give of themselves over and above the demands of the job that distinguishes the great from the merely adequate organization. ~ Peter Drucker

I have faith that the time will eventually come when employees and employers, as well as all mankind, will realize that they serve themselves best when they serve others most. ~ B.C. Forbes

## Organize

Don't agonize. Organize. ~ Florynce Kennedy

## Organized Crime

Organized crime in America takes in more than $40-billion a year and spends very little on office supplies. ~ Woody Allen

## Ovation

Usually, the standing ovation comes at the end of the show. I guess you're not sure I'm gonna make it that far. ~ 97-year-old comedian George Burns at Montreal's Just for Laughs Festival, 1993

## Owls

Owls teach us wisdom and sagacity and not to put our hands into hollow trees. ~ Will Cuppy, U.S. humorist, in paraphrase

## Ownership

Our life on Earth is, and ought to be, material and carnal. But we have not yet learned to manage our materialism and carnality properly; they are still entangled with the desire for ownership. ~ E.M. Forster

## Pace (of Life)

I grew up in a gentler, slower time. When Ike was president, Christmases were years apart, and now it's about five months from one to the next.
~ Garrison Keillor

## Painting

Painting is silent poetry, and poetry is painting that speaks.
~ Simonides

## Panic

We experience moments absolutely free from worry. These brief respites are called panic. ~ Cullen Hightower

## Paradise

The true paradises are the paradises that we have lost. ~ Marcel Proust

## Paranoids

I envy paranoids; they actually feel people are paying attention to them. ~ Susan Sontag, 1992

I think you're the opposite of a paranoid. I think you go around with the insane delusion that people like you. ~ Woody Allen

## Parent

A suspicious parent makes an artful child. ~ Thomas Chandler Haliburton

Parenthood remains the single greatest preserve of the amateur.
~ Alvin Toffler

There are times when parenthood seems nothing but feeding the hand that bites you. ~ Peter De Vries

The value to a child of poor role models is also underestimated.
Parents have the idea that it is their duty to set a good example, never
realizing that a bad one will do just as well, indeed better. ~ Jill Tweedie

## Parents

Ever since I lost mine, I've had my eye on other people's parents.
~ Ian McEwan, *The Cement Garden*

## Parkinson's Law

Work expands to fill the time available for its completion.
~ C. Northcote Parkinson

## Parties

Goodbye. I've barely said a word to you, but it's always like that at
parties – we never really see each other, we never say the things we
should like to: in fact it's the same everywhere in this life. Let's hope
that when we are dead, things will be better arranged. ~ Marcel Proust

## Party

Party is the madness of the many, for the gain of a few. ~ Alexander Pope

## Passion

The worst sin – perhaps the only sin – passion can commit is to be
joyless. ~ Dorothy L. Sayers

If we resist our passions, it is due more to their weakness than our own
strength. ~ La Rochefoucauld

The passions are the winds that fill the sails of the vessel. They sink it
at times, but without them it would be impossible to make way. Many
things that are dangerous here below are still necessary. ~ Voltaire

When the passions become masters, they are vices. ~ Blaise Pascal

## Passport

If you look like your passport photo, you're too ill to travel.
~ Will Kommen

## Past

When you are forty, half of you belongs to the past...And when you are
seventy, nearly all of you. ~ Jean Anouilh

What's past is prologue. ~ Shakespeare

The past is not simply the past, but a prism through which the subject filters his own changing self-image. ~ Doris Kearns Goodwin

Not to know what has been transacted in former times is to be always a child. If no use is made of the labours of the past, the world must remain always in the infancy of knowledge. ~ Cicero

Living in the past has one thing in its favour – it's cheaper. ~ Anonymous

You can't put the toothpaste back in the tube. ~ Richard Nixon

The past is still, for us, a place that is not yet safely settled.
~ Michael Ondaatje

Worshippers of light ancestral make the present light a crime.
~ James Russell Lowell

Nothing is said that has not been said before.
~ Terence (Publius Terentius Afer)

Even a god cannot change the past. ~ Agathon

The past is the only dead thing that smells sweet. ~ Edward Thomas

## Path

Some of necessity go astray, because for them there is no such thing as a right path. ~ Thomas Mann

Every path has its puddle. ~ English proverb

## Patience

Patience accomplishes its object, while hurry speeds to its ruin. ~ Sa'di

Patience and passage of time do more than strength and fury.
~ Jean de la Fontaine

With time and patience, and the mulberry leaf becomes a silk gown.
~ Chinese proverb

If you wait, there will come nectarlike fair weather. ~ Japanese proverb

Prayer of the modern American: Dear God, I pray for patience. And I want it RIGHT NOW! ~ Owen Arnold

Patience is a bitter plant but it has sweet fruit. ~ German proverb

He who has patience may accomplish anything. ~ Rabelais

Patience will come to he who waits for it. ~ Anonymous

The secret of patience: do something else in the meantime.
~ Anonymous

A handful of patience is worth more than a bushel of brains.
~ Dutch proverb

Our patience will achieve more than our force. ~ Edmund Burke

The strongest of all warriors are these two – Time and Patience.
~ Leo Tolstoy

Patience is passive, resignation is active. ~ Penelope Fitzgerald, *Innocence*

You must first have a lot of patience to learn to have patience.
~ Stanislaw J. Lec

Patience and diligence, like faith, remove mountains. ~ William Penn

The net of the sleeper catches fish. ~ Greek proverb

Patience, that blending of moral courage with physical timidity.
~ Thomas Hardy

Nothing comes of so many things, if you have patience.
~ Joyce Carol Oates

Whoever has no patience has no wisdom. ~ Sa'di

All things come round to him who will but wait.
~ Henry Wadsworth Longfellow

## Patients

It is much more important to know what sort of a patient has a disease than what sort of disease a patient has. ~ Sir William Osler

## Patriotism

Patriotism is often an arbitrary veneration of real estate over principles.
~ George Jean Nathan

## Pay

He who pays the piper may call the tune. ~ English proverb

One does not make "much of a showing" in the eyes of the large majority of people who one meets with, except by unremitting demonstration of ability to pay. ~ Thorstein Veblen

## Peace

Peace is not made at the council table or by treaties, but in the hearts of men. ~ Herbert Hoover

That they may have a little peace, even the best dogs are compelled to snarl occasionally. ~ William Feather

Peace, if it ever exists, will not be based on the fear of war, but on the love of peace. ~ Herman Wouk

Peace rules the day, where reason rules the mind. ~ William Collins

Looking for peace is like looking for a turtle with a mustache. You won't be able to find it. But when your heart is ready, peace will come looking for you. ~ Ajahn Chah

Righteousness and peace have kissed each other.
~ *Book of Common Prayer*

In the arts of peace man is a bungler. ~ George Bernard Shaw

## Pen

The pen is mightier than the sword. ~ Edward Bulwer-Lytton

## People

On the whole, people are rubbish, and they deserve to be wakened to the need to change and amend themselves not by some social factor or some force of circumstance but by conversion of their soul. ... All the problems of our society are caused by the false expectations of people who are led to suppose that they are entitled to these things.
~ Rev. Dr. Edward Norman, British academic

In numerous studies [social psychologists] have documented a deep paradox of human relations – persons get along, but people don't. Encounters among individuals are generally positive, supportive and rewarding, but those among groups are ordinarily unpleasant and confrontational. Even if people are randomly divided into groups, the groups will automatically discriminate against each other.
~ Atul Gawande in *Slate* magazine

One of the worst things about life is not how nasty the nasty people are. You know that already. It is how nasty the nice people can be.
~ Anthony Powell

People can be divided into three groups: those who make things happen, those who watch things happen, and those who wonder what happened. ~ John Newbern

People are like birds – from a distance, beautiful; from up close, those sharp beaks, those beady little eyes. ~ Richard J. Needham

## Perception

We don't see things as they are. We see things as we are. ~ Anais Nin

What I hear I forget. What I see I remember. What I do I know.
~ Chinese proverb

We must not allow other people's limited perceptions to define us.
~ Virginia Satir

When you are a Bear of Very Little Brain, and you Think of Things, you find sometimes that a Thing which seemed very Thingish inside you is quite different when it gets out into the open and has other people looking at it. ~ A.A. Milne in *House at Pooh Corner*

A blind man who sees is better than a seeing man who is blind.
~ Persian proverb

There is nothing either good or bad, but thinking makes it so.
~ Shakespeare

## Perfection

Have no fear of perfection – you'll never reach it. ~ Salvador Dali

The greater the emphasis on perfection the further it recedes.
~ Haridas Chaudhuri

People who strive for excellence tend to experience satisfaction. People who strive for perfection tend not to. ~ Paul Hewitt, psychologist

Doing a thing well is often a waste of time. ~ Robert Byrne

## Performance

There is no strong performance without a little fanatacism in the performer. ~ Ralph Waldo Emerson

A performance is not a contest but a love affair. ~ Glenn Gould

## Perseverance

Perseverance – a lowly virtue whereby mediocrity achieves an inglorious success. ~ Ambrose Bierce

## Persistence

Nothing in this world can take the place of persistence. Talent will not; nothing is more common than unsuccessful people with talent. Genius will not; unrewarded genius is almost a proverb. Education will not; the world is full of educated derelicts. Persistence and determination alone are omnipotent. The slogan "press on" has solved and always will solve the problems of the human race. ~ Calvin Coolidge

We are made to persist. That's how we find out who we are.
~ Tobias Wolff

The greatest oak was once a little nut who held its ground. ~ Unknown

Little strokes fell great oaks. ~ Benjamin Franklin

Fall seven times, stand up eight. ~ Japanese proverb

## Personality

If it weren't for caffeine, I'd have no personality whatsoever.
~ Anonymous

## Perspective

Go some distance away because the work appears much smaller and more of it can be taken in at a glance, and a lack of harmony or proportion is rapidly seen. ~ Leonardo da Vinci

Part of the reason for the ugliness of adults, in a child's eyes, is that the child is usually looking upwards, and few faces are at their best when seen from below. ~ George Orwell

The field cannot well be seen from within the field. ~ Ralph Waldo Emerson

Slight not what's near through aiming at what's far. ~ Euripides

## Persuasion

Persuasion is the only true intellectual process. ~ Matthew Arnold

You can persuade a man to believe almost anything provided he is clever enough, but it is much more difficult to persuade someone less clever. ~ Tom Stoppard

His tongue dropt manna, and could make the worse appear the better reason. ~ John Milton

## Pessimist

A pessimist is a man who has been compelled to live with an optimist.
~ Elbert Hubbard

The man who is a pessimist before forty-eight hours knows too much; if he is an optimist after it, he knows too little. ~ Mark Twain

There is no sadder sight than a young pessimist. ~ Mark Twain

A pessimist is one who builds dungeons in the air. ~ Walter Winchell

Things are always darkest just before they go pitch black. ~ Kelly Robinson

To a profound pessimist about life, being in danger is not depressing.
~ F. Scott Fitzgerald

A pessimist is a man who looks both ways before crossing a one-way street. ~ Laurence J. Peter

A pessimist is just a well-informed optimist. ~ Anonymous

## Peter Principle

In a hierarchy each employee tends to rise to his or her level of incompetence. ~ Laurence J. Peter

## Pettiness

How great in number are the little-minded men. ~ Plautus

## Philosophy

Philosophy is a battle against the bewitchment of our intelligence by means of language. ~ Ludwig Wittgenstein

It is easy to build a philosophy. It doesn't have to run. ~ Charles Kettering

In philosophizing we may not *terminate* a disease of thought. It must run its natural course and *slow* cure is all-important. ~ Ludwig Wittgenstein

The finding of arguments for a conclusion given in advance is not philosophy, but special pleading. ~ Bertrand Russell

Science is what you know, philosophy is what you don't know.
~ Bertrand Russell

## Photography

Most things in life are moments of pleasure and a lifetime of embarrassment; photography is a moment of embarrassment and a lifetime of pleasure. ~ Tony Benn, British politician

## Physicians

One of the first duties of the physician is to educate the masses not to take medicine. ~ Sir Willam Osler

## Pianists

The notes I handle no better than many pianists. But the pauses between the notes – ah, that is where the art resides!
~ Arthur Schnabel, 1958

## Piano

The piano is the easiest instrument to play in the beginning, and the hardest to master in the end. ~ Vladimir Horowitz

## Piety

Men always try to make virtues of their weaknesses. Fear of death and fear of life become piety. ~ H.L. Mencken

## Pioneers

There are two kinds of people in the world – those who pioneer and those who plod. The plodders always attack the pioneers. They say that the pioneers have gobbled up all the opportunity, when, as a plain matter of fact, the plodders would have nowhere to plod had the pioneers not first cleared the way. ~ Henry Ford

The one thing you don't hear mentioned about pioneers is that they are invariably, by their nature, messmakers.
~ Robert Pirsig, *Zen and the Art of Motorcycle Maintenance*

## Planning

Measure a thousand times and cut once. ~ Turkish proverb

I arise in the morning torn between a desire to improve (or save) the world and a desire to enjoy (or savour) the world. This makes it hard to plan the day. ~ E.B. White

The time to repair the roof is when the sun is shining. ~ John F. Kennedy

'Tis the part of a wise man to keep himself today for tomorrow, and not venture all his eggs in one basket. ~ Miguel de Cervantes

## Plans

Our plans miscarry because they have no aim. When a man does not know what harbour he is making for, no wind is the right wind. ~ Seneca

Plans get you into things, but you got to work your way out.
~ Will Rogers

He who is not a bird should not build his nest over abysses.
~ Friedrich Nietzsche

It's a bad plan that can't be changed. ~ Publilius Syrus

Burning the candle at both ends is the worst way to make ends meet.
~ Anonymous

The course of true anything does not run smooth. ~ Samuel Butler

In every affair consider what precedes and follows, and then
undertake it. ~ Epictetus

The more human beings proceed by plan, the more effectively they
may be hit by accident. ~ Friedrich Durrenmatt

Make no little plans; they have no magic to stir men's blood.
~ Daniel H. Burnham

I'll work on a new and original plan, said I to myself, said I.
~ William S. Gilbert

## Platitude

A platitude is simply a truth repeated until people get tired of hearing
it. ~ Stanley Baldwin, British statesman

## Platonic Relationships

Of course a platonic relationship is possible – but only between
husband and wife. ~ Ladies Home Journal, cited in The Macmillan Dictionary of
Contemporary Quotations

## Play

The true object of all human life is play. Earth is a task garden; heaven
is a playground. ~ G.K. Chesterton, 1908

To the art of working well a civilized race would add the art of playing
well. ~ George Santayana

Though this may be play to you, 'tis death to us. ~ Sir Roger L'Estrange

## Please

He is not yet born who can please everybody. ~ Danish proverb

He is a man whom it is impossible to please, because he is never pleased with himself. ~ Goethe

The art of pleasing consists of being pleased. ~ William Hazlitt

## Pleasure

Pleasure is very seldom found where it is sought; our brightest blazes of gladness are commonly kindled by unexpected sparks.
~ Samuel Johnson, *The Idler*

The test of pleasure is the memory it leaves behind. ~ Jean Paul Richter

Pleasure is a thief to business. ~ Daniel Defoe

## Plots

Plots, true or false, are necessary things,
To raise up commonwealths, and ruin kings. ~ John Dryden

## Poems

A well-rounded poem is like a sphere. It is impossible to view it completely. ~ John V. Hicks, 1987

## Poetry

You will not find poetry anywhere unless you bring some of it with you.
~ Joseph Joubert

There's no money in poetry, but then there's no poetry in money either.
~ Robert Graves

I know poetry is indispensable, but I don't know to what. ~ Victor Hugo

## Poets

The poet is the priest of the invisible. ~ Wallace Stevens

No poet or novelist wished he were the only one who ever lived, but most of them wish they were the only one alive, and quite a number fondly believe their wish has been granted. ~ W.H. Auden

People wish to be poets more than they wish to write poetry, and that's a mistake. One should wish to celebrate more than one wishes to be celebrated. ~ Lucille Clifton, U.S. poet/children's writer

Immature poets imitate; mature poets steal. ~ T.S. Eliot

I hate all Boets and Bainters.
~ George II, British King and elector of Hanover

Poets who know no better rhapsodize about the peace of nature, but a well-populated marsh is a cacophony. ~ Bern Keating, 1986

I have never yet known a poet who did not think himself super-excellent. ~ Cicero

To know how to say what others only know how to think is what makes men poets or sages; and to dare to say what others only dare to think makes men martyrs or reformers or both. ~ Elizabeth Charles

In spite of all romantic poets sing,
This gold, my dearest, is an useful thing. ~ Mary Leapor

## Poise

Ah, men do not know how much strength is in poise,
That he goes the farthest who goes far enough.
~ James Russell Lowell

## Politeness

A polite man is one who listens with interest to things he knows all about, when they are told him by a person who knows nothing about them. ~ Philippe de Mornay, French politician

Politeness is half good manners and half good lying. ~ Mary Wilson Little

Politeness is to goodness what words are to thought. ~ Joseph Joubert

## Political Correctness: Definitions

Acid rain: poorly buffered precipitation

Adultery: consensual non-monogamy

Aging (the): chronologically gifted persons; the experientially enhanced

Air crash (flying into the side of a mountain or other landscape feature – per ICAO): controlled flight into terrain

*Alcoholic: anti-sobriety activist

Boring speech: differently interesting address; charm-free oration

*Cannibalism: Intra-species dining

Cliché: previously enjoyed sound bite

*Corpse: permanently static post-human mass

Corrupt: ethically different; morally challenged

*Dead: actuarially mature

Drug addicts and alcoholics: the sobriety deprived; people of stupor

Education: children do not fail; they are merely "achieving a deficiency."
High school dropouts are "individuals with provisionally unmet
educational objectives."

Homeless: underhoused; involuntarily undomiciled

*Homelessness: mortgage-free living

Hunger: nutritional shortfall; caloric insufficiency

Lie: categorical inaccuracy; counterfactual proposition; strategic
misrepresentation; terminological inexactitude

Lobbyist: legislative advocate

Looters: nontraditional shoppers

Nerd: technically advantaged (*Globe & Mail* Nov. 19/93)

Panhandlers: unaffiliated applicants for private sector funding

*Plagiarism: previously owned prose

*Roadkill: vehicularly compressed maladapted life form

Sadomasochists: the differently pleasured

*Shoplifter: cost-of-living adjustment specialist

*Stabbing: social surgery

Toxic Dumping: deep ocean storage

*Vomiting: unplanned re-examination of recent food choices

~ Henry Beard, Christopher Cerf, *Int'l Herald Tribune* July 15, 1992
* *Globe & Mail* June 14, 1993, from *The Washington Post*

## Political Ideas

What matters most about political ideas is the underlying emotions, the
music, to which the ideas are mere libretto, often of very inferior
quality. ~ Sir Louis Naimer, *Personalities and Powers*

## Political Skills

The President of his country was a man of stunning political gifts. He had the courage of a lion and the tactical agility of a mongoose. It was a plan that he lacked. [Narmonov] had no idea where he was going and that was his weakness. ~ Tom Clancy, *The Sum of All Fears*

## Politicians

Politicians are the same all over. They promise to build bridges, even when there are no rivers. ~ Nikita Khrushchev

Any party which takes credit for the rain must not be surprised if its opponents blame it for the drought. ~ Dwight W. Morrow

Politicians make strange bedfellows, but they all share the same bunk. ~ Edgar A. Shoaff

Don't put it in writing if you can phone. Don't phone if you can meet. Don't speak if you can whisper. Don't whisper if you can nod. Don't nod if you can wink. ~ Earl Long, Louisiana governor

We are all mere petty provincial politicians at present; perhaps, by and by, some of us will rise to the level of national statesmen. ~ Sir John A. Macdonald

The thing about a politician is, you have to take the smooth with the smooth. ~ Susan Hill

Gladstone: I predict, Sir, that you will die either by hanging or of some vile disease.
Disraeli: That all depends, Sir, upon whether I embrace your principles or your mistress. ~ Exchange at a social gathering

To become the master, the politician poses as the servant. ~ Charles de Gaulle

Politicians can forgive almost everything in the way of abuse; they can forgive subversion, being contradicted, exposed as liars, even ridiculed, but they can never forgive being ignored. ~ Auberon Waugh

The more you are talked about, the more you will wish to be talked about. The condemned murderer who is allowed to see the account of his trial in the press is indignant if he finds a newspaper which has reported it inadequately. ... Politicians and literary men are in the same case. ~ Bertrand Russell

What this country needs is more unemployed politicians. ~ Edward Langley

## Politics

Life somehow finds a way of transcending politics. ~ Norman Cousins

Politics is the science of exigencies. ~ Theodore Parker

The difference between politics and statesmanship is philosophy.
~ Will and Ariel Durant

Politics is perhaps the only profession for which no preparation is thought necessary. ~ Robert Louis Stevenson

Three people marooned on a desert island would soon invent politics.
~ Mason Cooley

Politics is the art of the possible. ~ R.A. Butler

Politics in Canada has always been the art of the necessary possible.
~ Peter Newman

Politics is the art of helping oneself to people. ~ Henri de Montherlant

Culture is the backbone of society, politics merely its entertainment.
~ Eleanor Koldofsky, Canadian recording pioneer,

Politics is both fraud and vision. ~ Donald Horne

Great men don't bother with politics. ~ Albert Camus

Politics makes estranged bedfellows. ~ Goodman Ace

Politics is the skilled use of blunt objects. ~ Lester B. Pearson

Politics is applesauce. ~ Will Rogers

A sick society must think much about politics, as a sick man must think much about his digestion. ~ C.S. Lewis

In politics, if you want anything said, ask a man; if you want anything done, ask a woman. ~ Margaret Thatcher

There can be no greater error than to expect to calculate upon real favours from nation to nation. ~ George Washington

Politics is made up largely of irrelevancies. ~ Dalton Camp

In politics the middle way is none at all. ~ John Adams, 1776

Just because you do not take an interest in politics does not mean politics will not take an interest in you. ~ Pericles

In politics, an absurdity is not a handicap. ~ Napoleon Bonaparte

If you want to get along, go along. ~ Sam Rayburn

## Polls

One day the don't-knows will get in, and then where will we be?
~ Spike Milligan

The so-called science of poll-taking is not a science at all but a mere necromancy. People are unpredictable by nature, and although you can take a nation's pulse, you can't be sure that the nation hasn't just run up a flight of stairs. ~ E.B. White

## Poor

It is only the poor who pay cash, and that not from virtue, but because they are refused credit. ~ Anatole France, A *Cynic's Breviary*

It's no disgrace t' be poor, but it might as well be.
~ Kin Hubbard

## Pop Art

Pop art is the inedible raised to the unspeakable. ~ Leonard Baskin, 1965

## Popularity

Anyone who is popular is bound to be disliked. ~ Yogi Berra

## Portrait

It takes two people to make a good portrait. ~ Arnaud Magges

## Positive

Positive, *adj*. Mistaken at the top of one's voice. ~ Ambrose Bierce

## Possessions

The more a man possesses over and above what he uses, the more careworn he becomes. ~ George Bernard Shaw

You can't have everything. Where would you put it? ~ Steven Wright

People who get through life dependent on other people's possessions are always the first to lecture you on how little possessions count.
~ Ben Elton

People don't resent having nothing nearly as much as too little.
~ Ivy Compton-Burnett

## Posterity

Posterity is as likely to be as wrong as anyone else. ~ Heywood Broun

Posterity weaves no garlands for imitators. ~ Friedrich von Schiller

## Potential

Discussing the potential of a top prospect, "The guy is 21 right now and in ten years he has a good chance to be 31." ~ Casey Stengel

Man is as full of potentiality as he is of impotence. ~ George Santayana

It's never too late to be who you might have been. ~ George Eliot

## Poverty

He is now fast rising from affluence to poverty. ~ Mark Twain

I've never been poor, only broke. Being poor is a frame of mind.
~ Mike Todd

Poverty has its compensations – nobody begs of a poor man.
~ The Globe, 1877

Poverty eclipses the brightest virtues, and is the very sepulchre of brave designs, depriving a man of the means to accomplish what nature has fitted him for, and stifling the noblest thoughts in their embryo. Many illustrious souls may be said to have been dead among the living, or buried alive in the obscurity of their condition, whose perfections [might] have rendered them the darlings of Providence and the companion of angels. ~ Turkish Spy, pseudonym for a writer, circa 1700

Not he who has little, but he who wishes more, is poor. ~ Seneca

I come from a family where gravy is considered a beverage.
~ Erma Bombeck

Thousands upon thousands are yearly brought into a state of real poverty by their great anxiety not to be thought poor. ~ William Cobbett

## Power

The only prize much cared for by the powerful is power. The prize of the general is not a bigger tent, but command. ~ Oliver Wendell Holmes, Jr.

Power must never be trusted without a check. ~ John Adams

The measure of man is what he does with power. ~ Pittacus

Power can corrupt, but absolute power is absolutely delightful.
~ Anonymous

Power corrupts. Absolute power is kind of neat. ~ John Lehman

While nobody can seriously maintain that the greatest number must
have the greatest wisdom, or the greatest virtue, there is no denying
that, under modern social conditions, they are likely to have the most
power. ~ Walter Lippman

Power is the ability not to have to please. ~ Elizabeth Janeway

The distinction that really matters is not between violence and non-
violence but between having and not having the appetite for power.
~ George Orwell

Power is to have others listen to your silence. ~ Patrick Kelly

Power never takes a back step – only in the face of more power.
~ Malcolm X

## Practice

If I don't practise one day, I know it; two days, the critics know it; three
days, the public knows it. ~ Jascha Heifetz, 1971

However much thou art read in theory, if thou hast no practice thou art
ignorant. ~ Sa'di

## Pragmatism

The great weakness of pragmatism is that it ends up being of no use to
anybody. ~ T.S. Eliot

## Praise

The advantage of doing one's praising to oneself is that one can lay it
on so thick and exactly in the right places. ~ Samuel Butler

To praise oneself is considered improper, immodest; to praise one's
own sect, one's own philosophy, is considered the highest duty.
~ Leo Shestov

He who gladly does without the praise of the crowd will not miss the
opportunity of becoming his own fan. ~ Karl Kraus

He who refuses praise the first time that it is offered does so because
he would hear it a second time. ~ La Rochefoucauld

Among the smaller duties of life, I hardly know one more important
than that of not praising where praise is not due. ~ Sydney Smith

## Prayer

It's best to read the weather forecast before we pray for rain.
~ Mark Twain

It is folly for a man to pray to the gods for that which he has the power to obtain for himself. ~ Epicurus

## Pre-Menstrual Syndrome

Women complain about pre-menstrual syndrome, but I think of it as the only time of the month that I can be myself. ~ Roseanne Barr

Do you know why they call it "PMS"? Because mad cow disease was already taken. ~ Unknown

## Precautions

The chief danger in life is that you take too many precautions.
~ Alfred Adler

## Predictions

The wisest prophet makes sure of the event first. ~ Horace Walpole

You can only predict things after they've happened ~ Eugene Ionesco

A misty morning does not signify a cloudy day. ~ Proverb

The best way to predict your future is to make it. ~ Peter Drucker

I think the team that wins Game Five will win the series. Unless we lose Game Five. ~ Charles Barkley

## Pregnancy

If pregnancy were a book, they would cut the last two chapters.
~ Nora Ephron

## Prejudice

Prejudice is never easy unless it can pass itself off as reason.
~ William Hazlitt

No one who is Roman Catholic, left-handed and red haired has anything to learn about prejudice. ~ Paul Johnson, English historian

Without the aid of prejudice and custom, I should not be able to find my way across the room. ~ William Hazlitt

Prejudices are what fools use for reason ~ Voltaire

Prejudice is the child of ignorance. ~ William Hazlitt

A great many people think they are thinking when they are merely rearranging their prejudices. ~ William James

He had but one eye, and the popular prejudice runs in favour of two. ~ Charles Dickens

She was anxious to be someone, and, no one ever having voiced a prejudice in her hearing without impressing her, had come to associate prejudice with identity. You could not be a someone without disliking things. ~ Elizabeth Bowen in *The House in Paris*

I am free of all prejudices. I hate everyone equally. ~ W.C. Fields

## Preparation

If I had eight hours to chop down a tree I would spend six sharpening my axe. ~ Abraham Lincoln

The best preparation for tomorrow is to do today's work superbly well. ~ Sir William Osler

Failing to prepare is preparing to fail. ~ John Wooden

He who is not ready today, will be less ready tomorrow. ~ Ovid

It's a funny thing: the more I practise, the luckier I get. ~ Arnold Palmer

No matter how deep you dig your well, it affords poor refuge in times of flood. ~ Chinese proverb

## Presents

When thou makest presents, let them be of such things as will last long; to the end that they may be in some sort immortal and may frequently refresh the memory of the receiver. ~ Thomas Fuller

## President

In America any boy may become President and I suppose it's just one of the risks he takes. ~ Adlai Stevenson

Being President is like running a cemetery; you've got a lot of people under you and nobody's listening. ~ Bill Clinton

The things that bother the press about a President will ultimately bother the country. ~ David Halberstam

## Press

As the free press develops, the paramount point is whether the journalist, like the scientist or scholar, puts truth in the first place or the second. ~ Walter Lippman

Hastiness and superficiality are the psychic disease of the 20th century, and more than anywhere else this disease is reflected in the press. ~ Alexander Solzhenitsyn, 1978

I'm with you on the free press. It's the newspapers I can't stand. ~ Tom Stoppard

## Pressure

Pressure, pushing down on me, pressing down on you. ~ David Bowie

## Prestige

Prestige is the mainspring of all authority. Neither gods, kings nor women have ever reigned without it. ~ Gustave Le Bon, *The Crowd*

## Pretending

You can pretend to be serious. You can't pretend to be witty. ~ Sacha Guitry

## Pretty Face

It has been said that a pretty face is a passport. But it's not, it's a visa, and it runs out fast. ~ Julie Burchill

## Prevention

You can only cure retail but you can prevent wholesale. ~ Brock Chisholm

## Pride

Temper is what gets most of us in trouble. Pride is what keeps us there. ~ Unknown

Don't let your brains go to your head. ~ Unknown

Pride is generally censured and decried, but mainly by those who have nothing to be proud of. ~ Arthur Schopenhauer

Nature endowed us with pride to spare us the pain of knowing about our imperfections. ~ La Rochefoucauld

Pride does not wish to owe and vanity does not wish to pay. ~ La Rochefoucauld

## Principle

I am totally without principle – but not without interest. ~ Jim Lyons

It is often easier to fight for principles than live up to them.
~ Adlai Stevenson

He who merely knows right principles is not equal to him who loves
them. ~ Confucius

Nature imitates herself. A grain thrown into good ground brings forth
fruit; a principle thrown into a good mind brings forth fruit.
~ Blaise Pascal

Those who stand for nothing fall for anything. ~ Alexander Hamilton

The time has come for all good men to rise above principle. ~ Huey Long

Those are my principles, and if you don't like them – well, I have
others. ~ Groucho Marx

## Privacy

Privacy is one of those precious modern constructions that we've
dressed up as a fundamental right when it's really a frilly privilege that
comes with being so affluent that we can ignore the neighbours and
pretend that we don't need anyone else. In societies where folks have
to live on top of one another, there's not a lot of privacy. But there is
discretion. ... We've created a world of privacy without discretion, a
sort of inside-out Victorianism. God save anyone who dares to ask for
my Social Security number, but let's hear about my erectile
dysfunction! ~ Mark Fisher in *The Washington Post*

## Privilege

What men value in this world is not rights but privileges. ~ H.L. Mencken

## Probability

A reasonable probability is the only certainty. ~ Edgar Watson Howe

## Problems

Don't let us make imaginary evils, when we have so many real ones to
encounter. ~ Oliver Goldsmith

Problems are only opportunities in working clothes. ~ Henry J. Kaiser

If a problem is too difficult to solve, one cannot claim that it is solved
by pointing to all the efforts made to solve it. ~ Hannes Alfven, quoted in
*The New Anatomy of Britain*, 1982

The real problem is what to do with the problem solvers after the problems are solved. ~ Gay Talese, U.S. journalist

Some people approach every problem with an open mouth.
~ Adlai Stevenson

Problems cannot be solved by thinking within the framework in which the problems were created. ~ Albert Einstein

A problem is a chance for you to do your best. ~ Duke Ellington

People who are only good with hammers see every problem as a nail.
~ Abraham Maslow

No problem can withstand the assault of sustained thinking. ~ Voltaire

Every problem has a gift for you in its hands. ~ Richard Bach

It isn't that they can't see the solution. It is that they can't see the problem. ~ G.K. Chesterton

Problems worthy of attack prove their worth by hitting back. ~ Piet Hein

Repent what's past; avoid what is to come. ~ Shakespeare

We can face our problem. We can arrange our facts with order and method. ~ Agatha Christie

It is quite a three-pipe problem. ~ Arthur Conan Doyle

## Procrastination

Procrastination gives you something to look forward to. ~ Joan Konner

Procrastination is the art of keeping up with yesterday. ~ Don Marquis

Procrastination is opportunity's assassin. ~ Victor Kiam

If it weren't for the last minute, nothing would get done. ~ Anonymous

Never put off tomorrow what you can do the day after tomorrow.
~ Mark Twain

## Producer

Every man is a consumer and ought to be a producer.
~ Ralph Waldo Emerson

## Profanity

Profanity is the effort of a feeble mind to express itself forcefully.
~ Unknown

## Professionals

Professional are people who can do their job when they don't feel like it. Amateurs are people who can't do their job when they do feel like it. ~ *Bits & Pieces*

Being a professional is doing all the things you love to do on the days when you don't feel like doing them. ~ Julius Erving

The essence of a genuine professional man is that he cannot be bought. ~ H.L. Mencken

All professions are conspiracies against the laity. ~ George Bernard Shaw

## Profits

Nothing contributes so much to the prosperity and happiness of a country as high profits. ~ David Ricardo, 1820

Civilization and profits go hand in hand. ~ Calvin Coolidge

## Progress

The test of our progress is not whether we add more to the abundance of those who have much, it is whether we provide enough for those who have too little. ~ Franklin D. Roosevelt

Progress, therefore, is not an accident, but a necessity .... It is part of nature. ~ Herbert Spencer

It would take only one generation of forgetfulness to put us back intellectually several thousand years. ~ Dean Tollefson

Progress might have been all right once, but it's gone on too long. ~ Ogden Nash

Usually, terrible things that are done with the excuse that progress requires them are not really progress at all, but just terrible things. ~ Russell Baker

With every passing hour our solar system comes forty-three thousand miles closer to globular cluster M13 in the constellation Hercules, and still there are some misfits who continue to insist that there is no such thing as progress. ~ Ransom K. Ferm

What we call progress is the exchange of one nuisance for another nuisance. ~ Havelock Ellis

Habit creates the appearance of justice; progress has no greater enemy than habit. ~ José Martí

Those who speak the most of progress measure it by quantity and not by quality. ~ George Santayana

We're going to turn this team around 360 degrees.
~ Jason Kidd, upon being drafted by the Dallas Mavericks

Belief in progress is a doctrine of idlers and Belgians. It is the individual relying upon his neighbours to do his work. ~ Charles Beaudelaire

Technological progress is like an axe in the hands of a pathological criminal. ~ Albert Einstein

Progress imposes not only new possibilities for the future, but new restrictions. ~ Norbert Wiener

The chief obstacle to the progress of the human race is the human race. ~ Don Marquis

Civilization is impossible without traditions, and progress impossible without the destruction of those traditions. The difficulty, and it is an immense difficulty, is to find a proper equilibrium between stability and variability. ~ Gustave Le Bon, *The Crowd*, 1895

## Progression

Nothing in progression can rest on its original plan. We may as well think of rocking a grown man in the cradle of an infant. ~ Edmund Burke

## Proletariat

The proletariat are far more skilled at discovering what they want than what they need; so giving them power constituted giving them power to say what they want, not giving them objectivity to see what they need.
~ John Fowles

## Promise

Promise is most given when the least is said. ~ George Chapman

The promises of yesterday are the taxes of today.
~ William Lyon Mackenzie King

Better a friendly refusal than an unwitting promise. ~ German proverb

## Proof

"For example" is not proof. ~ Jewish proverb

## Propaganda

Why is propaganda so much more successful when it stirs up hatred than when it tries to stir up friendly feeling? ~ Bertrand Russell

## Prophecy

The art of prophecy is very difficult – especially with respect to the future. ~ Mark Twain

Prophecy is the most gratuitous form of error. ~ George Eliot, *Middlemarch*

Some people would take comfort from the end of the world, if only they had prophesied it. ~ Friedrich Hebbel

## Prosperity

Everything in the world may be endured except continued prosperity. ~ Goethe

## Protest

Protest long enough that you are right, and you will be wrong. ~ Yiddish proverb

## Proverbs

Solomon made a book of proverbs, but a book of proverbs never made a Solomon. ~ English proverb

A country can be judged by the quality of its proverbs. ~ German proverb

A proverb is one man's wit and all men's wisdom. ~ Lord John Russell

Even a proverb is no proverb to you until your life has illustrated it. ~ John Keats

## Provocation

To strike at a serpent that hisses may only cause it to spring. ~ Frank Moore

## Prudence

The eye of prudence may never shut. ~ Ralph Waldo Emerson

Affairs are easier of entrance than of exit, and it is but common prudence to see our way out before we venture in. ~ Aesop

## Psychiatrists

Psychiatrists pretend not to know everything. ~ Bob Kaufman, U.S. poet

## Psychoanalysis

Psychoanalysis makes quite simple people feel they're complex.
~ S.N. Behrman

## Psychology

The object of psychology is to give us a totally different idea of the things we know best. ~ Paul Valéry

## Public

The public do not know enough to be experts, yet know enough to decide between them. ~ Unknown

The public seldom forgive twice. ~ Johann Kaspar Lavater

The public will believe anything, so long as it is not founded on truth.
~ Edith Sitwell

## Public Interest

Everybody thinks chiefly of his own, hardly ever of the public, interest.
~ Aristotle

A democracy is badly served when newspapers and television focus so intensely on the personal joys and tragedies of famous people. This kind of "news" crowds out more serious issues, and there is an important difference ... between the public interest and what interests the public. ~ Cass Sunstein

## Public Life

Public life is the paradise of voluble windbags. ~ George Bernard Shaw

Public life is a situation of power and energy; he trespasses against his duty who sleeps upon his watch, as well as he who goes over to his enemy. ~ Edmund Burke

## Public Opinion

Public opinion is a compound of folly, weakness, prejudice, wrong feeling, right feeling, obstinacy, and newspaper paragraphs.
~ Sir Robert Peel, British Prime Minister

When the people have no tyrant, their own public opinion becomes one. ~ Edward Bulwer-Lytton

One should respect public opinion in so far as it is necessary to avoid starvation and keep out of prison, but anything that goes beyond this is a voluntary submission to an unnecessary tyranny. ~ Bertrand Russell

Your representative owes you, not his industry only, but his judgment; and he betrays instead of serving you if he sacrifices it to your opinion. ~ Edmund Burke

Because half-a-dozen grasshoppers under a fern make the field ring with their impudent chink, whilst thousands of great cattle, reposed beneath the shadow of the British oak, chew the cud and are silent, pray do not imagine that those who make the noise are the only inhabitants of the field; that, of course, they are many in number; or that, after all, they are other than the little, shrivelled, meagre, hopping, though loud and troubled *insects* of the hour. ~ Edmund Burke

When Princes break their miserable etiquette it is always in favour of some girl or jester, and never for a man of worth. When women make themselves conspicuous, it is never for an upright man, always for a *creature*. In a word, when we throw off the yoke of public opinion, it is seldom for the purpose of rising above it, but nearly always to fall below. ~ Sébastien Chamfort

## Public Service

Why is it that when people have no capacity for private usefulness they should be so anxious to serve the public? ~ Sara Jeanette Duncan

## Publicity

There's no bad publicity, except an obituary notice. ~ Brendan Behan

## Publishers

One of the signs of Napoleon's greatness is the fact that he once had a publisher shot. ~ Siegfried Unseld, 1980

## Punctuality

Punctuality is the virtue of the bored. ~ Evelyn Waugh

I have always been a quarter of an hour before my time, and it has made a man of me. ~ Lord Nelson

Punctuality is the politeness of princes. ~ Unknown

Punctuality has been defined as the art of guessing accurately just how late the other party may be. If you can manage to reach the appointed place first … you win. ~ Unknown

The trouble with being punctual is that nobody's there to appreciate it. ~ Unknown

If people are early, they're anxious. If they're on time, they're obsessive. If they're late, they're angry. ~ Unknown

The slogan of the Procrastinators Club of America is: "We're Behind You All the Way." ~ Unknown

## Pundit

A pundit is an expert on nothing but an authority on everything. ~ William Safire

## Pure

O Lord, help me to be pure, but not yet. ~ St. Augustine

Blessed are the pure in heart for they have so much to talk about. ~ Edith Wharton

I'm as pure as the driven slush. ~ Tallulah Bankhead

## Purpose

If a man hasn't discovered something he will die for, he isn't fit to live. ~ Martin Luther King, Jr.

All that we do is done with an eye to something else. ~ Aristotle

If you don't know where you are going, you will probably end up somewhere else. ~ Laurence J. Peter

The days come and go like muffled and veiled figures sent from a distant friendly party, but they say nothing, and if we do not use the gifts they bring, they carry them as silently away. ~ Ralph Waldo Emerson

If you're out to beat a dog, you're sure to find a stick. ~ Yiddish proverb

He who has a why to live can bear almost any how. ~ Friedrich Nietzsche

If one does not know to which port one is sailing, no wind is favourable. ~ Seneca

## Quality

The good composer is slowly discovered, the bad composer is slowly found out. ~ Ernest Newman

It is quality rather than quantity that matters. ~ Seneca

## Qantas Airways

Complaints logged by pilots and solutions logged by maintenance engineers:

Dead bugs on windshield. *Live bugs on back-order.*

Evidence of leak on right main landing gear. *Evidence removed.*

IFF inoperative. IFF *always inoperative in "off" mode.*

Aircraft handles funny. *Aircraft warned to straighten up, fly right, and be serious.*

Target radar hums. *Reprogrammed target radar with words.*

## Quarrels

Quarrels would not last long if the fault was only on one side.
~ La Rochefoucauld

The last sound on the worthless earth will be two human beings trying to launch a homemade space-ship and already quarrelling about where they are going next. ~ William Faulkner

Most quarrels amplify a misunderstanding. ~ André Gide

Let's not quarrel about the skin until we kill the bear.
~ Sir John A. Macdonald

It takes two to make a quarrel, but only one to end it. ~ Spanish proverb

A bad workman quarrels with the man who calls him that.
~ Ambrose Bierce

The test of a man or woman's breeding is how they behave in a quarrel.
~ George Bernard Shaw

There is a sort of man who goes through the world in a succession of quarrels, always able to make out that he is in the right, although he never ceases to put other men in the wrong. The least that can be said of such a person is that he has an unhappy aptitude for eliciting whatever evil there may be in the natures with which he comes in contact; and a man who is sure to cause injuries to him wherever he goes is almost as great an evil and inconvenience as if he were himself the wrongdoer. ~ Sir Henry Taylor, *The Statesman*, 1836

## Questions

No question is ever settled until it is settled right. ~ Ella Wheeler Wilcox

It is better to know some of the questions than to know all of the answers. ~ James Thurber

He who asks questions cannot avoid the answers. ~ Cameroonian proverb

Judge a man by his questions rather than his answers. ~ Voltaire

There aren't any embarrassing questions – just embarrassing answers.
~ Carl Rowan

A sudden bold, and unexpected question doth many times surprise a man and lay him open. ~ Francis Bacon

The important thing is not to stop questioning. ~ Albert Einstein

## Quiet

To be simple is the best thing in the world; to be modest is the next best thing. I am not so sure about being quiet. ~ G.K. Chesterton

## Quotations

On the rare occasions when I really didn't like a person, I quoted them verbatim. ~ Jay Scott, *Globe and Mail*, 1990

I hate quotations. Tell me what you know. ~ Ralph Waldo Emerson

It is a good thing for an uneducated man to read books of quotations.
~ Winston Churchill, *My Early Life*, 1930

By necessity, by proclivity – and by delight, we all quote.
~ Ralph Waldo Emerson

What's the use of a good quotation if you can't change it? ~ Doctor Who

Confound those who have said our remarks before us.
~ Aelius Donatus

## Race

The race is not to the swift, nor the battle to the strong. ~ Ecclesiastes

The race is to the swift;
The battle is to the strong. ~ John Davidson

The race is not always to the swift, nor the battle to the strong –
but that's the way to bet. ~ Damon Runyon

## Radicals

A radical man is a man with both feet firmly planted in the air.
~ Franklin D. Roosevelt

The radical of one century is the conservative of the next. The radical
invents the views. When he has worn them out the conservative adopts
them. ~ Mark Twain

## Rain

I hate all those weathermen [who] tell you that rain is bad weather.
There's no such thing as bad weather, just the wrong clothing.
~ Billy Connolly, comedian

It is impossible to live in a country which is continually under hatches
… Rain! Rain! Rain! ~ John Keats

## Rainbow

The way I see it, if you want the rainbow, you gotta put up with the rain.
~ Dolly Parton

## Rank

Rank is a great beautifier. ~ Edward Bulwer-Lytton

### Rashness

Rashness succeeds often, still more often fails. ~ Napoleon Bonaparte

You never saw a fish on the wall with its mouth shut. ~ Sally Berger

### Rat Race

The trouble with the rat race is that even if you win, you're still a rat.
~ Lily Tomlin

### Rationality

If rationality were the criterion for things being allowed to exist, the
world would be one gigantic field of soya beans. ~ Tom Stoppard

### Readiness

To be always ready, a man must be able to cut a knot, for not
everything can be untied. ~ Henri Frédéric Amiel

The readiness is all. ~ Shakespeare, *Hamlet*

### Reading

Men of power have no time to read; yet men who do not read are unfit
for power. ~ Bertrand Russell

Reading is to the mind what exercise is to the body.
~ Richard Steele

### Realist

The pessimist complains about the wind; the optimist expects it to
change; and the realist adjusts the sails. ~ William Ward

### Reality

Reality is something you rise above. ~ Liza Minnelli

The sky is not less blue because the blind man does not see it.
~ Danish proverb

All the mind's activity is easy if it is not subjected to reality.
~ Marcel Proust

I like reality. It tastes of bread. ~ Jean Anouilh

Not all things are black and white....the sooner we learn this, the
sooner we reach a better understanding of reality.
~ Alfred Charles Kinsey, American physician, author

Reality is what I see, not what you see. ~ Anthony Burgess

The dignity of man lies in his ability to face reality in all its
senselessness. ~ Martin Esslin

Reality's not strange, not unexpected. Reality doesn't reside in the
sudden hallucination of events. Reality is uneventfulness, vacancy,
flatness. Reality is that nothing happens. How many of the events of
history have occurred … for no other reason, fundamentally, than the
desire to make things happen? ~ Graham Swift

## Reason

If we live according to the guidance of reason, we shall desire for
others the good we seek for ourselves. ~ Baruch Spinoza

Ever since Kant divorced reason from reality, his intellectual
descendants have been diligently widening the breach. ~ Ayn Rand

We may take Fancy for a companion, but must follow Reason as our
guide. ~ Samuel Johnson

Reason can wrestle
And overthrow terror. ~ Euripides

Reason respects the differences, and imagination the similitudes of
things. ~ Percy Bysshe Shelley

Say first, of God above or man below,
What can we reason but from what we know? ~ Alexander Pope

Only reason can convince us of those three fundamental truths without
a recognition of which there can be no effective liberty: that what we
believe is not necessarily true; that what we like is not necessarily
good; and that all questions are open. ~ Clive Bell

If we would guide by the light of reason, we must let our minds be bold.
~ Louis D. Brandeis

There's a mighty big difference between good, sound reasons and
reasons that sound good. ~ Burton Hillis

Reason has always existed, but not always in a reasonable form.
~ Karl Marx

## Reasoning

Man is a reasoning rather than a reasonable animal. ~ Alexander Hamilton

Most of our so-called reasoning consists in finding arguments for going on believing as we already do. ~ James Harvey Robinson

## Recession

A recession is when your neighbour has to tighten his belt. A depression is when you have to tighten your belt. A panic is when you have no belt and your pants fall down. ~ Tommy Douglas

It is a recession when your neighbour loses his job; it's a depression when you lose yours. ~ Harry S. Truman, *Observer*, April 13, 1958

## Recipe

A recipe has a hidden side, like the moon. ~ James de Coquet

## Recollection

Recollection is the only paradise from which we cannot be turned out.
~Jean-Paul Richter, German humorist

## Reflection

Mirrors should reflect a little before throwing back images.
~ Jean Cocteau

To doubt everything and to believe everything are two equally convenient solutions; both free us from the necessity of reflection.
~ Henri Poincaré

## Reform

Every reform movement has a lunatic fringe. ~ Theodore Roosevelt

Reform yourself. That way there will be one less rascal in the world.
~ Thomas Carlyle, when asked by a young man how he should go about
~ reforming the world

But 'tis the talent of our English nation. Still to be plotting some new reformation. ~ John Dryden

## Regret

Never, never waste a minute on regret. It's a waste of time.
~ Harry S. Truman

My one regret in life is that I am not someone else. ~ Woody Allen

## Relationships

Relationships are hard. It's like a full time job and we should treat it like one. If your boyfriend or girlfriend wants to leave you, they should give you two weeks' notice. There should be severance pay and before they leave you, they should have to find you a temp. ~ Bob Ettinger

## Relatives

The normal man's antipathy to his relatives lies in the plain fact that every man sees in his relatives, and especially in his cousins, a series of grotesque caricatures of himself. They exhibit his qualities in disconcerting augmentation or diminution; they fill him with a disquieting feeling that this, perhaps, is the way he appears to the world. ~ H.L. Mencken

## Religions

I do benefits for all religions; I'd hate to blow the hereafter on a technicality. ~ Bob Hope

Doubt is part of all religion. All the religious thinkers were doubters. ~ Isaac Bashevis Singer, 1978

We must respect the other fellow's religion, but only in the sense and to the extent that we respect his theory that his wife is beautiful and that his children are smart. ~ H.L. Mencken (1880-1956)

Religion is the frozen thought of men, out of which they build temples. ~ Jiddu Krishnamurti

## Remedies

Focus on remedies, not faults. ~ Jack Nicklaus

He that will not apply new remedies must expect new evils; for time is the greatest innovator. ~ Sir Francis Bacon

## Remembrance

I would rather be remembered by a song than by a victory. ~ Alexander Smith

## Remorse

God has little patience with remorse. ~ Malcolm Lowry

## Remuneration

I was underpaid for the first half of my life; I don't mind being overpaid for the second half. ~ Pierre Berton, 1975

## Repetition

There is repetition everywhere, and nothing is found only once in the world. ~ Goethe

If a human being is condemned and restricted to perform the same functions over and over again, he will not even be a good ant, not to mention a good human being. ~ Norbert Wiener

It is sometimes necessary to repeat what we know. All mapmakers should place the Mississippi in the same location, and avoid originality. ~ Saul Bellow

## Repression

A cat pent up becomes a lion. ~ Italian proverb

## Reproach

The sting of a reproach is the truth of it. ~ Benjamin Franklin

## Reputation

A fellow doesn't last long on what he has done. He's got to keep delivering as he goes along. ~ Carl Hubbell

How many people live off the reputation of the reputation they might have made? ~ Oliver Wendell Holmes

I am not at all the sort of person you and I took me for.
~ Jane Carlyle, in a letter to Thomas Carlyle in 1822

Reputation is often got without merit and lost without fault.
~ English proverb

Getting better known has its risks. Everything that's in is on its way out.
~ Al Ries of Ries and Ries marketing consultants in Great Neck, N.Y., warns companies against overlicensing their name or trademark.

To get a name can happen to but a few: It is one of the few things that cannot be bought. It is the free gift of mankind, which must be deserved before it will be granted, and it is at last unwillingly bestowed.
~ Samuel Johnson

You can't build a reputation on what you are going to do. ~ Henry Ford

You can't build a reputation on what you intend to do. ~ Liz Smith

According to success do we gain a reputation for judgment. ~ Euripides

What people say behind your back is your standing in the community in which you live. ~ Edgar Watson Howe

The art of being able to make a good use of moderate abilities wins esteem, and often confers more reputation than real merit.
~ La Rochefoucauld

## Research

Enough research will tend to support your theory.
~ Murphy's Law of Research

## Reserve

Tell not all you know, believe not all you hear, do not all you are able.
~ Italian proverb

## Respect

I firmly believe that if you follow a path that interests you, not to the exclusion of love, sensitivity, and cooperation with others, but with the strength of conviction that you can move others by your own efforts, and do not make success or failure the criteria by which you live, the chances are you'll be a person worthy of your own respect.
~ Neil Simon, playwright

Follow the three R's: Respect for self, respect for others, responsibility for all your actions. ~ Dalai Lama

There is a vast difference in one's respect for the man who has made himself and the man who has only made his money.
~ Dinah Maria Mulock

## Restaurants

The problem with allowing only a select few into a restaurant is that when the select few decide to go somewhere else – and eventually they will – the restaurant has no replacement, no core of loyal [customers] to fill the tables. People generally don't come to the rescue of places that have refused to let them through the door. ~ Alan Richman in GQ Magazine

The secret of a successful restaurant is sharp knives. ~ George Orwell

## Results

Clapping with the right hand only will not produce a noise.
~ Malay proverb

One arrow does not bring down two birds. ~ Turkish proverb

## Retirement

We rarely find anyone who can say he has lived a happy life, and who, content with his life, can retire from the world like a satisfied guest.
~ Horace, *Satires*

Retirement means twice as much husband on half as much money
~ Anonymous

## Return on Equity

Achieving return on equity does not, as a goal, mobilize the most noble forces of our soul. ~ Lawrence Miller

## Revenge

Revenge is profitable, gratitude expensive.
~ Edward Gibbon in *Decline and Fall* II

A man that studieth revenge keeps his wounds green, which otherwise would heal and do well. ~ Francis Bacon

No more tears now; I will think about revenge. ~ Mary Queen of Scots

Life being what it is, one dreams of revenge. ~ Paul Gauguin

Live well. It is the greatest revenge. ~ *The Talmud*

Don't get mad – get even. ~ John F. Kennedy

## Reviewers

Professional reviewers read so many bad books in the course of duty that they get an unhealthy craving for arresting phrases.
~ Evelyn Waugh, 1981

## Revolution

Inferiors revolt in order that they may be equal, and equals that they may be superior. ~ Aristotle

Revolution…an abrupt change in the form of misgovernment.
~ Ambrose Bierce

Those who make peaceful revolution impossible will make violent revolution inevitable. ~ John F. Kennedy

Revolutions have never succeeded unless the establishment does three-quarters of the work. ~ Peter Ustinov

### Reward

The reward of a thing well done, is to have done it. ~ Ralph Waldo Emerson

Only the brave deserve the fair, but only the fat, rich, cowardly merchant can afford same. ~ Chinese proverb

### Rich

If you aren't rich, you should always look useful. ~ Louis-Ferdinand Céline

No man is rich enough to buy back his past. ~ Oscar Wilde

I've been poor and I've been rich. Rich is better. ~ Sophie Tucker

The only way for a rich man to be healthy is by exercise and abstinence, to live as if he were poor. ~ Sir William Temple

### Riches

A shortcut to riches is to subtract from our desires. ~ Petrarch

Riches serve a wise man but command a fool. ~ English proverb

Riches rather enlarge than satisfy appetites. ~ Thomas Fuller, M.D.

### Riddance

What belongs to a man he cannot get rid of, even though he throws it away. ~ Goethe

### Ridicule

Every nation ridicules other nations, and all are right.
~ Arthur Schopenhauer

### Ridiculous

Look for the ridiculous in everything, and you will find it. ~ Jules Renard

There is only one step from the sublime to the ridiculous.
~ Napoleon Bonaparte

There's only one step from the sublime to the ridiculous, but there's no road leading back from the ridiculous to the sublime. ~ Lion Feuchtwanger

### Right

When everyone is wrong, everyone is right.
~ Pierr-Claude Nivelle de la Chaussée

Chicken Little only has to be right once. ~ Anonymous

Always do right. This will gratify some people and astonish the rest.
~ Mark Twain

Be always sure you are right – then go ahead. ~ David Crockett

People don't ever seem to realize that doing what's right's no guarantee against misfortune. ~ William McFee

The right to be heard does not include the right to be taken seriously.
~ Hubert Humphrey

## Rise

Men think highly of those who rise rapidly in the world, whereas nothing rises quicker than dust, straw and feathers.
~ Augustus and Julius Hare, English clerics

## Risk

Only those who will risk going too far can possibly find out how far one can go. ~ T.S. Eliot

Take into account that great love and great achievements involve great risk. ~ Dalai Lama

Why not go out on a limb? Isn't that where the fruit is? ~ Frank Scully

If you are scared to go to the brink, you are lost. ~ John Foster Dulles

Come to the edge.
We might fall.
Come to the edge.
It is too high!
Come to the edge!
And they came,
and he pushed...
and they flew. ~ Christopher Logue

And the trouble is, if you don't risk anything, you risk even more.
~ Erica Jong

Avoiding danger is no safer in the long run than exposure. ~ Helen Keller

Take a big step if one is indicated: you can't cross a chasm in two steps. ~ David Lloyd George

Risk and reward travel side by side. Avoid one and the other will also pass you by. ~ Anonymous

To win without risk is to triumph without glory. ~ Pierre Corneille

Everything is sweetened by risk. ~ Alexander Smith

What is necessary is never a risk. ~ Cardinal de Retz

Take calculated risks. That is quite different from being rash.
~ George Smith Patton

Where there is no risk there can be no pride in achievement and consequently no happiness. ~ Ray Kroc, *Grinding It Out*, 1977

## Ritual

I am not a religious man, but I have a ritual that I perform every day: I wash my breakfast bowl. ... Most of what we do in our lives is frivolous – watching TV, fixing the car, reading books, waiting for the bus – but the washing of dishes is important: It is necessary. Washing dishes is part of being human. ~ Richard Nilsen in *The Arizona Republic*

## Rogues

I prefer rogues to imbeciles, because they sometimes take a rest.
~ Alexandre Dumas

## Romance

Romance without finance ain't got no chance. ~ Charlie (Bird) Parker

Romance is a love affair in other than domestic surroundings.
~ Sir Walter Raleigh, British poet

## Rope (End of)

When you get to the end of your rope, tie a knot and hang on.
~ Franklin Delano Roosevelt

## Routine

Men fall into a routine when they are tired and slack: it has all the appearance of activity with few of its burdens. ~ Walter Lippman

Routine, in an intelligent man, is a sign of ambition. ~ W.H. Auden

## Rudeness

Rudeness is the weak man's imitation of strength. ~ Eric Hoffer

## Ruins

What is a ruin but time easing itself of endurance? ~ Djuna Barnes, 1962

## Rule

No rule is so general, which admits not some exception. ~ Robert Burton

Learn the rules so you know how to break them properly. ~ Dalai Lama

Any fool can make a rule, and any fool will mind it. ~ Henry David Thoreau

The rule is, jam tomorrow and jam yesterday – but never jam today.
~ Lewis Carroll

To rule is easy, to govern difficult. ~ Goethe

## Rulers

The worst ruler is one who cannot rule himself. ~ Cato the Elder

Rulers are given to employing those they can teach rather than those
from whom they can learn. ~ Mencius

Those who rule us are like you and me. It is a frightening situation.
~ Brooks Atkinson, *Once Around the Sun*, 1951

## Rumour

A rumour without a leg to stand on will get around some other way.
~ John Tudor

The *Times* has published no rumours; it's only reported the facts,
namely, that other, less responsible papers are publishing certain
rumours. ~ Tom Stoppard in *Dirty Linen*

Rumour is a pipe blown by surmises, jealousies, conjectures, and of so
easy and plain a stop, that the blunt monster with uncounted heads,
the still-discordant wavering multitude, can play upon it. ~ Shakespeare

## Running

What's the use of running when you are on the wrong road? ~ Proverb

## Rush Hour

Why do they call it rush hour when nothing moves? ~ Robin Williams

## Russia

The two most powerful men in Russia were Czar Nicholas II and the last
man who spoke to him. ~ A.J.P. Taylor

## Rust

It is better to wear out than to rust out. ~ Bishop Richard Cumberland

## Sacrifice

Too long a sacrifice can make a stone of the heart. ~ W.B. Yeats

Upon such sacrifices, my Cordelia,
The gods themselves throw incense. ~ Shakespeare

It is a far, far better thing that I do, than I have ever done; it is a far, far better rest that I go to, than I have ever known.
~ Charles Dickens, A Tale of Two Cities

The Universe is so vast and so ageless that the life of one man can only be justified by the measure of his sacrifice. ~ V.A. Rosewarne

## Sad

This is the saddest story I have ever heard.
~ Ford Maddox Ford, The Good Soldier

## Safety

A ship in port is safe, but that is not what ships are built for.
~ Benazir Bhutto

To keep oneself safe does not mean to bury oneself. ~ Seneca

In skating over thin ice, our safety is in our speed. ~ Ralph Waldo Emerson

There is no safety in numbers, or in anything else. ~ James Thurber

## Saints

Saints should always be judged guilty until proven innocent.
~ George Orwell

## Salesmen

He's a man out there in the blue, ridin' on a smile and a shoeshine
... a salesman has got to dream, boys. ~ Arthur Miller

## Salvation

Work out your own salvation. Do not depend on others. ~ Buddha

Work out your salvation with diligence. ~ The Pali Canon

## Same

When two do the same thing, it is not the same thing after all.
~ Publilius Syrus

## Sand

A handful of sand is an anthology of the universe. ~ David McCord

## Sanity

Sanity is a matter of degree. ~ Aldous Huxley

Sanity is madness put to good use. ~ George Santayana

## Sappers

And, with a little pin, bores through his castle wall, and farewell king!
~ Shakespeare

## Satisfaction

There is more satisfaction in being a first-rate truck driver than in being
a tenth-rate executive. ~ B.C. Forbes

## Saving

A penny saved is ridiculous. ~ Unknown

We could have saved sixpence. We could have saved fivepence.
… But at what cost? ~ Samuel Beckett

## Scare

Anything scares me, anything scares anyone but really after all
considering how dangerous everything is nothing is really very
frightening. ~ Gertrude Stein in *Everybody's Autobiography*

## School

[School] reports always tell the truth. The problem for parents is to
know whether it is the truth about the pupil or the truth about the
teacher – or both." ~ John Rae, *Letters From School*, 1987

The school of hard knocks is an accelerated curriculum. ~ Menander

Remember in elementary school, you were told in case of fire you have to line up quietly in a single file line from smallest to tallest? What is the logic in that? Do tall people burn slower? ~ Warren Hutcherson

## School Boards

In the first place God made idiots. This was for practice.
Then he made school boards. ~ Mark Twain

## Schoolboy

And then the whining schoolboy, with his satchel,
And shining morning face, creeping like snail
Unwillingly to school. ~ T.S. Eliot, *Coriolanus*

## Science

Eve and the apple was the first great step in experimental science.
~ James Birdie

Science is built of facts the way a house is built of bricks; but an accumulation of facts is no more science than a pile of bricks is a house. ~ Jules Henri Poincaré, French mathematician

Science without religion is lame, religion without science is blind.
~ Albert Einstein

As soon as questions of will or decision or reason or choice of action arise, human science is at a loss. ~ Noam Chomsky

Science is an edged tool, with which men play like children.
~ Sir Arthur Eddington

A science which hesitates to forget its founders is lost.
~ Alfred North Whitehead (attributed)

Though many have tried, no one has ever yet explained away the decisive fact that science, which can do so much, cannot decide what it ought to do. ~ Joseph Wood Krutch

Do you really believe that the sciences would ever have originated and grown if the way had not been prepared by magicians, alchemists, astrologers and witches whose promises and pretensions first had to create a thirst, a hunger, a taste for hidden and forbidden powers?
~ Friedrich Nietzsche

## Scientists

Scientists are Peeping Toms at the keyhole of eternity. ~ Arthur Koestler

## Scorn

Of all the griefs that harass the distressed,
Sure the most bitter is a scornful jest. ~ Samuel Johnson

## Seafood

Why does Sea World have a seafood restaurant? I'm halfway through my fishburger and I realize, Oh my God, ...I could be eating a slow learner.
~ Lynda Montgomery

## Search

Nothing's so hard but search will find it out. ~ Robert Herrick

## Seasons

Live each season as it passes; breathe the air, drink the drink, taste the fruit, and resign yourself to the influence of each. ... Some men think that they are not well in spring, or summer, or autumn, or winter; it is only because they are not *well* in them. ~ Henry David Thoreau

To every thing there is a season, and a time to every purpose under the sun. ~ The Bible

## Second Thoughts

Second thoughts are ever wiser. ~ Euripides

## Secrecy

The art of secrecy lies in being so open about most things that the few things that matter are not even suspected to exist. ~ Basil H. Liddell Hart

## Secrets

Everyone old enough to have a secret is entitled to have some place to keep it. ~ Judith Martin

If you wish to preserve your secret, wrap it up in frankness.
~ Alexander Smith

Little secrets are commonly told again, but great ones generally kept.
~ Lord Chesterfield

The easiest way to keep a secret is without help. ~ Unknown

None are so fond of secrets as those who do not mean to keep them. Such persons covet secrets as spendthrifts do money, for the purpose of circulation. ~ Charles Caleb Colton

The man who can keep a secret may be wise, but he is not half as wise as the man with no secrets to keep. ~ Edgar Watson Howe

Three may keep a secret, if two of them are dead. ~ Benjamin Franklin

He that communicates his secret to another makes himself that other's slave. ~ Baltasar Gracian

I know that's a secret, for it's whispered everywhere. ~ William Congreve

## Security

Security does not exist in nature, nor do the children of men as a whole experience it. ~ Helen Keller

Security is a smile from a headwaiter. ~ Russell Baker, *New York Times* columnist

## Seeing

I shut my eyes in order to see. ~ Paul Gauguin

One may have good eyes and see nothing. ~ Italian proverb

Sight is a faculty; seeing is an art. ~ *Bits & Pieces*, December 5, 1995

What you see, yet cannot see over, is as good as infinite.
~ Thomas Carlyle

## Self-Absorption

When a man is all wrapped up in himself, he makes a pretty small package. ~ John Ruskin

If you are all wrapped up in yourself you are overdressed.
~ Katherine Halvorson

We would rather speak badly of ourselves than not talk about ourselves at all. ~ La Rochefoucauld

It is with narrow-souled people as with narrow-necked bottles:
the less they have in them, the more noise they make in pouring it out.
~ Alexander Pope

## Self-Conceit

Self-conceit may lead to self-destruction. ~ Aesop

## Self-Confidence

Trust yourself, you know more than you think you do.
~ Dr. Benjamin Spock

Let me listen to me, and not to them. ~ Gertrude Stein

Be yourself. Who else is better qualified? ~ Frank J. Giblin II

The privilege of a lifetime is being who you are. ~ Joseph Campbell

They can do all because they think they can. ~ Virgil

## Self-Control

He who conquers others is strong. He who conquers himself is mighty.
~ Lao-tzu

Not being able to govern events, I govern myself, and apply myself to
them, if they will not apply themselves to me. ~ Michel de Montaigne

He who says what he likes shall hear what he does not like.
~ English proverb

## Self-Criticism

Self-criticism is the secret weapon of democracy. ~ Adlai Stevenson

## Self-Defence

Self defence is nature's oldest law. ~ John Dryden

## Self-Disclosure

We like to read others but we do not like to be read. ~ La Rochefoucauld

## Self-Esteem

We do not think ourselves worse than the elephant for being smaller
and shorter-lived. ~ George Santayana

A man cannot be comfortable without his own approval. ~ Mark Twain

Be grateful for yourself ... be thankful. ~ William Saroyan

Self-esteem is regarding yourself as a grownup. ~ Susan Faludi

The only thing that does make us feel good about ourselves, if this is
what we are after, is doing things of which we feel proud or which we
deem to be worthwhile. In other words, self-esteem is a by-product of
action and can never be a goal in itself. ... Self-esteem is a red herring.
It comes, it goes. It gives us a nice feeling when we have it, but no
more, no less. ~ Virginia Ironside in *The Spectator*

The important thing is not what they think of me, it is what I think of
them. ~ Queen Victoria

Most people do not like themselves at all. They distrust themselves, put on masks and pomposities. They quarrel and boast and pretend and are jealous because they do not like themselves. ... If we could learn to like ourselves even a little, maybe our cruelties and angers might melt away. Maybe we would not have to hurt one another just to keep our ego chins above water. ~ John Steinbeck

## Self-Help

Men are made stronger on realization that the helping hand they need is at the end of their own right arm. ~ Sidney J. Phillips

The gods help them that help themselves. ~ Aesop

If a man wants to be of the greatest possible value to his fellow creatures, let him begin the long, solitary task of perfecting himself. ~ Robertson Davies

The proverb warns that, "You should not bite the hand that feeds you." But maybe you should, if it prevents you from feeding yourself. ~ Thomas Szasz

## Self-Interest

When tremendous dangers are involved, no one can be blamed for looking to his own interest. ~ Thucydides

Now is the time for all good men to come to the aid of themselves. ~ Felice Nelson

## Self-Knowledge

If you know the enemy and know yourself, you need not fear the result of a hundred battles. ~ Sun Tzu

It is in the ability to deceive oneself that the greatest talent is shown. ~ Anatole France

We know what we are, but know not what we may be. ~ Shakespeare

## Self-Love

Self-love so often seems unrequited. ~ Anthony Powell

One of the great drawbacks to self-centred passions is that they afford so little variety in life. The man who loves only himself cannot, it is true, be accused of promiscuity in his affections, but he is bound in the end to suffer intolerable boredom from the inevitable sameness of the object of his devotion. ~ Bertrand Russell

He who is in love with himself has at least this advantage – he won't encounter many rivals. ~ Georg Christoph Lichtenberg

## Self-Made Men

One thing wrong with a self-made man, he tends to worship his creator. ~ Morris Raphael Cohen

Luck is not something you can mention in the presence of self-made men. ~ E.B. White

## Self-Mastery

The mastery of nature is vainly believed to be an adequate substitute for self-mastery. ~ Reinhold Niebuhr

If you cannot mould yourself as you would wish, how can you expect other people to be entirely to your liking? ~ Thomas a Kempis

## Self-Opinion

I have often wondered why everyone loves himself more than everything else, but values his own opinion of himself less than that of others. ~ Marcus Aurelius

## Self-Pity

What poison is to food, self-pity is to life. ~ Oliver C. Wilson

## Self-Praise

Self-praise is no recommendation. ~ Proverb

## Self-Reliance

Every tub must stand upon its own bottom. ~ Thomas Fuller, M.D.

As we are, so we do; and as we do, so it is done to us; we are the builders of our fortunes. ~ Ralph Waldo Emerson

## Self-Understanding

Everything that irritates us about others can lead us to an understanding of ourselves. ~ Carl Jung

If you mean to know yourself, interline such of these amorphisms as affect you agreeably in reading, and set a mark to such as left a sense of uneasiness with you; and then show your copy to whom you please. ~ Johann Kaspar Lavater

The delights of self-discovery are always available. ~ Gail Sheehy

Know thyself? If I knew myself, I'd run away. ~ Goethe

Every man contains within himself a ghost continent – a place circled as warily as Antarctica was circled 200 years ago by Captain Cook.
~ Loren Eiseley in *The Unexpected Universe*

In the main, it is not by introspection but by reflecting on our living in common with others that we come to know ourselves.
~ Bernard Lonergan

Men never think their fortune too great, nor their wit too little.
~ Thomas Fuller, M.D.

## Selfish

A woman means by unselfishness chiefly taking trouble for others; a man means not giving trouble to others. Thus each sex regards the other as basically selfish. ~ C.S. Lewis

## Sense

There is nobody so irritating as somebody with less intelligence and more sense than we have. ~ Don Herold

## Senses

All credibility, all good conscience, all evidence of truth come only from the senses. ~ Friedrich Nietzsche

What can give us surer knowledge than our senses? With what else can we better distinguish the true from the false? ~ Lucretius

## Sentences

Backward ran sentences until reeled the mind. ~ Wolcottt Gibbs

## Sentimentalists

The barrenest of all mortals is the sentimentalist. ~ Thomas Carlyle

## Seriousness

Seriousness is the only refuge of the shallow. ~ Oscar Wilde

## Service (to others)

The service we render to others is really the rent we pay for our room on this earth. ~ Sir Wilfred Grenfell

## Sex

Sex is the lyricism of the masses. ~ Charles Beaudelaire, *Intimate Journals*, 1887

When you meet a human being, the first distinction you make is "male or female?" and you are accustomed to make the distinction with unhesitating certainty. ~ Sigmund Freud

Don't be so snobbish about the interest people show in [a sensational crime or trial] or so dismissive of its significance. After all, according to Genesis, when the Good Lord put us on this Earth just about the first two things that happened were a sex scandal and a murder. Great minds ever after have turned to these subjects, meditated on them, explored them. ~ Meg Greenfield, columnist for *Newsweek*

Women need a reason to have sex. Men just need a place.
~ Billy Crystal

## Sexes

I love the idea of there being two sexes, don't you?
~ James Thurber

There is more difference within the sexes than between them.
~ Ivy Compton-Burnett

## Shadow

What you are you do not see. What you see is your shadow.
~ Rabindranath Tagore

## Shakespeare

The remarkable thing about Shakespeare is that he is really very good – in spite of all the people who say he is very good. ~ Robert Graves

If I had any doubts at all about my dislike for Shakespeare, that doubt vanished completely. What a crude, immoral, vulgar, and senseless work *Hamlet* is…there is no rhyme or reason about it.
~ Leo Tolstoy in 1896

Alive today [Shakespeare] would undoubtedly have written and directed motion pictures, plays and God knows what. Instead of saying "This medium is not good," he would have used it and made it good.
~ Raymond Chandler in 1949

## Shame

One of the misfortunes of our time is that in getting rid of false shame, we have killed off so much real shame as well.
~ Louis Kronenberger, U.S. writer/critic

## Sharing

He who shareth honey with a bear hath the least part. ~ Proverb

## Sharks

If the shark sees clearly, then it doesn't bite you, it bites the bait.
~ Sarah Sams of Florida

## Shepherd

It is the part of a good shepherd to sheer his flock, not skin it.
~ Latin proverb

## Ships

Being in a ship is being in a jail, with the chance of being drowned.
~ Samuel Johnson

## Short Men

Short men have made millions, married beauties, ruled countries, founded universities and discovered cures for diseases. It's not exactly a handicap, okay? ... I suggest you take the cards you've been dealt and figure out a better way to play your hand.
~ Cherie Bennett, Advice columnist, to a U.S. teenager who signed himself Dwarf Boy

## Shortcut

It usually takes a long time to find a shorter way. ~ Anonymous

A shortcut is the longest distance between two points. ~ Charles Issawi

## Shyness

Shyness is just egotism out of its depth. ~ Penelope Keith, British actress

## Sick

There's nothing the matter with being sick that getting well can't fix.
~ Peg Bracken

## Sides

The reverse side also has a reverse side. ~ Japanese proverb

## Silence

People who make no noise are dangerous. ~ Jean de La Fontaine

Speech may be barren; but it is ridiculous to suppose that silence is always brooding on a nest full of eggs.
~ George Eliot (Mary Ann Evans, English novelist)

Better silent than stupid. ~ German proverb

Silence is the best substitute for brains ever invented. ~ Henry Ashurst

Of those who say nothing, few are silent. ~ Thomas Neill

In human intercourse the tragedy begins, not when there is misunderstanding about words, but when silence is not understood. ~ Henry David Thoreau

Silence is wisdom, when speaking is folly. ~ Thomas Fuller, M.D.

Silence is the virtue of fools. ~ Sir Francis Bacon

I have often regretted my speech, never my silence. ~ Publilius Syrus

When you have nothing to say, say nothing. ~ Charles Caleb Colton

Blessed is the man who, having nothing to say, abstains from giving in words evidence of the fact. ~ George Eliot

Silence is one of the hardest things to refute. ~ Josh Billings

The eternal silence of these infinite spaces terrifies me. ~ Blaise Pascal

## Simplicity

Simplicity is the mean between ostentation and rusticity.
~ Alexander Pope

Simplicity is the most deceitful mistress that ever betrayed man.
~ Henry Brooks Adams

Perfect simplicity is unconsciously audacious. ~ George Meredith

Teach us Delight in simple things,
And Mirth that has no bitter springs. ~ Rudyard Kipling

And all the loveliest things there be
Come simply, so, it seems to me. ~ Edna St. Vincent Millay

Nothing is as simple as we hope it will be. ~ Jim Horning

## Simplify

The ability to simplify means to eliminate the unnecessary so that the necessary can speak. ~ Hans Hoffmann

## Sin

Sin is a dangerous toy in the hands of the virtuous. It should be left to the congenitally sinful, who know when to play with it and when to let it alone. ~ H.L. Mencken, U.S. writer/critic

There's nothing so artificial as sinning nowadays.
I suppose it once was real. ~ D.H. Lawrence

We didn't invent sin; we are merely trying to perfect it. ~ Anonymous

We are not punished for our sins, but by them. ~ Elbert Hubbard

Some rise by sin, and some by virtue fall. ~ Shakespeare

The only deadly sin I know is cynicism. ~ Henry Lewis Stimson

Sins become more subtle as you grow older. You commit sins
of despair rather than lust. ~ Piers Paul Read

There is a great difference between a man who does not want to sin
and a man who does not know how to. ~ Seneca

It may be a sin to think evil of people, but it is seldom a mistake.
~ H.L. Mencken

Commit the oldest sins the newest kind of ways. ~ Shakespeare

## Sincerity

A deep, great, genuine sincerity is the first characteristic of all men in
any way heroic. ~ Thomas Carlyle

It is dangerous to be sincere unless you are also stupid.
~ George Bernard Shaw

## Sing

It is folly to sing twice to a deaf man. ~ English proverb

## Sisters

Never praise a sister to a sister, in the hope of your compliments
reaching the proper ears. ~ Rudyard Kipling

## Skepticism

Skepticism is the first step toward truth. ~ Denis Diderot

She believed in nothing: only her skepticism kept her from being an
atheist. ~ Jean-Paul Sartre

## Skill

'Tis skill, not strength, that governs a ship. ~ Thomas Fuller, M.D.

He that wrestles with us strengthens our nerves and sharpens our skill.
Our antagonist is our helper. ~ Edmund Burke

Skill and confidence are an unconquered army. ~ George Herbert

Politics and business can be settled by influence, cooks and doctors can only be promoted on their skill. ~ Penelope Fitzgerald

## Skydiving

If at first you don't succeed, so much for skydiving. ~ Unknown

## Slander

Slander is the revenge of a coward, and dissimulation his defence.
~ Samuel Johnson

It takes your enemy and your friend, working together, to hurt you to the heart; the one to slander you and the other to get the news to you.
~ Mark Twain

## Slang

Slang is a language that rolls up its sleeves, spits on its hands and goes to work. ~ Carl Sandburg

## Slavery

That state is a state of Slavery in which a man does what he likes to do in his spare time and in his working time that which is required of him.
~ Eric Gill

## Sleep

The sleep of a labouring man is sweet, whether he eat little or much; but the abundance of the rich will not suffer him to sleep. ~ Ecclesiastes

Oh Sleep! It is a gentle thing,
Beloved from pole to pole. ~ Samuel Taylor Coleridge

## Slowness

There is a slowness in affairs which ripens them, and a slowness which rots them. ~ Joseph Roux

## Sly

He's tough, ma'am, tough, is J.B. Tough and devilish sly. ~ Charles Dickens

## Smart

None of us is as smart as all of us. ~ Japanese proverb

## Smile

Start every day with a smile and get it over with. ~ W.C. Fields

A smile is a curve that sets things straight. ~ Proverb

## Smoking

Smoking is one of the leading causes of statistics. ~ Fletcher Knebel

I predict that ashtrays will become as obsolete as spittoons in our lifetime. ~ Arthur Black

## Soap

In Marseilles they make half the soap we consume in America, but the Marseillaise only have a vague theoretical idea of its use, which they have obtained from books of travel. ~ Mark Twain

## Sobriety

There's nothing wrong with sobriety in moderation. ~ John Ciardi

The worst thing about some men is that when they are not drunk they are sober. ~ William Butler Yeats

## Socialism

It is a socialist idea that making profits is a vice; I consider the real vice is making losses. ~ Winston Churchill

Under capitalism, man exploits man; under socialism, the reverse is true. ~ Polish proverb

## Society

Society cannot exist without law and order, and cannot advance except through vigorous innovators. ~ Bertrand Russell

Men would not long live in society were they not the dupes of one another. ~ La Rochefoucauld

Life cannot subsist in society without reciprocal concessions. ~ Samuel Johnson

A civilized society is one which tolerates eccentricity to the point of doubtful sanity. ~ Robert Frost

Society needs to condemn a little more and understand a little less. ~ John Major

## Soft-Headedness

I think there is only one quality worse than hardness of heart, and that is softness of head. ~ Theodore Roosevelt

## Software

If we built houses the way we build software, the first woodpecker to come along would destroy civilization. ~ John Hamre, U.S. Deputy Defence Secretary, believing that the Year 2000 problem had global implications "that we can't even comprehend."

## Soldiers

Soldiers are citizens of death's grey land. ~ Siegfried Sassoon

When soldiers have been baptized in the fire of a battlefield, they have all one rank in my eyes. ~ Napoleon Bonaparte

## Solitude

Whosoever is delighted in solitude is either a wild beast or a god. ~ Francis Bacon

The worst solitude is to be destitute of sincere friendship. ~ Francis Bacon

Man cannot long survive without air, water and sleep. Next in importance comes food. And close on its heels, solitude. ~ Thomas Szasz

## Solutions

Someone once said that for every problem there is a solution that is simple, attractive...and wrong. ~ Arthur C. Clarke

What we're saying today is that you're either part of the solution or you're part of the problem. ~ Eldridge Cleaver

It is not always by plugging away at a difficulty and sticking at it that one overcomes it; but, rather, often by working on the next one to it. Certain people and certain things require to be approached at an angle. ~ André Gide

There is always an easy solution to every human problem – neat, plausible, and wrong. ~ H.L. Mencken

The chief cause of problems is solutions. ~ Eric Sevareid

## Song

Anything too stupid to be said is sung. ~ Voltaire

## Sorrow

You cannot prevent the birds of sorrow from flying over your head, but you can prevent them from building nests in your hair. ~ Chinese proverb

We should feel sorrow, but not sink under its oppression; the heart of a wise man should resemble a mirror, which reflects every object without being sullied by any. ~ Confucius

## Soul

In the dark night of the soul it is always 3 o'clock in the morning. ~ F. Scott Fitzgerald

The lie in the soul is a true lie. ~ Benjamin Jowett

## Sounds

Not many sounds in life, and I include all urban and rural sounds, exceed in interest a knock at the door. ~ Charles Lamb

## Sovereign

The sovereign has ... three rights – the right to be consulted, the right to encourage, the right to warn. ~ Walter Bagehot

## Soviet Union

The Soviet empire did not fall apart because spooks had bugged the men's room in the Kremlin or put broken glass in Mrs. Brezhnev's bath but because running a huge, closed, repressive society in the 1980's had become – economically, socially, militarily and technologically – impossible. ~ John le Carré

## Space

Space isn't remote at all. It's only an hour's drive away if your car could go straight upwards. ~ Fred Hoyle

## Speaking Out

Don't be ashamed to say what you are not ashamed to think. ~ Michel de Montaigne

Speak, demon! What is it that you wish?
I wish you'd stop beating that damn gong. ~ Ron Goulart, Science-fiction author

It is terrible to speak well and be wrong. ~ Sophocles

## Special Status

Groups or segments of society who always want to be recognized as "special" risk forever being on the outside of the decision making looking in. ~ Stewart Kronberg

## Specialist

A specialist is one who knows everything about something and nothing about anything else. ~ Ambrose Bierce

## Speculation

There are two times in a man's life when he should not speculate: when he can't afford to, and when he can. ~ Mark Twain

## Speech

It usually takes me more than three weeks to prepare a good impromptu speech. ~ Mark Twain

## Spelling

He respects Owl, because you can't help respecting anybody who can spell Tuesday, even if he doesn't spell it right; but spelling isn't everything. There are days when spelling Tuesday simply doesn't count. ~ A.A. Milne in *The House at Pooh Corner*

## Sports

Sports do not build character. They reveal it.
~ Heywood Broun, U.S. journalist and founder of American Newspaper Guild

Everything about sport is derived from the hunt: there is no sport in existence that does not base itself either on the chase or on aiming, the two key elements of primeval hunting. ~ Desmond Morris

## Standing Still

Standing still is the fastest way of moving backwards in a rapidly changing world. ~ Unknown

Be not afraid of growing slowly, be afraid only of standing still.
~ Chinese proverb

## Stars

We emerged to see – once more – the stars. ~ Dante

All the atoms we are made of are forged from hydrogen in stars that died and exploded before our solar system formed. So if you are romantic, you can say we are literally stardust. If you're less romantic, you can say we're the nuclear waste from the fuel that makes stars shine. ~ Sir Martin Rees, Britain's astronomer royal

## Statesman

A statesman is any politician it's considered safe to name a school after. ~ Bill Vaughan

I don't for a minute flatter myself that I am a statesman or a diplomat, but I don't think it makes too much difference if I bring to this job a high sense of responsibility.
~ Lord Alexander, before being sworn in as G-G on April 12, 1947

The first requirement of a statesman is that he be dull. ~ Dean Acheson

## Statesmanship

The difference between politics and statesmanship is philosophy.
~ Will and Ariel Durant

## Statistics

Facts are stubborn things, but statistics are more pliable.
~ Laurence J. Peter

## Status Quo

Status quo. Latin for the mess we're in. ~ Jeve Moorman

## Stealing

A man who will steal *for* me will steal *from* me.
~ Theodore Roosevelt, upon firing one of his cowboys who had applied the Roosevelt brand to a steer belonging to a neighbouring ranch.

## Stigmas

Stigmas are the corollaries of values. If work, independence, responsibility, respectability are valued, then their converse must be devalued, seen as disreputable. The Victorians, taking their values seriously, also took seriously the need for social sanctions that would stigmatize and censure violations of those values.
~ Gertrude Himmelfarb in *The De-Moralization of Society*

## Stock Market

It will fluctuate. ~ J.P. Morgan, when asked what the stock market would do in the future

People who always try to play the market to its lowest point always miss it. ~ Earl Peattie, president of Mortgage News Co.

Never sell stocks when the sap is running up the tree.
~ Edwin Lefevre, 1923

The suckers haven't permanently deserted the stock market. They are merely waiting until the prices get too high again. ~ Unknown (American)

The secret of financial success is to buy sound stock, wait until it goes up and then sell it. If it does not go up, don't buy it. ~ Calvin Coolidge

## Strangers

The largest part of mankind are nowhere greater strangers than at home. ~ Samuel Taylor Coleridge

We were in some little time fixed in our seats, and sat with that dislike which people not too good-natured usually conceive of each other at first sight. ~ Joseph Addison and Sir Richard Steele, in *Days with Roger de Coverley*

Sometimes you have to get to know someone really well to realize you're really strangers. ~ Mary Tyler Moore

## Strategy

When you find a good move, look for a better one. ~ Bobby Fischer

The true aim is not so much to seek battle as to seek a strategic situation so advantageous that if it does not of itself produce the decision, its continuation by battle is sure to achieve this.
~ Basil H. Liddell Hart

## Strength

For the strength of the Pack is the Wolf,
and the strength of the Wolf is the Pack. ~ Rudyard Kipling

If we are strong, our strength will speak for itself.
If we are weak, words will be no help.
~ John F. Kennedy, from the address he was to give Nov. 22, 1963

We all have strength to endure the misfortunes of others.
~ La Rochefoucauld

May the strength of three be in your journey. ~ Irish proverb

It is the nature, and the advantage of strong people that they can bring out the crucial questions and form a clear opinion about them. The weak always have to decide between alternatives that are not their own. ~ Dietrich Bonhoeffer

## Strings

Yes, I had two strings to my bow; both golden ones, egad! and both cracked. ~ Henry Fielding

## Students

It is important that students bring a certain ragamuffin barefoot irreverence to their studies; they are not here to worship what is known, but to question it. ~ Jacob Bronowski in *The Ascent of Man*, 1975

Students achieving Oneness will move on to Twoness. ~ Woody Allen

## Stupidity

Against stupidity the gods themselves struggle in vain.
~ Friedrich von Schlegel

It is stupidity rather than courage to refuse to recognize danger when it is close upon you. ~ Sherlock Holmes to Dr. Watson, in *The Adventure of the Final Problem*, 1894

Stupidity does not consist in being without ideas. Such stupidity would be the sweet, blissful stupidity of animals, molluscs and the gods. Human stupidity consists in having lots of ideas, but stupid ones. ~ Henri de Montherlant, French novelist

The difference between genius and stupidity is that genius has its limits. ~ Unknown

There is nothing worse than aggressive stupidity. ~ Goethe

It's not getting any smarter out there. You have to come to terms with stupidity and make it work for you. ~ Frank Zappa

Only two things are infinite – the universe and human stupidity, and I'm not so sure about the universe. ~ Albert Einstein

The two most abundant things in the universe are hydrogen and stupidity. ~ Harlan Ellison

You can be sincere and still be stupid. ~ Charles F. Kettering

Even those honest enough to admit being wrong a thousand times are not honest enough to admit even once to being stupid. ~ David Kipp

As if there were safety in stupidity alone. ~ Henry David Thoreau

It is physically impossible for anybody to act intelligently even one-tenth as often as to act stupidly. ~ Walter Pitkin

The most dangerous form of stupidity is a sharp intellect.
~ Hugo von Hofmannsthal

## Style

There is no desolation so bleak that it cannot be made habitable by style. If we live inside a bad joke, it is up to us to learn, at best and worst, to tell it well. ~ Jonathan Raban

Know your limitations and call them your style. ~ Adam Scott

## Styrofoam

After they make Styrofoam, what do they ship it in? ~ Steven Wright

## Sublime

It is only a step from the sublime to the ridiculous.
~ Napoleon Bonaparte, following return from Moscow

## Submission

Oddly, submission to powerful, frightening, even terrible persons, like tyrants and generals, is not experienced as nearly so painful as is submission to unknown and uninteresting persons, which is what all luminaries of industry are. ~ Friedrich Nietzsche

## Substance

In arguing of the shadows, we forgo the substance. ~ John Lyly

Beware lest you lose the substance by grasping at the shadows. ~ Aesop

## Subtraction

A man has one hundred dollars and you leave him with two dollars; that's subtraction. ~ Mae West

## Succeed

Tell the truth or trump – but get the trick. ~ Mark Twain

## Success

Success is just a matter of luck. Ask any failure. ~ Earl Wilson

Success took me to her bosom like a maternal boa constrictor.
~ Noel Coward

The Lord gave us two ends – one to sit on and the other to think with. Success depends on which one we use the most. ~ Ann Landers

Nothing recedes like success. ~ Walter Winchell

There would be no triumph in success if there had been no hazard in failure. ~ Cardinal Newman

If there is any great secret of success in life, It lies in the ability to put yourself in the other person's place and to see things from his point of view – as well as your own. ~ Henry Ford

The world continues to offer glittering prizes to those who have stout hearts and sharp swords. ~ F.E. Smith, Earl of Birkenhead, 1923

The world is made of people who never quite get into the first team and who just miss the prizes at the flower show. ~ Jacob Bronowski, 1954

Success is never final. ~ Sir Winston Churchill

All you need in this life is ignorance and confidence, and then success is sure. ~ Mark Twain

Success is more dangerous than failure, the ripples break over a wider coastline. ~ Graham Greene

I owe my success to having listened respectfully to the very best advice and then going away and doing the exact opposite. ~ G.K. Chesterton

The toughest thing about success is that you've got to keep on being a success. ~ Irving Berlin

Success is that old A-B-C – ability, breaks and courage. ~ Charles Luckman

If people knew what they had to do to be successful, most people wouldn't. ~ Lord Thomson of Fleet

To deserve success is more important than to achieve it.
~ Lester B. Pearson

The secret of success is constancy to purpose. ~ Benjamin Disraeli

I cannot give you a formula for success, but I can give you a formula for failure; try to please everybody. ~ Herbert Bayward Swope

How can you say my life is not a success? Have I not for more than sixty years got enough to eat and escaped being eaten?
~ Logan Pearsall Smith, Last Words, 1933

One need not hope in order to undertake; nor succeed in order to persevere. ~ William the Silent

We may stop ourselves when going up, never when coming down.
~ Napoleon Bonaparte

The road up and the road down are the one and the same. ~ Heraclitus

Success in life is never to let your ego outstrip your talent. ~ Don Shebib

The common thought that success spoils people by making them vain, egotistic and self-complacent is erroneous; on the contrary it makes them, for the most part, humble, tolerant and kind. Failure makes people bitter and cruel. ~ W. Somerset Maugham

By the time we've made it, we've had it. ~ Malcolm Forbes

Success and failure are both difficult to endure. Along with success come drugs, divorce, fornication, bullying, travel, meditation, medication, depression, neurosis and suicide. With failure comes failure. ~ Joseph Heller, novelist

The only place where success comes before work is in the dictionary. ~ Vidal Sassoon

If at first you don't succeed, go back to bed. ~ Anonymous

The difference between failure and success is doing a thing nearly right and doing it exactly right. ~ Edward Simmons

By the time you've found the key to success, they've changed the lock. ~ Anonymous

Whenever an individual or business decides that success has been attained, progress stops. ~ Thomas Watson, Jr., IBM

It is not the going out of port, but the coming in, that determines the success of a voyage. ~ Henry Ward Beecher

The great secret of success is intense faith in oneself. ~ *The Globe*, May 23, 1865

Successful people are very lucky. Just ask any failure. ~ Michael Levine

Success is a great deodorant. ~ Elizabeth Taylor

This proverb flashes through his head,
The many fail, the one succeeds. ~ Alfred, Lord Tennyson

If I have seen further, it is standing on the shoulders of giants. ~ Isaac Newton

The line between failure and success is so fine that we scarcely know when we pass it: so fine that we are often on the line and do not know it. ~ Elbert Hubbard

Success is the realization of the estimate which you place upon yourself. ~ Elbert Hubbard

Success makes us intolerant of failure, and failure makes us intolerant of success. ~ William Feather

It's lonely at the top, but you eat better. ~ Robert Harrison

If at first you do succeed, try not to look astonished. ~ Anonymous

Success isn't permanent and failure isn't fatal. ~ Mike Ditka

Achieving high-level success requires the support and cooperation of others. Remember this: When you take over the leadership of a group, persons in that group immediately begin to adjust themselves to the standards you set. ~ Dr. David Schwartz, *The Magic of Thinking Big*

If at first you don't succeed, you're running about average.
~ M.H. Alderson

If A is a success in life, then A equals X plus Y plus Z. Work is X; Y is play; and Z is keeping your mouth shut. ~ Albert Einstein

It is often the fifth ace that makes all the difference between success and failure. ~ J.B. (Beachcomber) Morton

It is just as difficult to overcome success as it is to overcome failure.
~ Sir William Walton

Behind every successful man is a surprised woman. ~ Maryon Pearson

The penalty of success is to be bored by people who used to snub you.
~ Nancy Astor

Don't aim at success – the more you aim at it and make it a target, the more you are going to miss it. For success, like happiness, cannot be pursued; it must ensue … as the unintended side-effect of one's personal dedication to a course greater than oneself.
~ Viktor Frankl, *Man's Search for Meaning*

People who reach the top of the tree are only those who haven't got the qualifications to detain them at the bottom. ~ Peter Ustinov

Eighty per cent of success is showing up. ~ Woody Allen

Some people reach the top of the ladder only to find it is leaning against the wrong wall. ~ Anonymous

The only infallible criterion of wisdom to vulgar minds – success.
~ Edmund Burke

## Suffering

If suffer we must, let's suffer on the heights. ~ Victor Hugo

## Suicide

Anybody who has listened to certain kinds of music, or read certain kinds of poetry, or heard certain kinds of performances on the concertina, will admit that even suicide has its brighter aspects.
~ Stephen Leacock

## Sunbeams

If sunbeams were weapons of war, we would have had solar energy long ago. ~ Sir George Porter, Nobel laureate

## Sunday

For this is Sunday morning,
Fate's great bazaar. ~ Louis MacNeice

## Superiority

There is nothing noble about being superior to some other men. The true nobility is in being superior to your previous self.
~ Hindustani proverb

If you're one in a million, there are 5,000 people just like you.
~ Hal Rubenstein in *Paisley Goes With Nothing*

The superior man is firm in the right way, and not merely firm.
~ Confucius

## Superstitions

Natives who beat drums to drive off evil spirits are objects of scorn to smart Americans who blow horns to break up traffic jams.
~ Mary Ellen Kelly, cited in *Peter's Quotations: Ideas for Our Time*

It is the customary fate of new truths to begin as heresies and to end as superstitions. ~ Thomas Henry Huxley

## Surrender

Never give in, never give in, never, never, never – in nothing, great or small, large or petty – never give in except to convictions of honour and good sense. ~ Winston Churchill, address at Harrow School, October 29, 1941

Surrender is essentially an operation by means of which we set about explaining instead of acting. ~ Charles Peguy

The Guards die, but never surrender. ~ Pierre Jacques Etienne

## Survival

Oh, don't worry about Alan...Alan will always land on somebody's feet. ~ Dorothy Parker, U.S. writer, about her ex-husband

On the whole, I think we shall survive. The outlook is as bad as it ever has been, but thinking people realize that – and therein lies the hope of its getting better. ~ Jawaharlal Nehru

Rule of survival: pack your own parachute. ~ T.L. Hakala

It isn't important to come out on top; what matters is to be the one who comes out alive. ~ Bertolt Brecht

Survival is triumph enough. ~ Harry Crews

Survival of the fittest implies multiplication of the fittest. ~ Herbert Spencer

## Suspense

There is nothing to be gained by keeping the judge in suspense. ~ Paul M. Perell

## Suspicion

Suspicion is a thing very few people can entertain without letting the hypothesis turn, in their minds, into fact. ~ David Cort

## Sweater

Sweater: a garment worn by a child when his mother feels chilly. ~ Alma Denny

## Swim

My Mom said she learned how to swim when someone took her out on the lake and threw her off the boat. I said, "Mom, they weren't trying to teach you how to swim." ~ Paula Poundstone

## Sword

The sword is the axis of the world and its power is absolute. ~ Charles de Gaulle

### Sympathy

All sympathy not consistent with acknowledged virtues is but disguised selfishness. ~ Samuel Taylor Coleridge

I can sympathize with other people's pains, but not with their pleasures. There is something curiously boring about somebody else's happiness. ~ Aldous Huxley

### System

Unhappy the general who comes on the field of battle with a system.
~ Napoleon Bonaparte

The system doesn't have to be pure, but it does have to work.
~ Aminu Kano

I must create a system or be enslaved by another man's. ~ William Blake

### Systematic

It is best to do things systematically, since we are only human, and disorder is our worst enemy. ~ Hesiod

## Tabloid Headlines

Girl abandoned at birth raised by rattlesnakes ~ *Weekly World News*

Man who married Siamese twins jailed for bigamy ~ *Sun*

World leaders meet secretly with UFO aliens ~ *Sun*

That humming is UFO aliens tunnelling beneath Earth ~ *National Examiner*

Screaming corpse kicked out of cemetery ~ *Weekly World News*

It's me or the pig, wife says – and storms out of marriage ~ *Sun*

Noisy sneezers are Noisy Lovers ~ *Sun*

Singing Bat is Going on Concert Tour ~ *Weekly World News*

Eating hot dogs makes you smart. ~ *Sun*

Granny steals jet fighter for joy ride ~ *Sun*

Killer vultures attack graduation ceremony ~ *Weekly World News*

Squirrel holds 50 secretaries hostage ~ *Weekly World News*

Queen uses snake venom and arsenic to cure royal family ~ *Globe*

Aliens call off invasion of Earth ~ *Weekly World News*

Excited sports fan swallows TV remote control and changes channels every time he hiccups ~ *Sun*

Patients take on traits of organ donors ~ *National Examiner*

Take good care of that piece of my brother, Larry ~ *Star*

Men get heart attacks on purpose…as an excuse to rest, new research proves ~ *Weekly World News*

Big-eared guys are better in bed ~ *National Examiner*

Jealous cow kills bride ~ *Sun*

RICHARD W. POUND

Dragons stampede through Chinese village ~ *Weekly World News*

Time capsule buried in 1895 opened up – and a live cat jumps out
~ *Weekly World News*

Thousands discover they're descended from space aliens
~ *National Examiner*

Sailor is growing barnacles ~ *Sun*

Pet food company is run by a dog ~ *National Enquirer*

Vampire now ruled a saint ~ *Sun*

Worldwide pimple plague will strike millions of teens!
Greenhouse Effect means faces full of acne ~ *Weekly World News*

Fewer people are going to Hell, so Satan is laying off demons
~ *Weekly World News*

Beware! Bagels are dangerous ~ *National Examiner*

Bigfoot saves woman from car wreck ~ *Sun*

Single mother of triplets puts two up for adoption ~ *Weekly World News*

Paralyzed man kicked off social security –
for making money typing with his toes ~ *National Enquirer*

My idiotic Siamese twin is dying to get a sex change ~ *Weekly World News*

Poisonous snakes die after biting serpent handler ~ *Weekly World News*

$2-million lottery winner goes back to her job chasing fruit flies
~ *National Enquirer*

Mom spends $20-million to marry off her three daughters ~ *Star*

Boy, 9, raised by mountain goats ~ *Sun*

Trigger-happy cop gunned down my little Chihuahua ~ *National Enquirer*

Woman survives 53 days after plane crash – by living off her own
cellulite ~ *Weekly World News*

214 Chinese change their names to Elvis ~ *Weekly World News*

Man arrested for biting werewolf ~ *Weekly World News*

Boy, 8, behind bars because parents can't control his binge eating ~ *Sun*

Does your neighbour worship the devil? Telltale signs of a Satanist
~ *National Examiner*

Three out of five Americans are reincarnated in Brazil ~ *Weekly World News*

Blind golfer teed off: He's driven to sue pals who faked hole-in-one
~ *Sun*

Camel eats punk rocker's green hair because it looked like grass
~ *Weekly World News*

Macho duck hunters beaten to a pulp by bird-watching grannies
~ *Weekly World News*

Top plastic surgeon lets his wife do the carving, cops charge
~ *National Examiner*

GI gets laundry done by wife – by mail ~ *Sun*

101, but she still works a 60-hour week ~ *National Enquirer*

A pterodactyl bit my arm off…and I've still got the stump to prove it
~ *Weekly World News*

Space aliens hate dogs ~ *Weekly World News*

Marriage makes men healthier – instantly ~ *National Examiner*

Brothers take out each other's tonsils ~ *Sun*

Radioactive icebergs threaten you ~ *Sun*

Cannibalism runs rampant in Russia ~ *National Examiner*

Crazed sparrows attack bird-watcher and peck out her eyes
~ *Weekly World News*

Tidy burglar cleans up house ~ *National Examiner*

22 years in wheelchair – then I find I'm not paralyzed ~ *National Enquirer*

Think the Pilgrims had turkey for Thanksgiving? Baloney!
They gobbled down eels and swilled whiskey! ~ *Weekly World News*

I mooned a werewolf … and he nearly killed me ~ *Weekly World News*

Snoring dad suffocates as tot stuffs crayons up his nose ~ *Sun*

Husband kills nagging wife with booby-trapped cat ~ *Weekly World News*

## Tact

Tact is the ability to see others as they wish to be seen. ~ *Anonymous*

Tact: Ability to tell a man he's open-minded when he has a hole in his
head. ~ *F.G. Kernan*

Tact is after all a kind of mind-reading. ~ *Sarah Orne Jewett*

Being tactful in audacity is knowing how far one can go too far.
~ *Jean Cocteau*

## Tactics

With foxes we must play the fox. ~ Thomas Fuller, M.D.

In making tactical dispositions, the highest pitch you can attain is to conceal them; conceal your dispositions, and you will be safe from the prying of the subtlest spies, from the machinations of the wisest brains.
~ Sun Tzu

## Tale-Bearers

Tale-bearers are as bad as the tale-makers. ~ Richard Sheridan

## Talent

Talent is like money; you don't have to have some to talk about it.
~ Jules Renard

In the battle of existence, talent is the punch; tact is the clever footwork. ~ Wilson Mizner

There is no such thing as great talent without great willpower.
~ Honoré de Balzac

Everyone has talent. What is rare is the courage to follow the talent to the dark place where it leads. ~ Erica Jong

Everyone has talent at 25. The difficulty is to have it at 50. ~ Edgar Degas

All of us do not have equal talent, but all of us should have an equal opportunity to develop our talents. ~ John F. Kennedy

## Talk

Too much talk will include errors. ~ Burmese proverb

Talk low, talk slow, and don't say too much. ~ John Wayne

Talk is cheap because supply exceeds demand. ~ Unknown

If you do not wish a man to do a thing, you had better get him to talk about it; for the more men talk, the more likely they are to do nothing else. ~ Thomas Carlyle

## Talking

She probably laboured under the common delusion that you made things better by talking about them. ~ Rose Macaulay, English writer

Talk doesn't cook rice. ~ Chinese proverb

If to talk to oneself when alone is folly, it must be doubly unwise to listen to oneself in the presence of others. ~ Baltasar Gracian

## Tangents

All men are the same. They take no notice of the stag in the thicket because they are already chasing the hare. ~ Jean Giraudoux

## Tasks

No task is a long one but the task on which one dare not start. It becomes a nightmare. ~ Charles Beaudelaire

## Taste

I hate a man who swallows [food], affecting not to know what he is eating. I suspect his taste in higher matters. ~ Charles Lamb

## Tax Lawyers

A dog who thinks he is man's best friend is a dog who has obviously never met a tax lawyer. ~ Fred Lebowitz

## Tax Policy

Tax policies are the means of redistributing wealth among those who have the most political clout. ~ Jim Borden, humorist

## Taxes

The reward of energy, enterprise and thrift is taxes. ~ William Feather

The only difference between a tax man and a taxidermist is that the taxidermist leaves the skin. ~ Mark Twain

The politicians' promises of yesterday are the taxes of today.
~ William Lyon Mackenzie King

Why does a slight tax increase cost you two hundred dollars and a substantial tax cut save you thirty cents? ~ Peg Bracken

If Patrick Henry thought taxation without representation was bad, he should see it *with* representation. ~ Judge Earl R. Hoover

The taxes are indeed very heavy, and if those laid by the government were the only ones we had to pay, we might more easily discharge them; but we have many others, and much more grievous to some of us. We are taxed twice as much by our idleness, three times as much by our pride, and four times as much by our folly; and from these taxes the commissioners cannot ease or deliver us by allowing us an abatement. ~ Benjamin Franklin

Taxes are the price society pays for civilization. ~ Oliver Wendell Holmes, Jr.

Only the little people pay taxes. ~ Leona Helmsley

We contend that for a nation to try to tax itself into prosperity is like a man standing in a bucket and trying to lift himself up by the handle. ~ Winston Churchill

Why sir, there is every possibility that you will soon be able to tax it! ~ British scientist Michael Faraday, responding to William Gladstone as to the usefulness of electricity

## Taxis

No nice men are good at getting taxis. ~ Katharine Whitehorn

## Teachers

Make your friends your teachers and mingle the pleasures of conversation with the advantages of instruction. ~ Baltasar Gracian

A teacher is better than two books. ~ German proverb

## Teaching

Spoon feeding in the long run teaches us nothing but the shape of the spoon. ~ E.M. Forster

There is none who cannot teach somebody something, and there is none so excellent but he is excelled. ~ Baltasar Gracian

Most people do not care to be taught what they do not already know; it makes them feel ignorant. ~ Mary McCarthy

School is an institution built on the axiom that learning is the result of teaching. And institutional wisdom continues to accept this axiom, despite overwhelming evidence to the contrary. ~ Ivan Illich

Is there any college that puts a premium on good teaching? Is there any university that rewards – in pay and promotion – outstanding teachers? Always and everywhere in academia, recognition, promotion, tenure depend on what a faculty member publishes. Teaching? Exciting the minds of undergraduates? Turning them on to learning? Weighing pounds of print the way butchers weigh beef, faculty fathers more often butcher those who show brilliance in lecturing or in the classroom. Publish or perish is an option. Teach well and perish is for sure. ~ Malcolm S. Forbes, 1980

## Team Spirit

Team spirit is what gives so many companies an edge over their competitors. ~ George L. Clements

The main ingredient of stardom is the rest of the team. ~ John Wooden

## Tears

A tear dries quickly, especially when it is shed for the troubles of others. ~ Cicero

To make wail and lament for one's ill fortune, when one will win a tear from the audience, is well worthwhile. ~ Aeschylus

## Technology

Technology … the knack of so arranging the world that we need not experience it. ~ Max Frisch

## Tediousness

The man who suspects his own tediousness is yet to be born.
~ Thomas Bailey Aldrich

## Teenagers

Wierd clothing is de rigeur for teenagers, but today's generation is finding it difficult to be sufficiently wierd. [Those who] went through adolescence in the sixties and seventies used up practically all the available wierdness. ~ P.J. O'Rourke

## Telephone

Today the ringing of the telephone takes precedence over everything. It reaches a point of terrorism, particularly at dinnertime.
~ Niels Diffrient, 1986

If the phone doesn't ring, it's me. ~ Jimmy Buffet

## Television

He who is created by television can be destroyed by television.
~ Theodore H. White

Television is simply automated daydreaming. ~ Lee Loevinger, 1967

All television is children's television. ~ Richard P. Adler, 1987

Television has spread the habit of instant reaction and stimulated the hope of instant results. ~ Arthur M. Schlesinger, Jr., 1970

Television is not a visual medium. It is an acoustic medium.
~ Marshall McLuhan, 1984

Why should people go out and pay to see bad movies when they can stay home and see bad television for nothing? ~ *Observer*, Sept. 9, 1956

Television is inextricably woven into our lives, and television has so much spare time that everybody will be on it in the end. ~ Quentin Crisp

Television hangs on the questionable theory that whatever happens anywhere should be sensed everywhere. ~ E.B. White, in 1948

Television thrives on unreason and unreason thrives on television. It strikes at the emotions rather than the intellect. ~ Sir Robin Day, 1989

When I got my first television set, I stopped caring so much about having close relationships. ~ Andy Warhol

Television has raised writing to a new low. ~ Samuel Goldwyn (attributed)

There is a middlebrow snobbery in America that praises everything on public television and disdains everything on commercial television as a blight. ~ Henry Fairlie, 1982

[A television critic] is forced to be literate about the illiterate, witty about the witless and coherent about the incoherent. ~ John Crosby, 1955

Television, despite its enormous presence, turns out to have added pitifully few lines to the communal memory. ~ Justin Kaplan, 1991

The great networks are there to prove that ideas can be canned like spaghetti. ~ Frederic Raphael, British author, 1980

Television is the first truly democratic culture – the first culture available to everyone and entirely governed by what people want. The most terrifying thing is what people want. ~ Clive Barnes, 1969

Don't be deluded into believing that the titular heads of the networks control what appears on their networks. They all have better taste.
~ Edward R. Murrow, 1958

The world is going mad at an accelerating rate and television is the Typhoid Mary of this madness. ~ Edward Robb Ellis, 1981

Television probably has become the most evocative, widely observed signpost we have. ~ Robert McC. Adams, Smithsonian Institution, 1985

The human race is faced with a cruel choice; work or daytime television. ~ Unknown

Television has proved that people will look at anything rather than each other. ~ Ann Landers

I don't watch television, I think it destroys the art of talking about oneself. ~ Stephen Fry in *Paperweight*

The darkest spot in human history is a small luminous screen. ~ Regis Debray

Because television can make so much money doing its worst, it often cannot afford to do its best. ~ Fred Friendly, onetime CBS News president

Imitation is the sincerest form of television. ~ Fred Allen

There's so much comedy on television. Does that cause comedy in the streets? ~ Dick Cavett, on the subject of violence on television

Television is about performance. It is visual rather than verbal. It has little tolerance for argument, hypothesis or explanation, which is why frequent TV viewers don't either. Television encourages us to judge everything by one criterion alone: Is it entertaining? Unfortunately, much of what is important in life is not entertaining. ~ Neil Postman

Television has brought back murder into the home – where it belongs. ~ Alfred Hitchcock

Pure drivel tends to drive ordinary drivel off the TV screen. ~ Marvin Kitman

## Temper

Your temper is one of your more valuable possessions. Don't lose it. ~ *Bits & Pieces*, Nov. 1994

## Temptation

Don't worry about temptation – as you grow older, it starts avoiding you. ~ Old *Farmer's Almanac*

"Every man has his price." This is not true. But for every man there exists a bait which he cannot resist swallowing. ~ Friedrich Nietzsche

## Tenterhooks

Tenterhooks are the upholstery of the anxious seat. ~ Robert Sherwood

## Texas Talk

The engine's running, but ain't nobody driving.

It's so dry the trees are bribin' the dogs.

This ain't my first rodeo.

He looks like the dog's been keepin' him under the porch.

Time to paint your butt white and run with the antelope.

Don't that give you the saddle rash?

She could start a fight in an empty house.

He was so ugly his mother borrowed a baby to take to church.

Dumber than a barrel of hair.

Never sign nothin' by neon.

No matter how popular you are, the size of your funeral depends on the weather.

Denser than dog shit.

Two years older than dust.
~ Unknown

## Theatre

In the theatre, the audience want to be surprised – but by things they expect. ~ Tristan Bernard, French dramatist

## Theorize

It is a capital mistake to theorize before one has data.
~ Sir Arthur Conan Doyle

## Theory

Theory helps us to bear our ignorance of facts. ~ George Santayana

In theory, there is no difference between theory and practice. In practice, there is. ~ Jan van de Snepscheut

## Therapy

Many a patient, after countless sessions, has quit therapy, because he could detect no perceptible improvement in his shrink's condition.
~ Brendan Francis

## Things

The best things in life aren't things. ~ Art Buchwald

## Thinking

If you make people think they're thinking, they'll love you; but if you really make them think, they'll hate you. ~ Don Marquis

Thinking is the hardest work there is, which is the probable reason so few engage in it. ~ Henry Ford

To think is to differ. ~ Clarence S. Darrow

Do not ever mistake a clear view with a short distance. ~ Bill Gates

Thinking is hard work. One cannot bear burdens and ideas at the same time. ~ Remy de Gourmont

Think wrongly if you please, but in all cases think for yourself.
~ Doris Lessing

The mind is everything; what you think, you become. ~ Buddha

Those who have read about everything are thought to understand everything, too, but it is not always so. Reading furnishes the mind only with materials of knowledge; it is thinking that makes what we read ours. We are of the ruminating kind, and it is not enough to cram ourselves with a great load of collections. We must chew them over again. ~ William Channing

When the mind is thinking, it is talking to itself. ~ Plato

Those who have finished by making all others think with them, have usually been those who began by daring to think for themselves.
~ Charles Caleb Colton

Thinking doesn't seem to help very much. The human brain is too high-powered to have many practical uses in this particular universe.
~ Kurt Vonnegut

If a man sits down to think, he is immediately asked if he has a headache. ~ Ralph Waldo Emerson

Never be afraid to sit awhile and think. ~ Lorraine Hansberry

It is godlike ever to think on something beautiful and on something new. ~ Democritus

Beware when the great God lets loose a thinker on this planet.
~ Ralph Waldo Emerson

What is the hardest task in the world? To think. ~ Ralph Waldo Emerson

The real question is not whether machines think but whether men do.
~ B.F. Skinner

The shrewd guess, the fertile hypothesis, the courageous leap to a tentative conclusion – these are the most valuable coin of the thinker at work. ~ Jerome Bruner

Do not think what you want to think until you know what you ought to know. ~ John Crow

And if they think, they fasten their hands upon their hearts.
~ A.E. Housman

Many people would sooner die than think. In fact, they do.
~ Bertrand Russell

There is no expedient to which a man will not resort to avoid the real labour of thinking. ~ Sir Joshua Reynolds

To most people nothing is more troublesome than the effort of thinking. ~ James Bryce

We haven't got the money, so we've got to think. ~ Ernest Rutherford

## Thinking Ahead

It will be a shock to men when they realize that thoughts that were fast enough for today are not fast enough for tomorrow; but thinking tomorrow's thoughts today is one kind of future life. ~ Christopher Morley

## Thought

The brightest flashes in the world of thought are incomplete until they have been proved to have their counterparts in the world of fact.
~ John Tyndall

Not a hundredth part of the thoughts in my head have ever been or ever will be spoken or written – as long as I keep my senses, at least.
~ Jane Carlyle, Scottish poet

If you jot down every silly thought that pops into your mind, you will soon find out everything you most seriously believe. ~ Mignon McLaughlin

Many people have played themselves to death. Many people have eaten and drunk themselves to death. Nobody ever thought himself to death. ~ Gilbert Highet

Profundity of thought belongs to youth, clarity of thought to old age.
~ Friedrich Nietzsche

As soon as you have made a thought, laugh at It.
~ Lao-tzu, Chinese philosopher

A thought which does not result in an action is nothing much, and an action which does not proceed from a thought is nothing at all.
~ Georges Bernanos

Every thought has been thought of before, but the problem is to think of it again. ~ Goethe

From the moment of birth we are immersed in action, and can only fitfully guide it by taking thought. ~ Alfred North Whitehead

Action and faith enslave thought, both of them in order not to be troubled or inconvenienced by reflection, criticism and doubt.
~ Henri Frédéric Amiel

The highest possible stage in moral culture is when we recognize that we ought to control our thoughts. ~ Charles Darwin, *The Descent of Man*

When a thought is too weak to be expressed simply, simply drop it.
~ Marquis de Vauvenargues

I think that naught is worth a thought, and I'm a fool for thinking.
~ W.M. Praed

Along with thoughts which are unworthy of us, we have ones of which we are not worthy. ~ Edmond Rostand

## Thoughtless

The thoughtless are rarely wordless. ~ Howard K. Newton

## Threats

Threatened folks live longer. ~ Thomas Fuller, M.D.

## Thrift

It is thrifty to prepare today for the wants of tomorrow. ~ Aesop

## Tide

A single breaker may recede; but the tide is eventually coming in.
~ Lord Macaulay

## Time

It is an undoubted truth, that the less one has to do, the less time one finds to do it in. ~ Lord Chesterfield

Time is the small change of eternity. ~ Irving Layton

Time is the friend of the wonderful company, the enemy of the mediocre. ~ U.S. investor Warren Buffett

Vladimir: "That passed the time."
Estragon: "It would have passed in any case."
Vladimir: "Yes, but not so rapidly." ~ Samuel Beckett

Time spent getting even is better spent getting ahead. ~ Anonymous

Nothing, of course, begins at the time you think it did. ~ Lillian Hellman

Those who make the worst use of their time are the first to complain of its brevity. ~ Jean de la Bruyère

If you want to kill time, why not try working it to death? ~ Sam Levenson

For time will teach ye soon the truth. ~ Henry Wadsworth Longfellow

Dost thou love life, then do not squander time, for that's the stuff life is made of. ~ Benjamin Franklin

Half our life is spent trying to find something to do with the time we have rushed through life trying to save. ~ Will Rogers

Time's fun when you're having flies. ~ Kermit the Frog

Nothing really belongs to us but time, which even he has who has nothing else. ~ Baltasar Gracian

A stitch in time would have confused Einstein. ~ Frank Baer

If time be of all things most precious, wasting time must be the greatest prodigality, since lost time is never found again; and what we call time enough always proves little enough. Let us then be up and be doing, and doing to the purpose; so by diligence we shall do more with less perplexity. ~ Benjamin Franklin

The butterfly counts not months but moments and has time enough.
~ Rabindranath Tagore

Wait for the wisest of all counselors, time. ~ Pericles

Be ruled by time, the wisest counselor of all. ~ Plutarch

Again the shadow moveth o'er the dial-plate of time. ~ J.G. Whittier

There is never enough time, unless you are serving it. ~ Malcolm Forbes

The innocent and the beautiful
Have no enemy but time. ~ William Butler Yeats

Time hath a taming hand. ~ John Cardinal Newman

Time flies when you're having fun; even when you're not. ~ Ells MacNeil

A time to get, and a time to lose. ~ The Bible

Remember that time is money. ~ Benjamin Franklin

Time shall teach thee all things. ~ George Sharwood

Ah! The clock is always slow;
It is later than you think. ~ Robert Service

There must be something drastically wrong when a man starts wishing time away. Time was given us like jewels to spend, and it's the ultimate sacrilege to wish it away. ~ Sloan Wilson, *The Man in the Gray Flannel Suit*

## Timing

Observe due measure, for right timing is in all things the most important factor. ~ Hesiod

If you trap the moment before it's ripe,
The tears of repentance you'll certainly wipe;
But if once you let the ripe moment go,
You can never wipe off the tears of woe. ~ William Blake

## Tolerance

If it was necessary to tolerate in other people everything that one permits oneself, life would be unbearable.
~ Georges Courteline (Georges-Victor-Marcel Moineau, French writer)

When I was very young, I was disgracefully intolerant but when I passed the thirty mark I prided myself on having learned the beautiful lesson that all things were good, and equally good. That, however, was really laziness. Now, thank goodness, I've sorted out what matters and what doesn't. And I'm beginning to be intolerant again. ~ G.B. Stern

Tolerance merely means putting up with people, being able to stand things. ~ E.M. Forster

Tolerance is a tremendous virtue, but the immediate neighbours of tolerance are apathy and weakness. ~ Sir James Goldsmith

Say now Shibboleth; and he said Sibboleth, for he could not frame to pronounce it right. Then they took him and slew him. ~ The Bible

## Tomorrow

If you wait for tomorrow, tomorrow comes. If you don't wait for tomorrow, tomorrow comes. ~ Malinke (West African) proverb

When I consider life, 'tis all a cheat;
Yet, fooled with hope, men favour the deceit;
Trust on, and think tomorrow will repay.
Tomorrow's falser than the former day. ~ John Dryden

## Tools

Men have become the tools of their tools. ~ Henry David Thoreau

Look for a tough wedge for a tough job. ~ Publilius Syrus

Give us the tools and we will finish the job. ~ Winston Churchill

## Top

There is always room at the top. ~ Daniel Webster

## Toronto

This is the second time I have performed in Toronto, not counting my honeymoon. ~ Carol Lawrence

## Toupée

No matter how well a toupée blends in the back, in front it always looks like hell. ~ Leonard Louis Levinson

## Tradition

Tradition may be defined as an extension of the franchise. Tradition means giving votes to the most obscure of all classes, our ancestors....Democracy tells us not to neglect a good man's opinion, even if he is our groom; tradition asks us not to neglect a good man's opinion, even if he is our father. ~ G.K. Chesterton

Tradition is a guide and not a jailer. ~ W. Somerset Maugham

## Traditionalists

Traditionalists are pessimists about the future and optimists about the past. ~ Lewis Mumford

## Trap

I don't want the cheese; I just want to get out of the trap.
~ Latin American proverb

He who digs a hole for another may fall in himself. ~ Russian proverb

## Travel

Travelling is almost like talking with men of other centuries.
~ René Descartes

The use of travelling is to regulate imagination by reality, and, instead of thinking how things may be, to see them as they are. ~ Samuel Johnson

The person who finds his homeland sweet is still a tender beginning; the person to whom every soil is a native one is already strong; but he is perfect to whom every soil is as a foreign land.
~ Hugo of St. Victor, 12th century monk

The only aspect of our travels that is interesting to others is disaster.
~ Martha Gellman

## Trees

I like trees because they seem more resigned to the way they have to live than other things do. ~ Willa Cather, U.S. novelist/poet

## Trial (Fair)

The defendant is entitled to a fair trial before I hang him.
~ Hanging Judge Jeffreys

## Trifles

Trifles make the sum of human things,
And half our misery from our foibles springs. ~ Hannah Moore

To throw away the dearest thing he owned
As 'twere a careless trifle. ~ Shakespeare

## Triumph

Oh! Wherefore come ye forth in triumph from the north?
~ Thomas Babington Macaulay

If you can meet with Triumph and Disaster
And treat those two imposters just the same... ~ Rudyard Kipling

## Trouble

Most of the trouble in the world is caused by people wanting to be important. ~ T.S. Eliot

When an elephant is in trouble, even a frog will kick him. ~ Hindu proverb

Troubles hurt most when they prove self-inflicted. ~ Sophocles

It is a painful thing
To look at your own trouble and know
That you yourself and no one else has made it. ~ Sophocles

Many a man's tongue broke his nose. ~ Seumus MacManus

There's one thing said for inviting trouble:
it generally accepts. ~ May Maloo

People could survive their normal all right if it weren't for the trouble
they make for themselves. ~ Ogden Nash

Half the trouble in this world comes from saying "yes" too quick, and
"no" not soon enough. ~ American saying

## True

Be so true to thyself, as thou be not false to others. ~ Francis Bacon

This above all: to thine own self be true,
And it must follow as the night the day
Thou canst not then be false to any man. ~ Shakespeare, *Hamlet*

A thing is not necessarily true because it is badly uttered, nor false
because spoken magnificently. ~ St. Augustine

## Trust

Trust thyself only, and another shall not betray thee. ~ Thomas Fuller, M.D.

It's a vice to trust all, and equally a vice to trust none. ~ Seneca

We distrust our heart too much, and our head not enough. ~ Joseph Roux

A man who doesn't trust himself can never really trust anyone else.
~ Cardinal de Retz

I wonder men dare trust themselves with men. ~ Shakespeare

Put your trust in God, my boys, and keep your powder dry!
~ Valentine Blacker

Trust everybody, but cut the cards. ~ Finley Peter Dunne

## Truth

Ye shall know the truth, and the truth shall make you mad.
~ Aldous Huxley

Truth is mighty and will prevail. There is nothing the matter with this,
except that it ain't so. ~ Mark Twain

One has only to think of the sinister possibilities of the radio, state-controlled education and so forth, to realize that "truth is great and will prevail" is a prayer rather than an axiom. ~ George Orwell

What a word is *truth*. Slippery, tricky, unreliable. ~ Lillian Hellman, 1979

That which has always been accepted by everyone, everywhere, is almost certain to be false. ~ Paul Valéry

The (pure and simple) truth is rarely pure, and never simple.
~ Oscar Wilde, *The Importance of Being Earnest*

Artistic growth is, more than it is anything else, a refining of the sense of truthfulness. The stupid believe that to be truthful is easy; only the artist, the great artist, knows how difficult it is. ~ Willa S. Cather

Just as most issues are seldom black or white, so are most good solutions seldom black or white. Beware of the solution that requires one side to be totally the loser and the other side to be totally the winner. The reason there are two sides to begin with usually is because neither side has all the facts. Therefore, when the wise mediator effects a compromise, he is not acting from political motivation. Rather, he is acting from a deep sense of respect for the whole truth.
~ Stephen R. Schwambach

Beware of half-truths: you may have gotten the wrong half. ~ Unknown

Pure truth hath no man seen nor e'er shall know. ~ Xenophanes

I would rather offend with the truth, than please with adulation.
~ Seneca

Truth is more a stranger than fiction. ~ Mark Twain

Why *shouldn't* truth be stranger than fiction? Fiction, after all, has to make sense. ~ Mark Twain

Truth is stranger than fiction, but it is because fiction is obliged to stick to possibilities: truth isn't. ~ Mark Twain

Every violation of truth is not only a sort of suicide in the liar, but is a stab at the health of human society. ~ Ralph Waldo Emerson, 1841

It is hard to believe that a man is telling you the truth when you know that you would lie if you were in his place. ~ H.L. Mencken

The scornful nostril and the high head gather not the odours that lie on the track of truth. ~ George Eliot

Truth is the daughter of time.
~ Anonymous, cited in *The Fitzhenry & Whiteside Book of Quotations*

The truth is more important than the facts. ~ Frank Lloyd Wright

Whoever is careless with the truth in small matters cannot be trusted
with important matters. ~ Albert Einstein

A truth that's told with bad intent
Beats all the lies you can invent. ~ William Blake

Men stumble over the truth from time to time, but most pick
themselves up and hurry off as if nothing happened.
~ Sir Winston Churchill

Truth never damages a cause that is just. ~ Mahatma Gandhi

The truth would become more popular if it were not always
stating ugly facts. ~ Henry S. Haskins

Truth exists, only falsehood has to be invented. ~ Georges Braque

What probably distorts everything in life is that one is convinced that
one is speaking the truth because one says what one thinks.
~ Sacha Guitry

All truth is good, but not all truth is good to say. ~ African proverb

Opinion is a flitting thing,
But Truth outlasts the Sun -
If then we cannot own them both -
Possess the oldest one. ~ Emily Dickinson

If you always tell the truth you don't have to remember anything.
~ Mark Twain

Truth is the most valuable thing we have. Let us economize it.
~ Mark Twain

The dictum that truth always triumphs over persecution is one of those
pleasant falsehoods which men repeat after one another till they pass
into commonplace, but which all experience refutes. ~ John Stuart Mill

Every truth has two sides; it is well to look at both, before we commit
ourselves to either. ~ Aesop

Pushing any truth out very far, you are met by a counter-truth.
~ Henry Ward Beecher

We have reached an uncomfortable impasse. We need belief to make life meaningful, yet we cannot allow ourselves to believe in anything. Every faith, institution, political faction and ideal has proved at some level to be a tissue of hypocrisy. We decry our own cynicism, but recognize that, at some level, it is merely realism. Some [people] retreat into conventional orthodoxies; others free-float, aimless in an increasingly valueless society. But there is another alternative: starting from scratch to see if we may discover for ourselves something like universal truth and build the whole thing over again. ~ Richard Nilsen, columnist for *The Arizona Republic*

The greatest homage to truth is to use it. ~ Ralph Waldo Emerson

The pursuit of truth is like picking raspberries.
You miss a lot if you approach it from only one angle.
~ Randal Marlin, assoc. prof. of philosophy at Carleton University

All great truths begin as blasphemies. ~ George Bernard Shaw

Believe those who seek the truth. Doubt those who find it. ~ André Gide

Nobody speaks the truth when there is something they must have.
~ Elizabeth Bowen

Speak the truth, but leave immediately after. ~ Slovenian proverb

You can't win: if you tell lies, you'll be distrusted; if you tell the truth, you'll be disliked. ~ Jean Anouilh

There are certain persons for whom pure truth is a poison.
~ André Maurois

How often have I said to you that when you have eliminated the impossible, whatever remains, however improbable, must be the truth?
~ Sir Arthur Conan Doyle

In the long run, a harmful truth is better than a useful lie. ~ Thomas Mann

Something unpleasant is coming when men are anxious to tell the truth. ~ Benjamin Disraeli

## Trying

For us, there is only the trying. ~ T.S. Eliot

## T-Shirt Slogans

In this world it rains on the Just and the Unjust, but the Unjust have the Just's umbrella

RICHARD W. POUND

I'm out of estrogen and I have a gun

The purpose of art is to hold a mirror up to life. Clearly, life needs more sleep.

The secret is to find out what people really want and then call it self-awareness

## Two-Faced

If I were two-faced, would I be wearing this one? ~ Abraham Lincoln

## Tyranny

Where law ends, tyranny begins. ~ William Pitt

If they take you in the morning, they will be coming for us that night.
~ James Baldwin

## Tyrants

So long as men worship the Caesars and Napoléons,
Caesars and Napoléons will arise to make them miserable.
~ Aldous Huxley, *Ends and Means*

No man can terrorize a whole nation unless we are all his accomplices.
~ Edward R. Murrow, U.S. broadcaster

## Unanimity

You only find complete unanimity in a cemetery. ~ Abel Aganbegyan

## Uncertainty

All uncertainty is fruitful... so long as it is accompanied by the wish to understand. ~ Antonio Machado

## Unconstitutional

The illegal we can do right now; the unconstitutional will take a little longer. ~ Henry Kissinger

## Underdogs

You will never find an Englishmen among the underdogs – except in England, of course. ~ Evelyn Waugh

## Undergraduate

There is no more vulnerable human combination than an undergraduate. ~ John Sloan Dickey

## Understanding

One half of the world cannot understand the pleasures of the other. ~ Jane Austen

Understanding is a two-way street. ~ Eleanor Roosevelt

This has been a most wonderful evening. Gertrude [Stein] has said things tonight it will take her 10 years to understand. ~ Alice B. Toklas

I hear and I forget. I see and I remember. I do and I understand. ~ Chinese proverb

Seeing through is rarely seeing into. ~ Elizabeth Bibesco

Not only is there but one way of doing things rightly, but there is only one way of seeing them, and that is, seeing the whole of them.
~ John Ruskin

Too much light often blinds gentlemen of this sort. They cannot see the forest for the trees. ~ Christoph M. Wieland

It takes a long time to understand nothing. ~ Edward Dahlberg

To be surprised, to wonder, is to begin to understand.
~ José Ortega y Gasset

To be totally understanding makes one very indulgent. ~ Mme de Stael

## Unexplored

In everything there is an unexplored element because we are prone by habit to use our eyes only in combination with the memory of what others before us have thought about the thing we are looking at. The most insignificant thing contains some little unknown element. We must find it. ~ Guy de Maupassant

## Unhappiness

The most intelligent young people in Western countries tend to have that kind of unhappiness that comes of finding no adequate employment for their best talents.
~ Bertrand Russell, *The Conquest of Happiness*, 1930

Unhappiness is not knowing what we want and killing ourselves to get it. ~ Don Herold

## Uniqueness

Always remember that you are absolutely unique. Just like everyone else. ~ Margaret Mead

## Unity

When spider webs unite, they can tie up a lion. ~ Ethiopian proverb

## Universe

The universe is full of magical things, patiently waiting for our wits to grow sharper. ~ Eden Philpotts

To a man of the world, the universe is a suburb.
~ Elizabeth Bibesco, in *Haven*, 1951

The universe is a big place, perhaps the biggest. ~ Kurt Vonnegut

Suppose that I came to the outer limits of the universe. If I now thrust out a stick, what would I find? ~ Archytas, 4th century B.C.E. philosopher and commander-in-chief of city-state of Tarentum

## University

The university brings out all abilities, including stupidity. ~ Anton Chekhov

The first duty of a university is to teach wisdom, not a trade; character, not technicalities. We want a lot of engineers in the modern world, but we don't want a world of engineers. ~ Sir Winston Churchill, 1950

A university should be a place of light, of liberty and of learning. ~ Benjamin Disraeli

The most important function of the university in an age of reason is to protect reason from itself. ~ Allan Bloom

In my day, the principal concerns of university students were sex, smoking dope, rioting and learning. Learning was something you did only when the first three weren't available. ~ Bill Bryson

The quality of a university is measured more by the kind of student it turns out than the kind it takes in. ~ Robert Kibbee

Our major universities are now stuck with an army of pedestrian, toadying careerists, Fifties types who wave around Sixties banners to conceal their record of ruthless, beaverlike tunneling to the top. ~ Camille Paglia

At best, most college presidents are running something that is somewhere between a faltering corporation and a hotel. ~ Leon Botstein

University degrees are a bit like adultery: you may not want to get involved with that sort of thing, but you don't want to be thought incapable. ~ Peter Imbert

Is God a Yale man? ~ Wilmarth Lewis

I was a modest, good-humoured boy. It is Oxford that has made me insufferable. ~ Max Beerbohm

I often think how much easier the world would have been to manage if Herr Hitler and Signor Mussolini had been at Oxford. ~ Edward Wood

Four years was enough of Harvard. I still had a lot to learn, but had been given the liberating notion that now I could teach myself. ~ John Updike

## Unknown

Whoever starts out toward the unknown must consent to venture alone. ~ André Gide

To the man in the street, it has always seemed miraculous that anyone should turn aside from the beaten track with its known destinations, and strike out on the steep and narrow path leading into the unknown. Hence it was always believed that such a man, if not actually crazy, was possessed by a demon or a god; for the miracle of a man being able to act otherwise than as humanity has always acted could only be explained by the gift of demonic power or divine spirit. ~ Carl Jung

Give me a light that I may tread safely into the unknown.
~ Minnie Louise Haskins

## Unpredictability

Unpredictability, too, can become monotonous. ~ Eric Hoffer

There is many a slip 'twixt the cup and the lip. ~ Palladas

## Unseen

Greet the unseen with a cheer! ~ Robert Browning

## Unthinkable

We must dare to think about "unthinkable things," because when things become "unthinkable," thinking stops and action becomes mindless.
~ J. William Fulbright

## Upbringing

I was brought up to believe that the only thing worth doing was to add to the sum of accurate information in the world. ~ Margaret Mead, 1964

I think she must have been very strictly brought up, she's so desperately anxious to do the wrong thing correctly. ~ Saki (H.H. Munro)

## Useless

To be employed in useless things is half to be idle. ~ Thomas Fuller, M.D.

## Usury

No man of ripe years and of sound mind, acting freely, and with his eyes open, ought to be hindered ... from making such a bargain, in the way of obtaining money, as he sees fit.
~ Jeremy Bentham, 1787, *Defence of Usury*

## Vacuum

Living in a vacuum sucks. ~ Adrienne E. Gusoff

## Vagueness

There cannot be a precise answer to a vague question. ~ Samuel Johnson

If you can't be kind, at least be vague. ~ Judith Martin (Miss Manners)

Even vagueness can be explicit if it is explained well enough.
~ Dr. Edward J. Pfeiffer

## Valiant

I love the valiant, but it is not enough to wield a broadsword; one must also know against whom. ~ Friedrich Nietzsche

## Value

The only thing in the world of value is the active soul.
~ Ralph Waldo Emerson

The value of a sentiment is the amount of sacrifice you are prepared to make for it. ~ John Galsworthy

Everything is worth what its purchaser will pay for it.
~ Publilius Syrus, Maxim 865

## Values

Our scientific power has outrun our spiritual power. We have guided missiles and misguided men. ~ Dr. Martin Luther King, Jr.

## Vampires

The thing about vampires, is that they provide an opportunity to make a meditation on death. ~ Neil Jordan, director, 1994

## Vanity

The highest form of vanity is love of fame. ~ George Santayana

Vanity plays lurid tricks with our memory. ~ Joseph Conrad

Vanity makes men ridiculous, pride odious and ambition terrible.
~ Sir Richard Steele

Vanity and pride are different things, though the words are often used synonymously. A person may be proud without being vain. Pride relates more to our opinion of ourselves; vanity to what we would have others think of us. ~ Jane Austen

## Variety

No pleasure endures unseasoned by variety. ~ Publilius Syrus

## Vegetarian

I am not a vegetarian because I love animals; I am a vegetarian because I hate plants. ~ A. Whitney Brown

A vegetarian is a person who won't eat anything that can have children.
~ David Brenner

## Venice

Venice is like eating an entire box of chocolate liqueurs in one go.
~ Truman Capote, 1961

## Verbal Skills

A study in the *Washington Post* says that women have better verbal skills than men. I just want to say to the authors of that study: Duh.
~ Conan O'Brien

## Verbosity

Verbosity leads to unclear, inarticulate things. ~ Dan Quayle

## Verification

The meaning of a proposition is the method of its verification.
~ Moritz Schlick

## Vices

There will be vices as long as there are men. ~ Tacitus

Virtues and vices are of a strange nature; for the more we have, the fewer we think we have. ~ Anonymous, early 18th Century

It is the function of vice to keep virtue within reasonable bounds.
~ Samuel Butler

We make a ladder of our vices if we trample them underfoot.
~ St. Augustine

When the vices give us up we flatter ourselves that we are giving them up. ~ La Rochefoucauld

## Vicious

You can't expect a boy to be vicious till he's been to a good school. ~ Saki (H.H. Munro)

## Victims

I hate victims who respect their executioners. ~ Jean-Paul Sartre

## Victory

Victory is by nature insolent and haughty. ~ Cicero

The war horse is a vain hope for victory. ~ Psalm 33

Victory has a hundred fathers, but defeat is an orphan. ~ Count Galeazzo Ciano

## Viewpoint

How strange it is to see with how much passion
People see things only in their own fashion! ~ Molière

## Villain

... one may smile, and smile, and be a villain ... ~ Shakespeare, *Hamlet*

## Violence

Violence is the last refuge of the incompetent. ~ Salvor Hardin

Victory attained by violence is tantamount to a defeat, for it is momentary. ~ Mahatma Gandhi

Violence is not a knife in the hand. It grows like a poison tree inside other people who have not learned to value other human beings. ~ Frances Lawrence

## Virtue

Virtue has never been as respectable as money. ~ Mark Twain

Sincerity and truth are the basis of every virtue. ~ Confucius

Successful and fortunate crime is called virtue. ~ Seneca

Virtue is not left to stand alone. He who practises it will have neighbours. ~ Confucius

Search others for virtues, thyself for vices. ~ English proverb

A large part of virtue consists in good habits. ~ Barbara Paley

Amusements are to virtue, like breezes of air to the flame;
gentle ones will fan it, but strong ones will put it out.
~ David Thomas, 19th century U.S. writer

Fine words and an insinuating appearance are seldom associated with
true virtue. ~ Confucius

First secure an independent income, then practise virtue. ~ Greek saying

To be innocent is to be not guilty; but to be virtuous is to overcome
our evil inclinations. ~ William Penn

Virtue consists, not in abstaining from vice, but in not desiring it.
~ George Bernard Shaw

## Vision

Every man takes the limits of his own field of vision for the limits of the
world. ~ Arthur Schopenhauer

No man sees far; the most see no farther than their noses.
~ Thomas Carlyle

Vision is the art of seeing things invisible. ~ Jonathan Swift

## Visionary

Visionary people are visionary partly because of the very great many
things they don't see. ~ Berkeley Rice

## Visit

Once in a while you have to take a break and visit yourself.
~ Audrey Giorgi

Santa Claus has the right idea: visit people once a year. ~ Victor Borge

## Vocation

The test of a vocation is the love of the drudgery it involves.
~ Logan Pearsall Smith

## Voices

The black telephone's off at the root,
The voices just can't worm through. ~ Sylvia Plath, Daddy

### Voters

Your every voter, as surely as your chief magistrate, exercises a public trust. ~ Grover Cleveland

The voters have spoken. The bastards. ~ Morris Udall

### Votes

A straw vote only shows which way the hot air blows. ~ O. Henry

Voting is simply a way of determining which side is the stronger without putting it to the test of fighting. ~ H.L. Mencken

The vote means nothing to women. We should be armed. ~ Edna O'Brien

## Wages

If you pay peanuts, you get monkeys. ~ Sir James Goldsmith

## Waiting

Keeping another person waiting is a basic tactic for defining him as inferior and oneself as superior. ~ Thomas Szasz

All things come too late for those who wait. ~ Elbert Hubbard

## Walk

A vigorous five-mile walk will do more good for an unhappy but otherwise healthy adult than all the medicine and psychology in the world. ~ Paul Dudley White

Just walk. The road knows where you are going. ~ Arne Nyman

## Wander

Not all those who wander are lost. ~ J.R.R. Tolkien

## Wants

How few are our real wants! and how easy it is to satisfy them! Our imaginary ones are boundless and insatiable. ~ J.H. Hare and A.W. Hare

No man can have all he wants, but a man can refrain from wanting what he has not, and cheerfully make the best of the bird in the hand. ~ Seneca

Our necessities are few but our wants are endless. ~ Josh Billings

We are designed to want: with nothing to want, we are like windmills in a world without wind. ~ John Fowles

## War

When the war of giants is over, the wars of the pygmies will begin.
~ Sir Winston Churchill

War is like love, it always finds a way. ~ Bertolt Brecht

War doesn't determine who's right. War determines who's left.
~ Anonymous

There never was a good war or a bad peace. ~ Benjamin Franklin

Older men declare war, but it is youth that must fight and die.
~ Herbert Hoover

The tragedy of war is that it uses man's best to do man's worst.
~ Harry Emerson Fosdick

War would end if the dead could return. ~ Stanley Baldwin

Sometime they'll give a war and nobody will come. ~ Carl Sandburg

Throughout history, the world has been laid waste to ensure the
triumph of conceptions that are now as dead as the men that died for
them. ~ Henry de Montherlant, *Notebooks* 1930-1944

The first casualty of war, is truth. ~ Hiram Johnson, 1917

Blue is the smoke of war, white the bones of men. ~ Tu Fu

Mankind must put an end to war or war will put an end to mankind.
~ John F. Kennedy

Sometimes I think that war is God's way of teaching us geography.
~ Paul Rodriguez

War is a series of catastrophes that results in a victory.
~ Georges Clemenceau

After each war there is a little less democracy to save. ~ Brooks Atkinson

See that little stream – we could walk to it in two minutes. It took the
British a month to walk to it – a whole empire walking very slowly, dying
in the front and pushing forward behind. And another empire walked
very slowly backward a few inches a day, leaving dead like a million
bloody rugs. ~ F. Scott Fitzgerald, *Tender is the Night*

Against the beautiful and the clever and the successful, one can wage a
pitiless war, but not against the unattractive. ~ Graham Greene

The lamps are going out all over Europe. ~ Lord Grey of Fallodon

I hate war as only a soldier who has lived it can, only one who has seen its brutality, its futility, and its *stupidity*.
~ Dwight D. Eisenhower, 1946 speech in Ottawa

The truth about the war comes out 20 years after you died in it.
~ Richard J. Needham

# Warning

Take warning by the mischance of others, that others may not take warning of thine. ~ Sa'di

# Washington

Washington is a city of southern efficiency and northern charm.
~ John F. Kennedy

# Waste

And willful waste, depend upon't,
Brings, almost always, woeful want! ~ Ann Taylor

# Water

We never know the worth of water till the well is dry. ~ Thomas Fuller, M.D.

Thousands have lived without love, not one without water.
~ W.H. Auden

# Weak

In the process of tearing loose from nature, it was the weak who took the first steps. Chased out of the forest by the strong, they first essayed to walk erect, and in the intensity of their soul first uttered words, and first grabbed a stick to use as a weapon and tool. The weak's singular capacity for evolving substitutes for that which they lack suggests that they played a chief role in the evolvement of technology. ~ Eric Hoffer

# Weak Men

Like all weak men he laid an exaggerated stress on not changing one's mind. ~ W. Somerset Maugham

# Weakness

The highest point to which a weak but experienced mind can rise is detecting the weaknesses of better men. ~ Georg Christoph Lichtenberg

## Wealth

I wish to become rich, so that I can instruct the people and glorify honest poverty a little, like those kind-hearted, fat, benevolent people do. ~ Mark Twain

With luck and resolution and good guidance...the human mind can survive not only poverty, but even wealth. ~ Gilbert Highet

Nobody who has wealth to distribute ever omits himself. ~ Leon Trotsky

I am richer than [financier A. E.] Harriman. I have all the money I want and he doesn't. ~ John Muir, naturalist

Wealth is not without its advantages, and the case to the contrary, although it has often been made, has never proved widely persuasive. ~ John Kenneth Galbraith, *The Affluent Society*

## Weather

A change in the weather is sufficient to recreate the world and ourselves. ~ Marcel Proust, 1921

The weather is like the government, always in the wrong. ~ Jerome K. Jerome, 1899

Some are weather-wise, some are otherwise. ~ Benjamin Franklin

Don't knock the weather; nine-tenths of the people couldn't start a conversation if it didn't change once in a while. ~ Kin Hubbard

## Weekend

There aren't enough days in the weekend. ~ Steven Wright

## Weird

The weirder you are going to behave, the more normal you should look. It works in reverse, too. When I see a kid with three or four rings in his nose, I know there is absolutely nothing extraordinary about that person. ~ P.J. O'Rourke, U.S. humorist

## West

Comrade, look not on the west. It will have the heart out of your breast. ~ A.E. Housman

## White House

There can be no whitewash in the White House. ~ Richard M. Nixon

## Whole

The whole is always worth less than the sum of its parts.
~ David Russell

## Wickedness

Wickedness is always easier than virtue; for it takes the short cut to everything. ~ Samuel Johnson

## Wife

My first wife was a philosophy major. She would infuriate me by proving I didn't exist. ~ Woody Allen, in paraphrase

Basically, my wife was immature. I'd be at home in the bath and she'd come in and sink my boats. ~ Woody Allen

I tended to place my wife under a pedestal. ~ Woody Allen

## Wild

Serve the dinner backward, do anything – but for goodness sake, do something wild. ~ Elsa Maxwell, 1963

## Will

People do not lack strength; they lack will. ~ Victor Hugo

## Win

Anybody can win, unless there happens to be a second entry.
~ George Ade

## Wine

This wine is too good for toast-drinking, my dear. You don't want to mix emotions up with a wine like that. You lose the taste.
~ Ernest Hemingway, 1926

The dipsomaniac and the abstainer both make the same mistake: They both regard wine as a drug and not a drink. ~ G.K. Chesterton

Let us have wine and women, mirth and laughter,
Sermons and soda-water the day after. ~ Lord Byron in *Don Juan*

One of the disadvantages of wine is that it makes a man mistake words for thoughts. ~ Samuel Johnson

## Winning

If winning isn't everything, why do they keep score? ~ Vince Lombardi

I would be a winner because I was a loser! That's right, I dream of failure every night of my life, and that's my secret. ~ Donald Freed

## Winter

Winter is reality, summer is illusion. ~ Toivo Pekkanen

Winter makes us know new negatives: white darkness. ~ Douglas Barber

## Wisdom

The art of being wise is knowing what to overlook. ~ William James

The Chinese tell a story based on three or four thousand years of civilized wisdom. Two merchants were arguing heatedly in the midst of a crowd. A stranger, noting the depth of their anger, expressed surprise that no blows were being struck. His friend explained, "The man who strikes first admits that his ideas have given out."

Clever men are impressed in their differences from their fellows. Wise men are conscious of their resemblance to them.
~ R.H. Tawney, British historian

Life is a festival only to the wise. ~ Ralph Waldo Emerson

He who knows others is learned; he who knows himself is wise.
~ Chinese proverb

Wise men appreciate all men, for they see the good in each and know how hard it is to make anything good. ~ Baltasar Gracian

A wise man gets more use from his enemies than a fool from his friends. ~ Baltasar Gracian

The philosophies of one age have become the absurdities of the next, and the foolishness of yesterday has become the wisdom of tomorrow.
~ William Osler, 1902

To question a wise man is the beginning of wisdom. ~ German proverb

The beginning of wisdom is the definition of terms. ~ Socrates

A word to the wise ain't necessary – it's the stupid ones who need the advice. ~ Bill Cosby

Wise men say nothing in dangerous times. ~ John Selden

A wise man hears one word and understands two. ~ Yiddish proverb

A silent man is easily reputed wise. The unknown is always wonderful.
~ Frederick William Robertson

Wisdom and beauty form a very rare combination. ~ Petronius Arbiter

What is strength without a double share of wisdom? ~John Milton

Knowledge is a process of piling up facts; wisdom lies in their simplification. ~ Martin H. Fisher

Penny wise, pound foolish. ~ Robert Burton

Wisdom is knowing when you can't be wise. ~ Paul Engle

The wisest mind has something yet to learn. ~ George Santayana

'Tis not knowing much, but what is useful, that makes a wise man.
~ Thomas Fuller, M.D.

The wise man doesn't give the right answers, he poses the right question. ~ Claude Levi-Strauss

Any man can ride a train. Only a wise man knows when to get off.
~ Eric Hoffer

A wise man does not venture all his eggs in one basket.
~ Miguel de Cervantes

Wisdom denotes the pursuing of the best ends by the best means.
~ Francis Hutcheson

It is better to speak wisdom foolishly like the saints than to speak folly wisely like the deans. ~ G.K. Chesterton

Science is organized knowledge. Wisdom is organized life.
~ Immanuel Kant

## Wish

A wish is a desire without an attempt. ~ Frank Baur

We would often be sorry if our wishes were gratified. ~ Aesop

We are never further from our wishes than when we imagine that we possess what we have desired. ~ Goethe

## Wit

Wit is the only wall between us and the dark. ~ Mark Van Doren

## Witty

A witty saying proves nothing. ~ Voltaire

There's many witty men whose brains can't fill their bellies.
~ Benjamin Franklin

## Women

Give women the vote, and in five years there will be a crushing tax on bachelors. ~ George Bernard Shaw

It occurred to me when I was 13 and wearing white gloves and Mary Janes and going to dancing school that no one should have to dance backwards all their lives. ~ Jill Ruckelshaus, U.S. govt. official

Ginger Rogers did everything Fred Astaire did. She just did it backwards and in high heels. ~ Variously attributed to Faith Whittlesey, U.S. lawyer and politician, Linda Ellerbee, U.S. broadcast journalist and Ann Richards, governor of Texas

Do you know why God withheld the sense of humour from women? That we may love you instead of laughing at you.
~ Mrs. Patrick Campbell, British actress

Women should try to increase their size rather than decrease it, because I believe the bigger we are, the more space we'll take up, and the more we'll have to be reckoned with. I think every woman should be fat like me. ~ Roseanne Barr

Take my word for it, the silliest woman can manage a clever man; but it needs a very clever woman to manage a fool.
~ Rudyard Kipling, *Plain Tales From the Hills*

Some women are not beautiful – they only look as though they are.
~ Karl Kraus

Equal rights for the sexes will be achieved when mediocre women occupy high positions. ~ Françoise Giroud

You don't know a woman until you have had a letter from her.
~ Ada Leverson in *Tenterhooks*, 1912

You don't know anything about a woman until you meet her in court.
~ Norman Mailer

The majority of women (happily for them) are not very much troubled with sexual feelings of any kind. No nervous or feeble young man need, therefore, be deterred from marriage by an exaggerated notion of the duties required from him. ~ Dr. William Acton, who was popular in the 1860s

A woman's always younger than a man of equal years.
~ Elizabeth Barrett Browning

That is the worst thing about being a middle-class woman … you have more knowledge of yourself and the world: you are equipped to make choices, but there are none left to make. ~ Alison Lurie

Women sometimes forgive a man who forces the opportunity, but never a man who misses one. ~ Charles de Talleyrand-Perigord

No woman ever falls in love with a man unless she has a better opinion of him than he deserves. ~ Ed Howe

If a woman has to choose between catching a fly ball and saving an infant's life, she will choose to save the infant's life without even considering if there are men on base. ~ Dave Barry

When women are depressed they either eat or go shopping. Men invade another country. ~ Elayne Boosler

You see a lot of smart guys with dumb women, but you hardly ever see a smart woman with a dumb guy. ~ Erica Jong

Plain women know more about men than beautiful ones do.
~ Katharine Hepburn

Woman's virtue is man's greatest invention. ~ Cornelia Otis Skinner

The one certain way for a woman to hold a man is to leave him for religion. ~ Muriel Spark

Why are the needle and the pen thought incompatible by men?
~ Esther Lewis

A woman has to be twice as good as a man to go half as far.
~ Fannie Hurst

No person should be denied equal rights because of the shape of her skin. ~ Pat Paulsen

## Word (Printed)

The day of the printed word is far from ended. Swift as is the delivery of the radio bulletin, graphic as is television's eyewitness picture, the task of adding meaning and clarity remains urgent. People cannot and need not absorb meaning at the speed of light. ~ Erwin Canham

## Words

Use no word that under stress of emotion you could not actually say.
~ Ezra Pound, 1986

Man does not live by words alone, despite the fact that sometimes he has to eat them. ~ Adlai Stevenson

Words are all we have. ~ Samuel Beckett

Handle them carefully, for words have more power than atom bombs.
~ Pearl Strachan

Thanks to words, we have been able to rise above the brutes; and thanks to words, we have often sunk to the level of the demons.
~ Aldous Huxley, *Adonis and the Alphabet*

The words! I collected them in all shapes and sizes and hung them like bangles in my mind. ~ Hortense Calisher, 1964

A mean word like an arrow cannot be taken back. ~ Anonymous

Words that do not match deeds are not important. ~ Che Guevara

Words are, of course, the most powerful drug used by mankind.
~ Rudyard Kipling, cited in *The Oxford Dictionary of Literature*

Never use a big word when a diminutive phrase can be utilized.
~ Anonymous

As long as a word remains unspoken, you are its master; once you utter it, you are its slave. ~ Solomon ibn Gabirol, *The Choice of Pearls*, circa 1050

Check to see if you any words out. ~ Graffito

There is always time to add a word, never to withdraw one.
~ Baltasar Gracian

Words are wise men's counters, they do but reckon with them; but they are the money of fools. ~ Thomas Hobbes

When ideas fail, words come in very handy. ~ Goethe

And once sent out, a word takes wing beyond recall. ~ Horace

If the advocate cannot justify the presence of a word, then that word should be deleted from his or her prose. ~ Paul M. Perell

A multitude of words is no proof of a prudent mind. ~ Thales

## Work

It is an article of faith in my creed to pick the man who does not take himself seriously, but does take his work seriously. ~ Michael C. Cahill

Work is much more fun than fun. ~ Noel Coward

The more I want to get something done, the less I call it work.
~ Richard Bach, 1977

My grandfather once told me that there are two kinds of people: those who do the work and those who take the credit. He told me to try to be in the first group; there was less competition there. ~ Indira Gandhi

By working faithfully eight hours a day you may eventually get to be a boss and work 12 hours a day. ~ Robert Frost

The biggest mistake you can ever make is to believe that you are working for someone else. ~ Anonymous

For one person who dreams of making 50,000 pounds, a hundred people dream of being left 50,000 pounds. ~ A.A. Milne

Choose a job you love, and you will never have to work a day in your life. ~ Confucius

Most people like hard work, particularly when they're paying for it.
~ Franklin P. Jones

The one important thing I have learned over the years is the difference between taking one's work seriously and taking one's self seriously. The first is imperative, the second disastrous. ~ Margot Fonteyn

Thunder is good, thunder is impressive, but it is the lightning that does the work. ~ Mark Twain

Roasted pigeons will not fly into one's mouth. ~ Pennsylvania Dutch proverb

Chop your own wood and it will warm you twice. ~ Proverb

Every man is the son of his own works. ~ Miguel de Cervantes

It is the privilege of any human work which is well done to invest the doer with a certain haughtiness. He can well afford not to conciliate, whose faithful work will answer for him. ~ Ralph Waldo Emerson

The bitter and the sweet come from the outside, the hard from within, from one's own efforts. ~ Albert Einstein

If there is no wind, row. ~ Latin proverb

Work is a fine thing if it doesn't take too much of your spare time.
~ Anonymous

I've met a few people in my time who were enthusiastic about hard work. And it was just my luck that all of them happened to be men I was working for at the time. ~ Bill Gold

Work to become, not to acquire. ~ Elbert Hubbard

When your work speaks for itself, don't interrupt. ~ Henry J. Kaiser

One beats the bush; another catches the bird. ~ German proverb

Nothing you can't spell will ever work. ~ Will Rogers

Blessed is he who has found his work; let him ask no other blessedness. ~ Thomas Carlyle

If people really liked to work, we'd still be plowing the ground with sticks and transporting goods on our backs. ~ William Feather

When work is a pleasure, life is a joy. When work is a duty, life is slavery.
~ Maxim Gorky, *The Lower Depths*

I have long been of the opinion that if work were such a splendid thing, the rich would have kept more of it for themselves. ~ Bruce Grocott

Any man can do any amount of work, provided it isn't the work he's supposed to be doing. ~ Robert Benchley

Work is delegated down to the level at which it cannot be competently carried out. ~ Christopher Bradshaw

Every morning I get up and look through the Forbes list of the richest people in America. If I'm not there, I go to work.
~ Robert Orben, American humorist

## Working Classes

Imagine...the universal outcry that would occur if every year several corporate headquarters routinely collapsed like mines, crushing 60 or 70 executives. ... Try to imagine the horror...if thousands of university professors were deafened every year or lost fingers, hands, sometimes eyes, while on their jobs. ~ Andrew Levison, *The Working-Class Majority*, 1974

The worst fault of the working classes is telling their children they're not going to succeed, saying "There is life, but it's not for you."
~ John Mortimer

## World

The world is extremely interesting to a joyful soul. ~ Alexandra Stoddard

The world belongs to the enthusiast who keeps his cool. ~ William McFee

It's a small world but I wouldn't want to paint it. ~ Steven Wright

As for the just and noble idea that nations, as well as individuals, are parts of one wondrous whole, it has hardly passed the lips or pen of any but religious men and poets. ~ Harriet Martineau, English author

The world is my lobster. ~ Henry J. Tillman

All the world's a cage. ~ Jeanne Phillips

The most incomprehensible thing about the world is that it is comprehensible. ~ Albert Einstein

The world is a force, not a presence. ~ Wallace Stevens

## Worry

Worry is the interest paid on trouble before it falls due. ~ W. R. Inge

If there be no remedy, why worry? ~ Spanish proverb

Worrying helps you some. It seems as if you are doing something when you are worrying. ~ Lucy Maud Montgomery

The reason worry kills more people than work is that more people worry than work. ~ Robert Frost

## Writers

For a writer only one form of patriotism exists; his attitude toward language. ~ Joseph Brodsky, 1972

Writers really live in the mind and in the hotels of the soul.
~ Edna O'Brien, 1985

The creations of a great writer are little more than the moods and passions of his own heart, given surnames and Christian names, and sent to walk the earth. ~ W.B.Yeats, 1895

My idea is always to reach my generation. The wise writer... writes for the youth of his own generation, the critics of the next and the schoolmasters of ever afterward. ~ F. Scott Fitzgerald, 1924

For a country to have a great writer is like having a second government. That is why no regime has ever loved great writers, only minor ones.
~ Alexander Solzhenitsyn, 1976

A writer who takes political, social or literary positions must act only with the means that are his. These means are the written words.
~ Jean-Paul Sartre, 1964

The shelf life of the modern hardback writer is somewhere between the milk and the yoghurt. ~ John Mortimer, 1987

Life can't ever defeat a writer who is in love with writing, for life itself is a writer's lover until death. ~ Edna Ferber

A writer is, after all, only half his book. The other half is the reader and from the reader the writer learns. ~ P.L. Travers, 1978

It takes more than a mastery of words to be an excellent writer. First, good writers thoroughly understand the point they are trying to make, or the impression they are trying to convey. Then they get to it quickly. When it is accomplished, they get off the page. They never hang around wasting time and taking bows. ~ John L. Beckley, founder of *The Economic Press*

Writers, like teeth, are divided into incisors and grinders. ~ Walter Bagehot

A publisher offers you $30,000 to write a 350-page guidebook. Thirty thousand dollars! Congratulations! Guess what? You're about to go broke. ~ Tom Brosnahan, author of *Lonely Planet*

It would be dangerous for a writer instantly to think of a global audience because he may be robbing himself of his own voice.
~ Pico Iyer

Why do writers write? Because it isn't there. ~ Thomas Berger

The most essential gift for a good writer is a built-in shock-proof shit-detector. ~ Ernest Hemingway

If writers were good businessmen, they'd have too much sense to be writers. ~ Irvin S. Cobb

## Writing

The art of writing requires a constant plunging back into the shadow of the past where time hovers ghost-like. ~ Ralph Ellison, 1963

All good writing is swimming under water and holding your breath.
~ F. Scott Fitzgerald

If Thomas Wolfe sold, I'd write like Thomas Wolfe. ~ Mickey Spillane

An old tutor of a college said to one of his pupils: Read over your compositions, and whenever you meet with a passage which you think is particularly fine, strike it out. ~ Samuel Johnson

It took me fifteen years to discover I had no talent for writing, but I couldn't give it up because by that time I was too famous. ~ Robert Benchley

I have learned in my 30-odd years of serious writing only one sure lesson: Stories, like whiskey, must be allowed to mature in the cask. ~ Sean O'Faolain, 1956

A playwright must be his own audience. A novelist may lose his readers for a few pages; a playwright never dares lose his audience for a minute. ~ Terence Rattigan, 1956

Sometimes I think [my writing] sounds like I walked out of the room and left the typewriter running. ~ Gene Fowler

Nothing matters but the writing. There has been nothing else worthwhile...a stain upon the silence. ~ Samuel Beckett, 1986

It's none of their business that you have to learn how to write. Let them think you were born that way. ~ Ernest Hemingway

No tears in the writer, no tears in the reader. ~ Robert Frost

It is a sobering thought that each of us gives his hearers and his readers a chance to look into the inner working of his mind when he speaks or writes. ~ J.M. Barker

My writing goes well when there is something out there that amazes me or fascinates me – and it is a big damn world. ~ Tim Cahill

You must write for children the same way as you write for adults, only better. ~ Maxim Gorky

The secret of popular writing is never to put more on a given page than the common reader can lap off it with no strain whatsoever on his habitually slack attention. ~ Ezra Pound

## Wrong

The wrong way always seems the more reasonable. ~ George Moore

## Wrong Number

Well, if I called the wrong number, why did you answer the phone?

~ James Thurber

## Wrongs

Two wrongs don't make a right, but they make a good excuse.

~ Thomas Szasz

## Yearning

A little yearning is a dangerous thing. ~ Graffito

## "Yes Men"

I don't want any yes-men in this firm. I want people who speak their minds, even if it does cost them their jobs. ~ Sam Goldwyn

## Youth

You're only young once, but you can be immature forever.
~ *Globe & Mail*, Aug. 29,1992

We must view young people not as empty bottles to be filled, but as candles to be lit. ~ Robert H. Shaffer

Young men are apt to think themselves wise enough, as drunken men are apt to think themselves sober enough. ~ Lord Chesterfield

Don't laugh at a youth for his affectations; he is only trying on one face after another till he finds his own. ~ Logan Pearsall Smith, U.S. writer

It is better to waste one's youth than to do nothing with it at all.
~ Georges Courteline

As for me, except for an occasional heart attack – I feel as young as I ever did. ~ Robert Benchley

Youth is a malady of which one becomes cured a little every day.
~ Benito Mussolini

Blessed are the young, for they shall inherit the national debt.
~ Herbert Hoover, (former) U.S. President

I am not young enough to know everything. ~ Oscar Wilde

It is fitting that we should hold the young in awe. ... Only when a man reaches the age of 40 or 50 without distinguishing himself in any way can one say, I suppose, that he does not deserve to be held in awe.
~ Confucius

Youth is glorious, but it isn't a career. ~ Unknown

There is a strong disposition in youth, from which some individuals never escape, to suppose that everyone else is having a much more enjoyable time than we are ourselves. ~ Anthony Powell, A Buyer's Market

If men and women are to understand each other, to enter into each other's nature with mutual sympathy, and to become capable of genuine comradeship, the foundation must be laid in youth.
~ Havelock Ellis

Youth would be an ideal state if it came a little later in life.
~ Herbert Henry Asquith

Youth is wholly experimental. ~ Robert Louis Stevenson

# INDEX

RICHARD W. POUND

Camus, Albert, 16, 26, 114, 128, 148, 150, 164, 177, 185, 233, 258
"Canadian Tax Highlights," 146
Canham, Erwin, 355
Cantinflas, 190
Capek, Josef, 96
Capio, Oliver, 106
Capone, Al, 50, 150
Capote, Truman, 343
Carey, Drew, 183
Carlin, George, 111
Carlyle, Jane, 281, 327
Carlyle, Thomas, 124, 159, 160, 176, 221, 241, 279, 292, 296, 300, 319, 345, 358
Carnegie, Andrew, 10
Carpenter, Liz, 15
Carrel, Alexis, 178
Carroll, Lewis, 25, 41, 92, 218, 226, 287
Carson, Johnny, 105
Carter, Bunk, 172
Case, Mary, 91
Casey, Douglas, 130
Casselman, Bill, 127
Cate, Henry, VII, 183
Cather, Willa, 159, 332, 334
Cato the Elder, 68, 287
Cato the Younger, 135
Caulfield, Holden, 9
Cavafy, Constantine, 34
Cavett, Dick, 324
Cecil, Richard, 104
Céline, Louis-Ferdinand, 284
Cellini, Benvenuto, 132
Cerf, Christopher, 255, 256
Cervantes, Miguel de, 75, 83, 163, 218, 252, 353, 357
Cezanne, Paul, 200
Chah, Ajahn, 248
Chamberlain, Neville, 179
Chamfort, Sébastien, 23, 73, 178, 271
Chamson, Andre, 137
Chandler, Raymond, 180, 297
Chanel, Coco, 104
Channing, William, 326
Chaplin, Charlie, 121, 138
Chapman, George, 130, 148, 268
Char, René, 130
Charles, Elizabeth, 255
Chartier, Emile-Auguste, 166
Chase, Alexander, 170, 218
Chase, Ilka, 119
Chaucer, Geoffrey, 150
Chaudhuri, Haridas, 249
Chaussée, Pierr-Claude Nivelle de la, 284
Chazal, Malcolm de, 167
Chekhov, Anton, 25, 36, 94,

213, 340
Cheng, Matthew, 135
Cheops, 59
Chesterfield, Fourth Earl of, 44
Chesterfield, Lord, 7, 14, 47, 94, 163, 177, 184, 224, 291, 328, 363
Chesterton, G.K., 20, 22, 23, 88, 95, 123, 126, 154, 162, 165, 207, 212, 225, 253, 266, 274, 310, 331, 351, 353
Chief Justice of Ontario, 239
Chisholm, Brock, 264
Chomsky, Noam, 133, 290
Chopin, Frederick, 68
Christie, Agatha, 172, 207, 231, 266
Christina of Sweden, 15
Churchill, Winston, 17, 29, 52, 79, 91, 105, 129, 132, 159, 193, 200, 274, 302, 310, 313, 321, 331, 335, 340, 348
Ciano, Count Galeazzo, 87, 344
Ciardi, John, 19, 125, 302
Cicero, 92, 169, 187, 191, 223, 246, 255, 322, 344
Clancy, Tom, 257
Clare, Anthony, 43
Clare, John, 10
Clark, Karen Kaiser, 199
Clarke, Arthur C., 172, 179, 303
Claxton, Guy, 43
Clay, Henry, 57
Cleaver, Eldridge, 16, 303
Clemenceau, Georges, 348
Clements, George L., 322
Cleveland, Grover, 346
Clifton, Lucille, 254
Clinton, Bill, 263
Cobb, Irvin S., 360
Cobbett, William, 260
Cockburn, Bruce, 233
Cockburn, Claud, 89
Cocks, Barnett, 64
Cocteau, Jean, 279, 318
Cohen, Leonard, 226
Cohen, Morris Raphael, 295
Coleridge, Samuel Taylor, 214, 221, 301, 307, 315
Colette, 59, 113, 182, 183
Collins, John Churton, 111, 223
Collins, William, 248
Colton, Charles Caleb, 17, 18, 65, 88, 112, 132, 151, 188, 222, 291, 299, 326
Commoner, Barry, 31
Compton-Burnett, Ivy, 259, 297

Confucius, 53, 101, 124, 131, 140, 141, 189, 265, 304, 313, 344, 345, 357, 364
Congreve, William, 153, 292
Connolly, Billy, 188, 276
Connolly, Cyril, 62, 204, 212
Conrad, Joseph, 10, 81, 169, 193, 342
Cook, Peter, 25
Cooley, Mason, 135, 258
Coolidge, Calvin, 204, 250, 267, 307
Coote, George, 139
Copland, Aaron, 228
Coquet, James de, 279
Corelli, Marie, 214
Corinthians, 120
Corneille, Pierre, 78, 141, 285
Cort, David, 314
Cosby, Bill, 352
Courteline, Georges, 330, 363
Cousins, Norman, 84, 159, 196, 258
Coward, Noel, 15, 16, 62, 226, 309, 357
Cowley, Malcolm, 139
Cowper, William, 75, 216
Crane, Stephen, 63
Creighton, Bishop Mandell, 154
Creighton, Donald, 158
Crews, Harry, 314
Crimmons, Cathy, 152
Crisp, Quentin, 142, 155, 323
Crockett, David, 285
Cronkite, Walter, 111
Crosby, John, 323
Crosby, Norm, 76
Crosby, Philip, 8
Cross, Amanda, 150
Crow, John, 327
Crowquill, Alfred, 167
Cruickshank, Ken, 65
Crystal, Billy, 297
Cumberland, Bishop Richard, 287
cummings, e.e., 191
Cuppy, Will, 243
Curtis, Charles P., 171
Curtis, Richard, 63
Czar Nicholas I, 46

D
da Vinci, Leonardo, 125, 132, 178, 237, 250
Dad, 225
Dahlberg, Edward, 156, 339
Dalai Lama, 90, 135, 194, 223, 282, 285, 287
Dali, Salvador, 145, 211, 249
Dalrymple, Dr. Theodore, 33
The Dancing Wu Li Masters: An Overview of the New

Physics, 233
Dane, Frank, 197
Daniels, Anthony, 143
Dante, 21, 72, 119, 204, 232, 305
Darrow, Clarence S., 326
Darwin, Charles, 154, 173
Darwin, Erasmus, 241
Davidson, John, 276
Davies, Robertson, 163, 214, 294
Davies, Sir John, 131
Davis, Elmer, 125
Davis, Evan, 232
Davis, Miles, 228
Davitz, Lois and Joel, 163
Dawkins, Richard, 44, 202
Day, Clarence, 115
Day, Sir Robin, 323
de Gaulle, Charles, 257, 314
De Voto, Bernard, 215
De Vries, Peter, 109, 114, 201, 234, 244
Debray, Regis, 324
Deffand, Marquise du, 95
Defoe, Daniel, 130, 254
Degas, Edgar, 26, 319
DeGeorge, Joe, 112
Delacroix, Eugene, 115, 212
Delillo, Don, 126
The Deltones, 16
Deming, W. Edwards, 193
Democritus, 9, 53, 83, 153, 326
Denny, Alma, 314
Descartes, René, 332
Destouches, Philippe Nericault, 7
Dewar, Thomas R., 173, 206
Dewey, John, 169
Dickens, Charles, 22, 72, 94, 263, 288, 301
Dickey, John Sloan, 338
Dickinson, Emily, 55, 335
Diderot, Denis, 211, 300
Diefenbaker, John, 76
Dieterle, William, 210
Dietrich, Marlene, 134
Diffrient, Niels, 322
Diller, Phyllis, 72, 161
Dimnet, Ernest, 198
Diogenes, 211
Dirksen, Everett M., 201
Disch, Thomas, 77
Disney, Walt, 97, 172
Disraeli, Benjamin, 22, 42, 57, 61, 79, 85, 107, 116, 197, 310, 336, 340
D'Israeli, Isaac, 148
Ditka, Mike, 312
Divac, Vlade, 175
Dizick, Missy, 52
Dollar, Robert, 8

Donatus, Aelius, 275
Dostoevsky, Fyodor, 55, 232
Doughty, Arthur, 24
Douglas, Norman, 13, 185
Douglas, Tommy, 279
Doyle, Sir Arthur Conan, 75, 90, 170, 266, 325, 336
Drucker, Peter, 148, 213, 242, 262
Dryden, John, 32, 254, 279, 293, 331
du Gard, Maurice Martin, 179
Duckworth, Keith, 175
Dudek, Louis, 81
Duell, Charles H., 180
Duhamel, Georges, 109
Dulles, John Foster, 285
Dumas, Alexandre, 138, 286
Duncan, Isadora, 41
Duncan, Sara Jeanette, 271
Dunham, David, 103
Dunn, Alan, 36
Dunne, Finley Peter, 333
Duppa, Richard, 190
Duran, Richard, 138
Durant, Will, 62, 92, 103, 159, 195, 226, 234
Durant, Will and Ariel, 258, 306
Durrenmatt, Friedrich, 253
Dworkin, Ronald, 150

E
Eagan, J.W., 42
Earhart, Amelia, 76
Easterbrook, Greg, 69
Eastwood, Clint, 215
Eban, Abba, 35
Ebner-Eschenbach, Marie von, 71, 73, 187
Ecclesiastes, 276, 301
Eddington, Sir Arthur, 290
Edison, Thomas Alva, 35, 119, 175, 210
Edwards, Bob, 16
Einstein, Albert, 81, 104, 108, 136, 142, 151, 165, 170, 173, 180, 187, 216, 230, 266, 268, 274, 290, 308, 312, 335, 357, 359
Eiseley, Loren, 296
Eisenhower, Dwight D., 177, 349
Eisner, Thomas, 45
Elias, Maurice, 148
Eliot, George, 12, 14, 22, 87, 114, 141, 183, 260, 269, 298, 299, 334
Eliot, T.S., 9, 101, 105, 166, 254, 261, 285, 290, 332, 336
Ellerbee, Linda, 122, 354
Ellington, Duke, 266

Ellis, Dr. Albert, 206
Ellis, Edward Robb, 323
Ellis, Havelock, 28, 73, 141, 242, 267, 364
Ellison, Harlan, 308
Ellison, Ralph, 360
Elmer-De Witt, Philip, 155
Elton, Ben, 259
Emerson, Ralph Waldo, 9, 10, 11, 36, 49, 56, 57, 58, 60, 62, 63, 65, 79, 87, 106, 115, 120, 140, 144, 156, 157, 158, 170, 174, 180, 185, 202, 204, 209, 216, 226, 237, 241, 249, 250, 266, 269, 272, 274, 275, 284, 288, 295, 326, 334, 336, 342, 352, 357
Engle, Paul, 353
Eno, Brian, 209
Ephron, Nora, 74, 262
Epictetus, 79, 102, 125, 153, 253
Epicurus, 94, 107, 134, 221, 262
Epstein, Joseph, 224
Erasmus, 151
Ertz, Susan, 171
Erving, Julius, 267
Esslin, Martin, 278
Etienne, Pierre Jacques, 314
Ettinger, Bob, 280
Ettore, Barbara, 61
Euripides, 75, 76, 84, 133, 134, 141, 184, 250, 278, 281, 291
Evenius, 80
Eysenck, Hans, 16

F
Fadiman, Clifton, 114
Fairlie, Henry, 323
Falkland, Lord, 87
Fallodon, Lord Grey of, 349
Fallon, Pat, 170
Faludi, Susan, 293
Faraday, Michael, 321
Faulkner, William, 133, 273
Feather, William, 58, 171, 248, 312, 320, 358
Feesch, Rudolph, 77
Feiffer, Jules, 216
Ferber, Edna, 360
Ferdinand I, Emperor, 185
Ferguson, Bill, 238
Ferm, Ransom K., 267
Fernandez-Armesto, Felipe, 117
Feuchtwanger, Lion, 284
Fiedler, Edgar, 101, 130
Fielding, Henry, 82, 98, 307
Fields, W.C., 61, 176, 263, 301
Finley, John, 216

RICHARD W. POUND

173, 202, 205, 213, 234, 300, 344, 360
Sassoon, Siegfried, 303
Sassoon, Vidal, 311
Satie, Eric, 210
Satir, Virginia, 249
Sauget, John, 103
Saurin, Jacques, 191
Sayers, Dorothy L., 245
Schelling, Friedrich von, 23
Schiller, Johann Friedrich von, 83, 110, 133, 159, 260
Schlegel, Friedrich von, 158, 308
Schlesinger, Arthur M., Jr., 322
Schlick, Moritz, 343
Schlitz, Don, 116
Schmidt, Walt, 13
Schnabel, Arthur, 252
Schnitzler, Arthur, 197
Schopenhauer, Arthur, 42, 85, 171, 203, 217, 224, 264, 284, 345
Schulz, Charles M., 45, 200
Schumacher, E.F., 113
Schwanbach, Stephen R., 334
Schwartz, Dr. David, 192, 312
Schwarzenegger, Arnold, 9
Schweitzer, Albert, 188
Sciascia, Leonardo, 78
Scott, Adam, 309
Scott, F.R., 133
Scott, Jay, 274
Scott, Walter, 191
Scruton, Roger, 154
Scully, Frank, 285
Seaward, Brian, 163
Sedgwick, Ellery, 31
Segal, Erich, 208
Seinden, Morton Irving, 150
Seinfeld, Jerry, 127
Selden, John, 72, 112, 352
Seneca, 9, 12, 13, 28, 76, 90, 93, 123, 197, 208, 209, 252, 260, 272, 273, 288, 300, 333, 334, 344, 347
serial killer, Kansas, 186
Service, Robert, 330
Sevareid, Eric, 78, 303
Shadwell, Thomas, 129
Shaffer, Robert H., 363
Shakespeare, 11, 18, 22, 60, 63, 91, 94, 113, 118, 123, 124, 129, 130, 132, 140, 143, 154, 155, 160, 196, 210, 219, 231, 241, 245, 249, 266, 277, 287, 288, 289, 294, 300, 332, 333, 344
Sharwood, George, 330
Shaw, George Bernard, 16, 26, 35, 41, 80, 82, 86, 97, 101, 114, 115, 120, 127, 143,

147, 159, 170, 174, 190, 193, 194, 195, 207, 221, 225, 248, 259, 267, 270, 274, 300, 336, 345, 354
Shebib, Don, 311
Sheehy, Gail, 55, 295
Sheen, Fulton J., 126
Shelley, Percy Bysshe, 278
Shepard, Sam, 207
Sheridan, Richard, 218, 319
Sherman, John, 136
Sherwood, Robert, 324
Shestov, Leo, 261
Shirley, James, 123
Shoaff, Edgar A., 257
Shoaff, Olga, 169
Siegel, Henry, 77
Sigismund, Holy Roman Emperor, 155
Simak, Clifford, 108
Simic, Charles, 177
Simmons, Edward, 311
Simon, Neil, 282
Simonides, 244
Sinatra, Frank, 97
Singer, Isaac Bashevis, 133, 280
Sitwell, Dame Edith, 145, 270
Skinner, B.F., 102, 327
Skinner, Cornelia Otis, 355
Slick, Grace, 34
Slick, Sam, 61
Smiles, Samuel, 67, 93, 209
Smith, Alexander, 280, 286, 291
Smith, Alfred Emanuel, 33, 89
Smith, F.E., Earl of Birkenhead, 310
Smith, Jaime, 32
Smith, Liz, 281
Smith, Logan Pearsall, 30, 40, 134, 154, 198, 222, 229, 310, 345, 363
Smith, Russell R.W., 190
Smith, Stevie, 22, 85
Smith, Sydney, 131, 180, 221, 261
Smith, Will, 225
Smythe, Conn, 66
Snepscheut, Jan van de, 325
Snow, Carmel, 104
Sobran, Joseph, 103, 146
Socrates, 90, 222, 352
Solon, 191
Solzhenitsyn, Alexander, 205, 223, 264, 360
Sondheim, Stephen, 232
Sontag, Susan, 25, 169, 179, 244
Sophocles, 43, 85, 105, 185, 304, 332, 333
Sorensen, Janet, 60
Spark, Muriel, 355

Spencer, Herbert, 128, 187, 267, 314
Spielmann, Rudolph, 228
Spillane, Mickey, 361
Spinoza, Baruch, 69, 110, 118, 278
Spock, Dr. Benjamin, 292
Spock, Mr., 199
Sproles, Judy, 240
Squire, J.C., 142
St. Augustine, 208, 272, 333, 343
St. Clement of Alexandria, 161
St. Jerome, 64
de Stael, Mme, 201, 240, 339
Star, 316, 317
Star, Alexander, 181
Starnes, Richard, 50
Stauff, Elaine, 18
Steele, Sir Richard, 98, 277, 307, 343
Steffens, Lincoln, 26
Stein, Ben, 78
Stein, Gertrude, 65, 289, 293
Steinbeck, John, 13, 219, 294
Steinem, Gloria, 126, 214, 227
Steiner, George, 162
Stekel, Wilhelm, 171
Stendahl, 62
Stengel, Casey, 14, 213, 260
Stengel, Richard, 48
Stephens, James, 81
Stern, Bill, 104
Stern, G.B., 330
Stern, Laurence, 178
Stevens, Wallace, 254, 359
Stevenson, Adlai, 18, 72, 94, 127, 132, 147, 159, 161, 232, 263, 265, 266, 293, 356
Stevenson, Robert Louis, 47, 60, 134, 144, 176, 197, 214, 226, 227, 258, 364
Stimson, Henry Lewis, 300
Stockman, Ralph, 111
Stoddard, Alexandra, 359
Stolberg, Benjamin, 116
Stoppard, Tom, 52, 64, 89, 92, 180, 200, 250, 264, 277, 287
Storr, Anthony, 60, 176
Strachan, Pearl, 356
Strauss, Richard, 68
Stravinsky, Igor, 59, 204, 228
Strindberg, August, 95, 123
Strunsky, Simeon, 88, 92
Sulzberger, Arthur Hays, 184, 221
Summerskill, Baroness Edith, 230
Sumner, William, 167
Sun, 316, 317, 318
Sun Tzu, 12, 17, 71, 106, 112,

RICHARD W. POUND